The Children's Illustrated

Bible Dictionary

WITH SCRIPTURE INDEX

COMPILED AND EDITED BY

V. GILBERT BEERS, Ph.D., Th.D.

Publishers since 1798

THOMAS NELSON INC., PUBLISHERS
Nashville, Tennessee / New York, New York

Library of Congress Cataloging in Publication Data
Beers, Gil, 1928-
    The Children's Illustrated Bible Dictionary.
    Includes index.
    SUMMARY: Short definitions, scripture references, and a topical guide
identifies personal names, cities, and other terms in the Bible.
    1. Bible—Dictionaries, Juvenile. [1. Bible—Dictionaries] I. Title.
BS440.B46   220′.3   77-12650

2 3 4 5 6 7 8 9 0 — 80 79

Preface

A dictionary is commonly associated with word definition. Thus the very word "dictionary" often suggests a factual reference work with little concern for reading pleasure.

Since the Children's Illustrated Bible Dictionary is a Bible dictionary for children, its purpose goes beyond word definition. The volume does define terms, but in a style designed for ease of reading and heightened interest value. A primary purpose of this work is to motivate the reader to search the Scriptures further and to discover a sense of adventure and delight in them.

A full color illustration is included with each entry to reinforce the visual dimension of learning. Learning comes easier and lasts longer when a person or object can be visualized. This is especially true of Bible learning since the cultural gap is so wide between then and now.

Scripture references are included at the close of each entry, directing the reader to selected parts of the Bible which relate to the topic at hand. In addition, a Scriptural guide is provided in the back of the volume, directing the reader from the Scriptures to the topics or entries in this work which are related.

A topical guide in the back directs the reader from one topic to other related topics. Thus he may use it to provide topical help as he studies the Bible or as a cross reference among entries in this work.

Parents, teachers and others who work with children should find this volume invaluable in helping them build a lifelong desire to study the Scriptures. Adult habits of Bible study are formed in childhood, primarily through the pleasant times the child has shared with parents or teachers.

While the audience for this work is primarily children, it is certain that many adults will find the Children's Illustrated Bible Dictionary stimulating and helpful for their own Bible study. Adults should find a most rewarding experience as they use this volume in studying God's Word with the children whom God has entrusted into their care.

A

Aaron

Moses' older brother, Aaron, was raised by his parents, Amram and Jochebed. Moses was raised in Pharaoh's palace by Pharaoh's daughter. When Moses wanted to take his people from Egypt, Aaron spoke to Pharaoh for him. Later, when the Hebrews lived in the wilderness, Aaron served as their High Priest. (Exod. 4:10ff; Num. 26:59.)

Abel

Abel and Cain were brothers, sons of Adam and Eve. Cain, the older, was a farmer and Abel was a shepherd. When God accepted Abel's offering, but rejected Cain's, Cain murdered his brother Abel. The Bible tells us that Abel's works were righteous and acceptable to God, but Cain's works were evil. (Gen. 4:1–8; I John 3:12.)

Abiathar

When the priests of Nob gave David a hiding place from King Saul, the king became angry and murdered eighty-five of them. Abiathar, son of Ahimelech, the high priest, was the only one to escape. Later, when David became king, Abiathar helped him bring the Ark of the Covenant back to Jerusalem. He also served as King David's adviser. (I Sam. 22:20–23; I Chron. 15:11.)

Abigail

While running away from King Saul, David hid with his men in the Carmel area. Nearby, a rude man named Nabal had come to shear his sheep. When David asked for food, Nabal went into a fit of anger and refused. But Nabal's beautiful wife Abigail heard of this and brought food to David. Later, when Nabal died, David married Abigail. (I Sam. 25; II Sam. 3:3.)

Abijah

For three years Abijah reigned over Judah while Jeroboam was king of Israel. Abijah was Rehoboam's son and Solomon's grandson, having inherited the throne from them. During his reign he tried to gain control of the ten tribes of Israel. In a speech on Mt. Ephraim, he asked Jeroboam not to fight because God was with them. God gave Abijah a great victory. (II Chron. 12:16—14:1.)

Abimelech

When Abraham and Sarah moved to Gerar, Abimelech, the Philistine king, fell in love with Sarah. Abraham was afraid Abimelech would kill him to get Sarah, so he said that Sarah was his sister. But when Abimelech tried to marry Sarah, he was warned by God in a dream and he gave Sarah back to Abraham. (Gen. 20:1–18.)

Abinadab

When the Philistines captured the Ark of the Covenant from the Israelites, it brought them so much trouble that they sent it back. The Ark was put into the house of a Levite of Kirjathjearim named Abinadab. His son Eleazar was given charge of the Ark and he cared for it for twenty years until David carried it to Jerusalem. (I Sam. 7:1, 2; II Sam. 6:3; I Chron. 13:7.)

Abishai

One of King David's bravest warriors was his nephew Abishai. Throughout his lifetime he was loyal to David. On one occasion he went with David into Saul's enemy camp and suggested that they kill King Saul while he slept. He also helped Joab murder Abner as revenge for killing their brother Asahel. (II Sam. 3:30; 21:17; I Chron. 11:20; 18:12, 13.)

Abner

King Saul's cousin Abner was an outstanding warrior and commander-in-chief of his army. After David's victory over Goliath, Abner brought him to King Saul. But when Saul chased David to kill him, Abner went with Saul to help him. Saul thought so highly of Abner that he invited him to eat with him at the king's table. (I Sam. 14:50–58; 17:55–58.)

Abraham

Marching under God's command, Abraham moved his family and possessions from his childhood home at Ur of the Chaldees to a new land called Canaan. There he and his wife Sarah had a son when they were almost 100 years old. It was through this son Isaac that God fulfilled His promise to make Abraham the father of a great nation. (Gen. 11:27—24:9; 25:1–8; Rom. 4:11.)

Absalom

Absalom, King David's third son, was the most handsome young man in the land, with thick hair and winning ways among the people. But he brought about the murder of his half-brother Amnon and later revolted against his own father. He tried to take the kingdom from David. Yet through it all, David loved his son greatly. (II Sam. 13—18.)

Aceldama, Akeldama

The priests who had paid Judas to betray Jesus had a problem. When Judas threw the thirty pieces of silver on the Temple floor, they did not know what to do with it. It was blood money, so they would not use it in the Temple. "Buy a Potter's Field and use it as a cemetery," someone suggested. The field they bought became known as Aceldama, or Akeldama, the Field of Blood. (Matt. 27:3–10; Acts 1:18, 19.)

Achan

When the people of Israel attacked Jericho, God warned them not to take anything for themselves and to destroy all that was in the city. But Achan stole some silver and gold and a beautiful robe and buried them under his tent. Because of his sin, Israel was defeated when they tried to take Ai. When Achan's sin was discovered, he was put to death. (Josh. 7.)

Achish

The jealous King Saul tried to kill David, forcing him to flee for his life. David fled to Achish of Gath, a Philistine king, for protection, but he ran away when Achish's officers became suspicious. Later David lived with Achish for a while. Achish wanted David to help him fight Saul. But the Philistine officers were again suspicious, and so David was sent back home. (I Sam. 21:10–15; 29:1–11.)

Achor

In their first battle at Ai, the Israelites were defeated because there was sin in their camp. Achan had kept silver, gold, and a beautiful robe in the battle for Jericho, even though God had commanded the Israelites not to do this. For his sin and the trouble he brought to Israel, Achan was stoned to death in the Valley of Achor. The name Achor means "trouble." (Josh. 7:24–26; 15:7.)

Achsah

So anxious was Caleb to capture Kirjath-sepher, or Debir, as it was later called, that he offered his daughter Achsah in marriage to the man who took it. Othniel was the victor, and so Achsah became his bride. Then Achsah asked her father Caleb for some springs of water and some lands as her wedding gift. (Josh. 15:16–19; Judg. 1:12–15.)

Acropolis

Within some Greek cities, a fortified hill with a citadel or castle rose above the rest of the buildings. Philippi, Corinth, and Samaria each had an acropolis, as this hill was called, but the most famous acropolis of all was at Athens. Paul preached at Mars' Hill, part of the acropolis area of Athens, when he visited the city. (Acts 17:15—18:1.)

Acts

The Acts of the Apostles, the fifth book of the New Testament, could be called The Acts of the Holy Spirit because it tells of His work through the apostles. The first part of Acts tells of Peter's ministry; the last part tells of Paul's ministry. The physician Luke, who also wrote the Gospel by his name, was the author of the Book of Acts. (The Book of Acts.)

Adam

On the sixth day of creation, God made the first man from the soil and named him Adam. The name is actually the Hebrew word which means "the earth." Adam was placed over all of God's other creation. God gave him the task of naming the birds and animals and taking care of the garden which God had made. When Adam and his wife Eve sinned, God made them leave the garden forever. (Gen. 1 and 2.)

Adoni-zedek

Not only had Joshua defeated Jericho and Ai, but he had also made a truce with Gibeon. This frightened Adoni-zedek, King of Jerusalem, so he led four other Amorite kings against Gibeon to destroy it. But Joshua came to Gibeon's rescue. In his battle against Adoni-zedek and the other four kings, Joshua commanded the sun and moon to stand still. (Josh. 10:1–27.)

Adoption

When a child is brought into a family, loved and cared for as though it were part of that family and given all the rights and privileges of that family, it is said to be adopted. Moses was adopted by Pharaoh's daughter. Esther was adopted by her cousin Mordecai. Christians are those people whom God adopts into His own family and calls His children. (Rom. 8:15, 16.)

Adoration

How can a man show that he is worshiping? One way is by kneeling or falling down before the one he worships. Some men lie face down before idols to show their worship for those gods. But God alone is to receive our worship or adoration. To adore means to worship. Adoration is the way a person shows he is worshiping. (Dan. 3:5, 6; Luke 4:8; Rev. 19:10.)

Adullam

While fighting the Philistines, David and his men used a large limestone cave near the city of Adullam in Judah as headquarters. One day David longed for a drink from the well in Bethlehem, and so three of his bravest men fought their way to the well for some water. David would not drink it, but poured it out as an offering to the Lord because the men had risked their lives to get it. (II Sam. 23:13–17.)

Adversary

Our greatest enemy or adversary is the devil, who seeks to destroy the work of God and take people with him to his final destruction. Another name for the devil is Satan, a Hebrew word meaning "adversary." Satan is like an enemy soldier, trying to destroy us. Therefore we should be on our guard against his attacks. (I Tim. 5:14, 15; I Pet. 5:8.)

Advocate

When a lawyer stands before the judge, he pleads the case for another. In doing so, he speaks as an advocate on behalf of that person. He explains in the best way possible that person's point of view to the judge. Jesus and the Holy Spirit are our advocates, for They speak to God the Father on our behalf. (John 14:16, 26; I John 2:1.)

Aeneas

Lying in bed for eight years with the palsy, Aeneas was a hopeless cripple who lived in Lydda. But one day Peter visited Lydda and stopped at Aeneas' house to see him. "Jesus Christ has healed you," Peter told Aeneas. "Get up." Aeneas stood up immediately. This miracle caused many in Lydda and the nearby Plain of Sharon to turn to Christ. (Acts 9:32–35.)

Agabus

While Paul and Barnabas were in Antioch, a Christian prophet named Agabus told of a famine that was coming. This caused many Christians to collect money for the poor Christians of Judea. Later, Agabus warned Paul that he would be made a prisoner in Jerusalem. As a sign, he bound his own hands with Paul's belt. (Acts 11:27–30; 21:10, 11.)

Agag

King Saul marched forth under God's command to completely destroy the Amalekites and Agag, their king. But Saul disobeyed God and kept some of the spoils of battle and spared Agag. When Samuel arrived, he cut King Agag into pieces and told Saul that God had rejected him as Israel's king, for God must have a king who obeys Him. (I Sam. 15:32, 33.)

Agrippa I

To please the Jews, King Herod Agrippa I, grandson of Herod the Great, began to persecute the church. He was a strict observer of the Jewish law. First he killed James, the brother of John, and then he put Peter in prison, planning to kill him after the Passover. Agrippa I died of worms when the people of Tyre and Sidon called him a god. (Acts 12:1–23.)

Agrippa II

At Caesarea, Paul was brought before King Agrippa to be judged. Agrippa and his sister Bernice had come to visit the Roman governor Festus. Son of Herod Agrippa I, King Agrippa was seventh and last of the kings of the Herod family. He was born in 27 A.D. and was great-grandson of Herod the Great who ruled during the time of Jesus' birth. (Acts 25:13—26:32.)

Ahab

For 22 years, the wicked King Ahab ruled over Israel. When he married Jezebel, a very wicked Sidonian princess, he let her bring her gods into Israel. He encouraged the Israelites to worship them, especially the god Baal. Elijah the Prophet opposed Ahab and Jezebel. Ahab was fatally wounded by a stray arrow as he stood in his chariot in a battle at Ramoth–gilead. (I Kings 16–22.)

Ahasuerus

From the most beautiful young ladies of the land, Esther was chosen to be the bride of the Persian king, Ahasuerus. When her cousin Mordecai saved the king's life, an account was written in the royal records. Ahasuerus, also known as Xerxes, later rewarded Mordecai. At Esther's request, he also saved the Jews from Haman's mass murder plot. (The Book of Esther.)

Ahaz

When Jotham, King of Judah, died in 735 B.C., his son Ahaz became king in his place. The kings of Israel and Syria wanted Ahaz to help them fight Assyria, but he refused. And so they invaded Judah and Ahaz was defeated. Isaiah the Prophet tried in vain to persuade Ahaz to trust God, but Ahaz sought help from Assyria instead. (Isa. 7:1–9; II Chron. 28.)

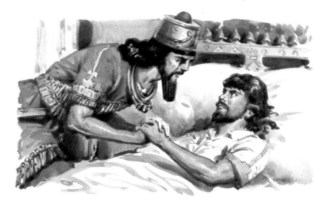

Ahaziah of Israel

Ahaziah ruled as the eighth king over Israel from 851–850 B.C. Like his parents Ahab and Jezebel, Ahaziah was an evil king. While he was king, Moab rebelled against Israel. When he fell through a lattice in his upper room, he was badly injured. He sought help from Baalzebub, god of Ekron, but the prophet Elijah warned that he would die. (II Kings 1.)

Ahaziah of Judah

When Ahaziah became king of Judah at 22, he followed the wicked ways of his father and mother, King Jehoram of Judah and Athaliah. He joined with his uncle, King Jehoram of Israel, to fight the Syrians. After Jehoram was shot in battle, Ahaziah went to visit him. Jehu followed and mortally wounded him. Ahaziah returned to Megiddo where he died. (II Kings 8:25–29; 9:11–27.)

Ahijah

One day Jonathan bravely attacked a Philistine camp without telling his father, King Saul, or Saul's army. The noise of battle reached Saul's camp, but he did not know what it was. Saul quickly called for the priest Ahijah, grandson of Eli, to bring the Ark of God and ask God about this. But Saul rushed to battle with the Philistines before Ahijah gave God's answer. (I Sam. 14:1–23.)

Ahimaaz

After Absalom rebelled against his father David, Ahimaaz, a son of Zadok the High Priest, helped David. To escape from Absalom's men, he hid in a well. He learned what Absalom planned to do and then reported it to David. When Absalom was finally killed, Ahimaaz ran to David with the news that the war had been won. (II Sam. 15:24–27; 17:15–22; 18:27.)

Ahimelech

In the days when David fled from King Saul, the Tabernacle was located at Nob. David went there and asked for bread and a sword, which Ahimelech, the High Priest, gave him. Saul was so angry when he heard about this that he killed Ahimelech and eighty-four other priests. Ahimelech's son, Abiathar, was the only member of the family to escape. (I Sam. 21–22.)

Ahithophel

When King David's son Absalom rebelled against his father, Ahithophel became Absalom's adviser. But David's friend Hushai pretended to go with Absalom also. When Ahithophel advised Absalom to pursue David and his men immediately, Hushai advised him to wait. Absalom listened to Hushai's advice and Ahithophel went home and hanged himself. (II Sam. 16:15—17:23.)

Ai

After Joshua captured Jericho, the next place to be attacked was Ai. As it was only a little town, Joshua sent a small army. To Joshua's surprise, the people of Israel were defeated by the men of Ai. When Joshua asked God why, he was told that someone had disobeyed God's orders and Israel was being punished. After the sinner had been found, Joshua's army destroyed Ai. (Josh. 7:1—8:29.)

Aijalon

After the city of Gibeon signed a peace treaty with Joshua, the neighboring Amorite kings became afraid and attacked Gibeon. Because of the treaty, Joshua was forced to fight for Gibeon. But time ran out and in an hour of great need, Joshua commanded the sun and moon to stand still as he stood in the Valley of Aijalon. In the long day that followed, Joshua won a great victory. (Josh. 10:12–14.)

Alabaster

One day Jesus sat with his friends in the house of Simon the Leper in Bethany. A woman came to Jesus with an alabaster flask filled with expensive ointment and poured it lovingly on Jesus. Alabaster is a beautiful white stone, with yellow and brown veins through it. It was used for making jars for keeping perfumes. (Matt. 26:7; Mark 14:3; Luke 7:37.)

Alexandria

The chief grain port of Rome, Alexandria sent its grain ships across the Mediterranean Sea. Paul sailed from Myra on one of these ships, bound for Rome. The city, which was in Egypt, was founded in 332 B.C. by Alexander the Great and gained fame for its lighthouse, its library of 700,000 books, and for the Septuagint, the Hebrew Old Testament translated into Greek by Jewish scholars. (Acts 27:6.)

Almond Tree

As early as January, the pink blossoms of the almond tree appear before its leaves. Its Hebrew name means "awakener" for it is the first tree to wake up from winter. The almond nuts were used for food or made into oil. When Jacob's sons went to Egypt for grain, Jacob sent almond nuts as gifts for the governor. When Aaron's rod budded, it produced almonds. (Gen. 43:11.)

Almug Tree

When Solomon began to build the great Temple in Jerusalem, he imported almug wood to make pillars. The fleet of Hiram, king of Tyre, brought the timber from Ophir, together with gold and precious stones for God's House. The sweet-scented wood, which was black outside and ruby red inside, was also used for harps and other musical instruments for the Temple players. (I Kings 10:11, 12.)

Alms

Every Sabbath day, alms of money and food were collected in the synagogues. Officials distributed these alms or gifts to the poor. Beggars asked for alms in the streets as people passed by. One day a lame beggar asked Peter and John for alms at the Beautiful Gate of the Temple. But instead, Peter healed the man in the name of Jesus. (Acts 3.)

Alpha and Omega

The first letter of the Greek alphabet was alpha, the last letter was omega. New Testament writers often used alpha and omega to speak of first and last. In the Book of Revelation God is called Alpha and Omega. As Alpha He is Creator, the beginning and source of all life. As Omega He is the end, the final hope of every believer. (Rev. 1:8–11; 21:6; 22:13.)

Altar

Great men of God, such as Abraham, Isaac, and Jacob, often built altars at a place where they heard the voice of God. Animals were sacrificed to God on these altars. That is, the meat of the animals was burned on the altars as an act of worship. Some altars were made from stones piled together, others were carved from rock. (Gen. 8:20; 12:7.)

Amalekites

On their way through the wilderness, the Israelites were attacked by the Amalekites. As long as Moses held up his hands, Israel had victory. But he soon grew tired and Aaron and Hur held up his hands until sunset when the battle was won. Years later God commanded Saul to destroy the Amalekites, but Saul disobeyed and kept King Agag alive. (Exod. 17:8–16; I Sam. 15:8ff; 30:18; II Sam. 1:8ff.)

Amasa

Amasa was David's nephew, son of his sister Abigail. However, he joined with Absalom in revolting against David. Amasa led Absalom's forces against David, and was defeated by Joab. David later made him captain of his forces instead of Joab because Joab killed Absalom. Joab also killed Amasa when they met at Gibeon. (II Sam. 17:25; 18:6ff; 19:13; 20:8–10.)

Amaziah

Amaziah, King of Judah, hired Israelite soldiers to help him capture Edom. But a man of God warned him not to use them, so he sent them home. Angered by this, the Israelites attacked some cities of Judah and later captured Amaziah. For 15 years, he lived as a prisoner in Jerusalem, then escaped to Lachish where he was killed. (II Kings 14; II Chron. 25.)

Ambassador

An ambassador was an envoy or representative, usually of high rank, who took personal messages from one ruler to another. Ambassadors were usually treated with respect when they went to foreign countries. The New Testament describes Christians as ambassadors for Christ because they take His Word to the world in His name. (II Cor. 5:20; Eph. 6:20.)

Ammon, Ammonites

The Ammonites were descended from Lot's younger son, Ammon, and were thus related to the Israelites. However, they were constant enemies of Israel. When Nehemiah and his workmen rebuilt the walls of Jerusalem, the Ammonites made fun of their work and tried to stop them. They worshiped idols and offered human sacrifices to their god, Molech. (Gen. 19:38; Deut. 2:19: I Sam. 11:2.)

Amnon

As the oldest of David's sons, Amnon was the prince next in line to become king. But when he mistreated his half-sister, Tamar, her brother Absalom made plans to kill him. Two years later Absalom gave a great banquet and invited Amnon. When Amnon was drunk with wine, Absalom ordered his servants to kill him. (II Sam. 3:2; 13:1ff; I Chron. 3:1.)

Amon

Named for one of the Egyptian gods, Amon was the son of Manasseh, King of Judah. At the age of twenty-two, Amon became king in his father's place. Like his father, he worshiped idols instead of the true God. He had been king only two years when his own servants plotted his death, killing him in his own house. (II Kings 21:19–26; II Chron. 33:21–25.)

Amorites

When the people of Israel invaded the Promised Land, two Amorite kings, Og and Sihon, were the first to be defeated. Later, Joshua defeated five Amorite kings and ended Amorite opposition to Israel. In the days of Solomon, the Amorites were slaves, quarrying stone for Solomon's buildings. (Deut. 3:1–13; Josh. 10:1—11:14; I Sam. 7:14; I Kings 9:20, 21.)

Amos

Amos was a shepherd of Tekoa, a little village just south of Bethlehem. He was called by God to go north to Samaria to preach. His message, mostly about the sin of God's people, may be found in the Book of Amos. He lived about 780–745 B.C. Besides his work as shepherd and prophet, Amos also took care of sycamore fig trees. (The Book of Amos.)

Amram

Amram, Moses' father, lived and worked in Egypt as a slave. Both he and his wife, Jochebed, descended from Jacob's son Levi. Amram was also the father of Aaron and Miriam. The Amramites, descendants of Amram, had charge of the Tabernacle, watching over the ark, table, candlestick and other furnishings. (Exod. 6:20; Num. 26:59; I Chron. 26:23.)

Amulets

People in Bible times sometimes wore small charms, earrings, or necklaces called amulets. They thought these would keep them safe from evil spirits, sickness, or accident. These small ornaments were often gems, stones, or clay figures of gods. Sometimes they had on them words which were to keep the wearer from evil. (Exod. 32:2ff; Isa. 3:16–26.)

15

Ananias

The Christians in the early church at Jerusalem had begun selling their land and giving the money for the Lord's work. Ananias and his wife, Sapphira, decided they would also do this, but lie about the amount they were giving. Peter knew about this lie. When he scolded Ananias, then Sapphira, each fell dead at his feet. (Acts 5:1–11.)

Anathoth

About three miles, or five kilometers, north of Jerusalem was a little town called Anathoth. Here Jeremiah purchased a field as God commanded. It was not only Jeremiah's home, but also the home of two of David's great soldiers, Abiezer and Jehu, and the home of Abiathar the priest. (II Sam. 23:27; I Kings 2:26; I Chron. 12:3; Jer. 1:1; 32:7ff.)

Anchors

Bible-time ships often carried several anchors, used to slow the movement of the ship or to keep it from moving. Early anchors were large stones with holes in them or fitted with handles through which the anchor rope was passed. At first, iron anchors were T-shaped. Later the arms of the T were bent forward to grip the ocean floor better. (Acts 27:29, 30, 40.)

Andrew

At first Andrew was a disciple of John the Baptist. But John pointed him to Jesus, the Lamb of God who would take away the sins of the world. As soon as Andrew decided to follow Jesus, he brought his brother Simon Peter to Jesus also. Andrew came from Bethsaida in Galilee, but later lived with Peter at Capernaum, where the two fishermen were partners with James and John. (John 1:40.)

16

Angels

There are countless angels that move about from heaven to earth, serving as God's special messengers. God created angels higher than men to worship Him, help Him, and take care of His people. They never marry and never die for they are spirits without bodies like ours. Angels spoke to the shepherds at Bethlehem, to Philip at Samaria, and to Paul at Corinth. (Ps. 91:11; Dan. 3:28; II Pet. 2:4; Jude 6.)

Anna

Although the prophetess Anna was 84 years old, she faithfully attended the morning and evening services in the Temple. Like Simeon, she waited eagerly for the coming of the Messiah, God's Son. When Mary and Joseph brought the Baby Jesus to the Temple, Anna and Simeon recognized that He was the Messiah for whom they had waited. (Luke 2:36–38.)

Annas

Annas was appointed High Priest in 6 A.D. by Quirinius, the same man who was governor of Syria when Jesus was born. Nine years later, the Romans forced him from office, but the Jews considered a High Priest to be one for life. Five of Annas' sons and his son-in-law Caiaphas all became High Priests. Annas asked the first question when Jesus was arrested. (Luke 3:2; John 18:13.)

Annunciation

When some great event is announced, it is an annunciation. The Annunciation is the term usually given to the greatest announcement ever made, that the Savior would be born. The Angel Gabriel made this announcement to the Virgin Mary while she was living in Nazareth, telling her that she would give birth to the Savior. (Luke 1:26–38.)

Anointing

Anointing meant to pour oil, usually made from olives, on the skin. The sick or wounded were anointed with oil for healing and the dead were anointed for burial. The Epistle of James speaks of the elders of the church anointing the sick. Priests and kings were dedicated to God's service by anointing them with oil. (I Sam. 9:16; II Sam. 2:7; Luke 10:34; James 5:14.)

Antioch Near Pisidia

Like Antioch in Syria, this Antioch was founded by Seleucus and named in honor of his father, Antiochus. Pisidian Antioch, as it is sometimes called, was in Phrygia, part of Galatia. A strong Roman garrison was headquartered there. Paul and Barnabas preached there on their first missionary journey and probably also on their second and third journeys. (Acts 13:14–50; 14:19–24; 16:6.)

Antioch in Syria

Around 300 B.C. Seleucus built at least sixteen cities which he called Antioch to honor his father, Antiochus. Seleucus was one of Alexander's officers who ruled after his death. Antioch in Syria was the most famous city of that name. It was here that the disciples were first called Christians. This Antioch was on the River Orontes at the foot of Mt. Sylphus. (Acts 6:5; 11:19–26.)

Apollos

Like Paul, Apollos was a Jew with great knowledge of the Old Testament, who was also a good speaker. When Apollos visited Ephesus, Priscilla and Aquila helped him come to know Christ and taught him much about the Gospel. Later Apollos became a preacher of the gospel. He and Paul worked in Corinth to build up the church there. (Acts 18:24–28; I Cor. 3:4; 16:12; Titus 3:13.)

Apostle

An apostle is someone sent with a special message. Jesus chose twelve of His disciples to be His special messengers, His apostles, to share the Gospel after He returned to heaven. Matthias was chosen to replace Judas. Later, Paul became an apostle, sent by the risen Christ to take the Gospel to the Gentiles. (Luke 6:13; Acts 1:8; I Cor. 4:9.)

Aquila and Priscilla

When the Emperor Claudius expelled the Jews from Rome in 49 A.D., Aquila and his wife Priscilla settled in Corinth and worked as tentmakers. Paul, also a tentmaker, was drawn to them and lived in their home for a year and a half. They traveled with Paul to Ephesus and remained there. Apollos came to Christ because of their witness. (Acts 18:2, 18, 26; Rom. 16:3; I Cor. 16:19; II Tim. 4:19.)

Appii Forum

On his way to Rome as a prisoner, Paul was met by Roman Christians at the market town of Appii Forum, about 39 miles, or 65 kilometers, south of Rome. The name meant "the market place of Appius." It was built at the end of a canal through the Pontiac marshes. The Latin poet Horace complained that the town was packed with barges and cheating innkeepers. (Acts 28:15.)

Arabia

Kings from Arabia, a peninsula in southwest Asia, brought gold and spices to Solomon. Later, Arabians brought tribute to King Jehoshaphat. When King Jehoram fought the Philistines, the Arabians joined the Philistines to defeat Jehoram. Shortly after Paul came to Christ, he went to Arabia to think and pray. (I Kings 10:15; II Chron. 17:11; 21:16—22: 1; Gal. 1:17.)

Aramaic

Although the Hebrew and Aramaic languages were somewhat alike, they had differences which kept persons who spoke one language from understanding the other. In late Old Testament times, officials used Aramaic. Parts of Jeremiah, Ezra, and Daniel were written in this language of the officials. By New Testament times, most Jews could speak Aramaic.

Ararat

In the northern part of Armenia, now within Turkey, lies a mountainous tableland known as Ararat. On these mountains Noah's ark came to rest after the flood. The sons of Sennacherib fled to this land after murdering their father. Mt. Ararat is the tallest of the mountains, rising to a height of 17,000 feet or 5,100 meters. (Gen. 8:4; Jer. 51:27.)

Araunah

Seventy thousand men died in the great plague that swept across the land, for David had displeased God by counting His people. When the plague ended, David bought a threshing floor and oxen from a Jebusite named Araunah and built an altar on a great rock there. The place later became the site for the Temple in Jerusalem. (II Sam. 24:15–25.)

Archangel

Although the Bible speaks of millions of angels, "ten thousand times ten thousand," and thousands of thousands, it mentions one as the chief of all angels. The chief angel, or archangel, is named Michael. The archangel argued with the devil over the body of Moses, yet never spoke abusive language to him. (Jude 9; Rev. 12:7.)

Archelaus

After Herod the Great died, his son Archelaus ruled in Judea for eight years, from 4 B.C. to 4 A.D. Archelaus had the worst reputation of any of Herod's sons. At last some Jewish leaders went to Rome to warn Augustus that there would be a revolt if Archelaus continued to rule. During the reign of Archelaus, Mary and Joseph returned to Nazareth with Jesus. (Matt. 2:22.)

Areopagus

The city council of Athens met on a rocky hill called the Areopagus. The name meant "the hill of Ares," Greek god of war, although it was sometimes called Mars' Hill. Mars was the Roman god of war. Paul was invited to tell the council about God and His Son, Jesus. But when he told of the resurrection, some laughed and refused to listen. (Acts 17:19, 34.)

Ark, Noah's

The world was so filled with sin that God decided to destroy it. But He was pleased with Noah and his family, for Noah obeyed God and honored Him. God told Noah to make a large boat, called an ark, where his family could live during a great flood that God would send upon the earth. Noah also took animals and birds into the ark to continue life on earth. (Gen. 6:14—8:19.)

Ark of the Covenant

Throughout the long journey from Sinai to the Promised Land, the people of Israel carried a golden box or chest. Inside were the tablets of stone on which God wrote with His finger on Mt. Sinai. The Ark was made of acacia wood and covered with pure gold inside and outside. It was a sign that God was with His people, guiding them at all times. (Exod. 25:1–22; Deut. 10:2–5; Num. 10:33; Josh. 3; 4:7–11.)

Armageddon

The world's last great battle will be fought at Armageddon, the Mount of Megiddo. Many great battles have been fought in this broad plain, the Plain of Esdraelon or Jezreel. Gideon defeated the Midianites here, Deborah and Barak won a great victory here, and Saul died near here, at the Mount of Gilboa, as his forces were defeated by the Philistines. (Judg. 5:19, 20; 6:33; I Sam. 31; Rev. 16:16.)

Armor

Before the days of the Israelite kings, only a few officers could afford armor, the heavy garments worn in battle. It was made only of leather or quilted material. Much of the armor in the time of David and Saul was taken from conquered enemies. When David learned how to make iron from conquered Philistines, metal armor became more common. (I Sam. 13:19–23; 17:38ff.)

Armor-bearer

A general or important warrior usually chose a soldier to carry his armor and stand by him in times of need. In battle the armor-bearer also helped to kill enemies who had been struck down. Saul chose David as his armor-bearer because he was so fond of him. Goliath brought an armor-bearer with him when he fought David in the Valley of Elah. (I Sam. 16:21; 17:41.)

Army

There was no regular army in Israel until Saul formed one when he became king. Every man over 20 years of age, except Levites, could be drafted into the army, to fight for the country as needed. But those who had been married only a short time and those who had recently built a house or planted a vineyard were excused for a while. Each tribe had to provide men during a war. (Num. 1; II Sam. 24:9.)

Arnon

From the mountains of Gilead, the Arnon River rushed down toward the Dead Sea. Its name meant "rushing torrent," for it rushed through a deep gorge of red and yellow sandstone, forming in early times a boundary between the kingdoms of King Sihon of the Amorites and the Moabites. Later it formed the Southern boundary of the territory of the tribe of Reuben. (Num. 21:13; 22:36.)

Arrows

The earliest arrowheads were made of flint or stone. Later, bronze or iron was used. The shaft of an arrow was made from a reed or light wood. Arrows were stored in a quiver, usually on the archer's left side, and were used in very early Bible times. Ishmael was an archer. Jonathan used arrows to warn David that Saul wanted to kill him. (Gen. 21:20; I Sam. 20.)

Artaxerxes

Artaxerxes was the son of Xerxes, Queen Esther's husband. He ruled as king of Persia from 465 to 423 B.C. and decreed that Ezra and the Jews could go back to the Promised Land. His cupbearer was Nehemiah, who tasted the king's wine to be sure it was not poisoned. Artaxerxes gave Nehemiah permission to return to Jerusalem to rebuild the walls of the city. (Ezra 7:1—8:1; Neh. 2:1; 5:14; 13:6.)

Asa

Throughout most of his reign as the third king of Judah, Asa was faithful to God. He destroyed the idols which his grandmother Maacah, Absalom's daughter, had set up. When a vast army from Ethiopia invaded Judah, Asa asked God for help and won a great victory at Mareshah. Asa ruled Judah for 41 years. (I Kings 15:2–22; II Chron. 14:9–15; 15:1–13; 16:1–14.)

23

Asaph

Twelve beautiful psalms were written by Asaph, a Levite musician. He was a good singer and player of cymbals. He was one of the musicians who performed when the Ark was brought to Jerusalem. David put him in charge of the choirs who led the service of praise to God. The sons of Asaph continued to be the leading musicians of the land. (I Chron. 15:16–19; Ps. 50; 73—83.)

Ascension

As Jesus came from heaven to die for our sins and show us the way to God, so He also returned to heaven to sit at God's right hand and act as our Mediator. After promising that He would send the Holy Spirit, Jesus rose from the Mount of Olives while His disciples watched. This return to heaven is called The Ascension. (Mark 16:19; Luke 24:50–52; Acts 1:6–11.)

Asenath

Before the great famine began in Egypt, Pharaoh gave Asenath to Joseph to become his wife. Asenath was the daughter of Potipherah, Priest of On, now known as Heliopolis. Asenath was the mother of Ephraim and Manasseh, heads of the two half-tribes of Israel. (Gen. 41:45–50.)

Ashdod

After the Philistines' victory over Israel at Ebenezer, they captured the Ark of the Covenant and carried it in triumph back to Ashdod. It remained there a short time and was sent to Gath. Ashdod was one of the five principal cities of the Philistines. The others were Gaza, Ashkelon, Gath, and Ekron. Ashdod was a center for the worship of Dagon, a fish god. (Josh. 13:3; I Sam. 5:1–7.)

Asher

"Women will call me happy now," Leah exclaimed when her maid Zilpah gave birth to her second son. Leah claimed the son as her own and named him Asher. This was Jacob's eighth son. Later Asher went with the rest of his family to Egypt, where Joseph cared for him during the great famine. He became the head of one of the twelve tribes of Israel. (Gen. 30:12, 13; Exod. 1:1–4.)

Ashkelon

Overlooking the Mediterranean Sea about 12 miles or 19 kilometers north of Gaza, Ashkelon was one of the five chief cities of the Philistines. One time Samson raided the city and killed thirty Philistines. The city was taken by the tribe of Judah. Herod the Great was born here and later built beautiful courts and colonnades. (Judg. 14:19; II Sam. 1:20; Amos 1:6–8.)

Ashes

As a sign of humiliation and grief or mourning, an Israelite often dressed in coarse sackcloth and sat in ashes. He also sprinkled ashes upon his head and smeared them over his skin. Mordecai, Queen Esther's cousin, put on sackcloth and ashes when his people, the Jews, were condemned by Haman to die. (II Sam. 13:19; Esther 4:1; Job 2:8; Luke 10:13.)

Ashtoreth, Ashtaroth

Ashtoreth, sometimes called Astarte, was the chief Canaanite goddess of love and war and the wife of Baal. After the Israelites came to live in Canaan, they began to turn from God and worship Ashtoreth. When Saul was killed by the Philistines, his armor was placed in the temple of Ashtoreth at Bethshan. Ashtaroth is the plural name. (Judg. 2:13; I Kings 11:5.)

Asia

In the New Testament Asia is not the continent we call by that name today, but a Roman province in the west of Asia Minor. Ephesus, where both John and Paul shared the Gospel, was its capital. The seven churches mentioned in Revelation were in Asia. Paul worked throughout Asia in his missionary journeys, and was almost killed there a number of times. (Acts 18:19ff; Rev. 1:11.)

Ass

A man's wealth was often measured by the number of asses he owned. The ass was the name used for the donkey. It was used for transportation, to carry loads, to pull a plow, and to haul a threshing sled. White asses were used by the rich and by royalty, but even the poor could own the others. Jesus rode on the colt or foal of an ass into Jerusalem. (II Sam. 16:1; John 12:14.)

Assos

On his third missionary journey, Paul walked to Assos to board a ship. From there he sailed to Ephesus and then to Jerusalem. Assos was a seaport of Mysia in Asia Minor, about 20 miles or 33 kilometers south of Troas. Its granite buildings were perched on a high rock with steps leading to the sea. (Acts 20:13, 14.)

Assyria

Northeast of the land of Israel, along the Tigris and Euphrates Rivers, lay the empire of Assyria, sometimes called Asshur or Assur. Assyria waged many battles against Israel and Judah. Because God's people did not trust Him to lead them, they often lost and had to pay tribute to Assyria. God once sent Jonah to Nineveh, Assyria's capital, to preach and the people repented. (II Kings 17; 18.)

Astrologer

Although many ancient people sought their guidance for the future from astrologers, God's people were to seek theirs from Him directly. An astrologer tried to "read" the stars, and from their movements and positions tell what would happen. But a man of God learned the future by prayer and seeking the Lord's will. (Isa. 47:12ff; Dan. 2:10.)

Atad

From Egypt, the funeral procession went across the land carrying the body of Jacob to a threshing floor at Atad. For a week, Jacob's family and their Egyptian friends mourned his death there and then went on to Hebron where they buried him. Atad was east of the Jordan River and north of the Dead Sea. The Canaanites called it Abel-mizraim. (Gen. 50:11.)

Athaliah

Only once did a woman rule over Judah. That woman was the wicked queen Athaliah, daughter of Ahab and Jezebel. She killed her grandsons who were heirs to the throne so that she could rule. But one grandson, Joash, was hidden and later crowned as king. Athaliah was then killed by her own guards. (II Kings 8:18, 25–28; 11:1–20.)

Athens

It was in Athens, chief city of ancient Greece, that Paul discovered a monument to the unknown god. There he preached to the leaders of the city, both in the market place and on Mars' Hill. He told them about God and the Gospel of the Lord Jesus. The men of Athens were anxious to hear new ideas, but most refused to believe. (Acts 17:16–34.)

Atonement

The word may be taken apart for its meaning, at-one-ment, or "making at one." Through atonement, God unites people with Himself. In the Old Testament, the High Priest atoned for the sins of the people through the sin offering. But Christ has atoned for our sins by dying on the cross. As we confess our sins and seek His forgiveness, we may be made one with Him. (Lev. 4:20; Rom. 5:11.)

Augustus Caesar

For four generations the name Gaius Octavius had been in the family. But when the great-uncle of young Gaius Octavius was murdered, the new ruler of the Roman republic changed his name to Augustus Caesar. He took over the power to be emperor, starting the Roman Empire. Augustus gave orders for the census to be taken which sent Mary and Joseph to Bethlehem. (Luke 2:1.)

Avenger

When a man was murdered, the nearest relative became the avenger, hunting for the murderer to take his life. In this way the murderer would be punished. If the murderer could reach a city of refuge, he was safe until a fair trial could be arranged. An avenger also paid back evildoers for other injuries they had done. (Num. 35:11–34; I Thess. 4:6.)

Azariah

At least 22 men of the Old Testament were named Azariah. Some of the notable men of this name included two sons of King Jehoshaphat, a son of King Jehu, a High Priest who rebuked King Uzziah for doing work assigned to a priest, and King Uzziah himself, who had the other name Azariah. (I Chron. 2:38; II Chron. 26:16–20; II Kings 14:21.)

B

Baal

When the people of Israel came into the Promised Land, they found the Canaanites worshiping a god named Baal. Each district had its own Baal, but the chief Baal was a storm-god. On Mt. Carmel, Elijah challenged the prophets of Baal to send fire on an altar. When they failed, God sent fire and proved that He was God, not Baal. (I Kings 16:32; 18:17–40.)

Baanah and Rechab

While Saul's son Ish-bosheth lay on his bed during the mid-day rest, two of his servants, Baanah and Rechab, slipped into his house and murdered him. The two brothers cut off his head and took it to David, thinking that he would reward them for killing the one man who could become king instead of David. But David was not pleased with the murder and had both brothers executed. (II Sam. 4.)

Baasha

For 24 years Baasha ruled as the third king of Israel. But Baasha worshiped golden calves instead of the Lord. To become king he murdered Jeroboam's son Nadab and then killed Jeroboam's other descendants. Baasha carried on a long war with King Asa of Judah. When he died, his son and the other members of his family were murdered. (I Kings 15; 16; II Chron. 16:1–6.)

Babylon

About 50 miles, or 80 kilometers, south of modern Baghdad in Iraq the great city of Babylon once stood. It was a city of huge walls and gates, truly a wonder of the ancient world. The Jews, including Daniel, were carried there during the captivity. There Daniel became influential in the affairs of the land. Nebuchadnezzar was a king of Babylon. (Dan. 1:1; 2:5–49; 4:7–33.)

Bahurim

On the road from Jerusalem to the Jordan River, not far from the Mount of Olives, was a village of Judah named Bahurim. During Absalom's rebellion, two of David's supporters stayed behind to keep in touch with things as they happened. One day they were discovered but hid in a well at Bahurim. Shimei, who cursed David as he escaped, lived at Bahurim. (II Sam. 16:5; 17:18; 19:16; I Kings 2:8.)

Balaam

After their victory over Sihon and Og, the people of Israel pitched their tents in the plains of Moab. Frightened, the king of Moab offered rewards to the Midianite prophet, Balaam, to curse Israel. Instead Balaam blessed Israel. One day as Balaam rode on his donkey, an angel appeared with a sword. The angel warned Balaam to obey God. (Num. 22:2—24:25; 31:8, 16.)

Balak

With the people of Israel camped nearby, Balak, King of Moab, feared that the Israelites they would conquer him as they had done with Og and Sihon. He tried to bribe Balaam to curse Israel, but instead Balaam blessed them because God told him to. Later, through Balaam's advice, he helped lead Israel into idolatry. (Num. 22—24; Judg. 11:25; Mic. 6:5.)

Balance

Ancient balances were used to weigh things. From a center beam, two pans were suspended. Weights were placed in one pan and the goods to be weighed in the other pan. Moses commanded the Israelites to keep accurate weights and measures, but the prophets often denounced cheating merchants who used false weights and balances. (Prov. 16:11; Dan. 5:27.)

Balm

From a bush of Gilead came a sweet-smelling gum or resin called balm. It was prized, but plentiful, and was sent to surrounding lands. Balm was used for healing, cosmetics, and embalming. The Ishmaelite traders who bought Joseph carried balm. Later, when Jacob sent gifts to Joseph, he included balm with honey, spices, myrrh, and nuts. (Gen. 37:25; 43:11; Jer. 8:22; Ezek. 27:17.)

Banner

Lift up the banner! A banner might be lifted to rally troops during a battle or for a religious festival. Sometimes banners were signs in the shapes of animals but always were objects to be lifted high for all to see. The Israelites, the Assyrians, the Egyptians, and other nations used banners. One banner or standard was found in a royal tomb at Ur and is 5,000 years old. (Num. 2:2; Isa. 5:26; 11:10; Jer. 4:21.)

Banquet

Banquets were great dinners held at the religious festivals and on special family occasions such as birthdays, weddings, and funerals. The end of sheepshearing and harvest were celebrated with banquets, as was the arrival of old friends and travelers. Jesus attended a number of feasts or banquets. (Gen. 29:22; Esther 5:4–14; Dan. 5:10; Matt. 22:24; Luke 14:17.)

Baptism

The Scriptures teach that people should turn from their sins, seek forgiveness, and ask God to give them a new life in Christ. When that happens, our sins are "washed away" and we are "cleansed" from them by the blood of Jesus. Baptism is a sign or symbol of this cleansing or washing, showing others of the change that has happened inside our lives. (Matt. 3:16; Acts 2:38.)

Barabbas

Captured by the Romans, the bandit and murderer Barabbas sat in prison awaiting execution. But each year during the Passover the Romans pleased the Jews by releasing one prisoner of their choice. During Jesus' trial, Pilate asked the crowd to choose which prisoner should go free, Jesus the Christ or Jesus Barabbas. The crowd chose Barabbas. (Matt. 27:16ff.)

Barak

For 20 years the Canaanites oppressed Israel, stealing harvest, terrorizing the people, and taking their weapons. Then Deborah, a prophetess, called Barak to lead Israel against Sisera and his forces. God sent a great rain which bogged down the Canaanite chariots. Sisera escaped to the tent of Jael, but when Barak arrived, Jael had already killed Sisera. (Judg. 4.)

Barbarian

To the Greeks, all non-Greek-speaking people were barbarians. They were given this name by the Greeks because foreign languages sounded like "bar-bar-bar." When Paul was shipwrecked on Malta, he was welcomed by the islanders. Because they did not speak Greek, Luke calls them barbarians when he mentions their kindness to Paul and those with him. (Acts 28:2, 4; Rom. 1:14.)

Barnabas

When Paul accepted Christ into his life, the Jerusalem Christians were suspicious. But Barnabas assured them that Paul was a changed man. Barnabas was later sent to Antioch to lead the Christian work there and then joined Paul on his first missionary journey. The Bible describes him as a good man, full of the Holy Spirit and faith. (Acts 4:36ff; 11:22–30; 13:2, 3; 14:14.)

Bartholomew

Imagine Bartholomew's surprise when Jesus told him that he had been sitting under a fig tree earlier! Philip had brought his friend Bartholomew, also known as Nathanael, to Jesus. From now on, he would follow Jesus completely as one of the twelve disciples. Bartholomew came from Cana of Galilee. (Mark 3:18; John 1:45, 46; Acts 1:13.)

Bartimaeus

Beside the road near Jericho sat a blind beggar. He was there when Jesus passed by on His last journey to Jerusalem. As the crowd became excited, blind Bartimaeus asked why and learned that Jesus was near. Bartimaeus called out for Jesus to help him. Although men told him to be quiet, he kept calling until Jesus stopped and healed him. (Luke 18:35–43.)

Baruch

While the prophet Jeremiah dictated God's warnings, his close friend and scribe, Baruch, wrote them on a scroll. Jeremiah then told Baruch to go to the Temple and read the scroll. When King Jehoiakim heard about it, he angrily burned the scroll and tried to arrest Baruch and Jeremiah. But they escaped and put God's warnings on another scroll. (Jer. 36; 43:3–6.)

Barzillai

King David had escaped across the Jordan River, running from his rebellious son Absalom. In need of supplies, David and his forces were met by Barzillai and two other men who brought food, beds, and pottery. Later, after Absalom had died, David returned home. Barzillai crossed the Jordan with him but refused David's invitation to live in the palace. (II Sam. 17:27–29; 19:31–40; I Kings 2:7.)

Bashan

North of Gilead and east of the Jordan River lay a land named Bashan. It was a place of great oaks, grain fields, and cattle. The Israelites defeated Og, the last king of a race of people in this land, called the Rephaim. The territory was then assigned to the half tribe of Manasseh. When Jesus was born, it was part of the kingdom of Herod the Great. (Deut. 3:13; I Kings 4:13; II Kings 10:33.)

Basin

Various kinds of bowls were called basins, but usually the word meant a wide hollow bowl that held water for washing. The great bowl that caught the blood of the sacrifices in the Temple was called a basin. Some basins were bronze and others silver. Hiram made 100 basins of gold to use in Solomon's Temple services. (Exod. 12:21, 22; 24:6; Zech. 9:15; John 13:5.)

Basket

What did the people of Bible times use to carry fruit or bread, cake or meat, or perhaps some clay to make bricks? The answer is baskets, small and large, all sizes and shapes, with or without handles or lids. Baskets were made of leaves, reeds, rushes, ropes, or twigs. When Jesus fed the 5,000, there were twelve baskets of food left. (Gen. 40:17; Deut. 26:2; Matt. 14:20.)

Bathsheba

King David fell in love with the beautiful Bathsheba, but she was already married. So David ordered her husband, Uriah, to a dangerous place in a battle at Rabbah where he would be killed. David married Bathsheba, but God was displeased with David's sin. As punishment, David and Bathsheba's first baby died. Another son, Solomon, became king after David. (II Sam. 11; 12:14ff.)

Battering Ram

Not many gates or walls could stand after repeated pounding by a battering ram. This weapon was a heavy wooden beam, tipped with an iron head that looked like the head of a ram. It was thrust again and again until a gate or wall crumbled. Attackers using the battering ram were protected by wooden shelters or movable high towers. (II Sam. 20:15; Ezek. 4:2; 21:22.)

Beard

Most ancient men, including the Hebrews, wore beards. But Roman and Greek men shaved their faces and Egyptians usually shaved both head and face. Egyptian kings often wore an artificial beard as a mark of royalty. Even Queen Hatshepsut wore such a beard. It was an insult to cut a Hebrew's beard as Hanun did to David's servants. (Lev. 19:27; II Sam. 10:4.)

Beatitudes

"Nine Ways to Be Happy" could be a title for the Beatitudes. Jesus gave these nine rules for happiness to His disciples at the beginning of the Sermon on the Mount. The word "beatitude" means "made happy" or "blessed." They are meant for those who seek happiness in Christian living, even though life on earth may bring trouble and sorrow. (Matt. 5:3–12; Luke 6:20–23.)

Beautiful Gate

One day Peter and John approached the Beautiful Gate of the Temple. There a lame man was begging. Instead of giving the man money, they healed him. The Beautiful Gate was the most beautiful of all Temple gates as well as the largest. It was thickly plated with silver and gold and was so heavy that it took 20 men to move it. (Acts 3:1–7.)

Beeroth

Travelers to and from Jerusalem often stopped for the night at the little village of Beeroth, about nine miles or 15 kilometers north of Jerusalem. True to its name, which means "wells," the village had plenty of water for washing and drinking. What a welcome sight the wells and springs of Beeroth were to weary travelers who had spent the long day on hot dusty roads! (II Sam. 4:2; 23:37.)

Bed

The law forbade an outer garment to be kept as a pledge after sunset because it was the only bed a poor man may have had. Sometimes the poor had a mat or rug for a bed which was laid on the floor near a wall. Rich people had beds on legs and some made their beds of ivory, gold, or silver with expensive coverings or cushions. (Deut. 24:12; Esther 1:6; Prov. 7:16, 17; Amos 6:4.)

Beersheba

The flocks of Abraham, Isaac, and Jacob all watered at the wells of Beersheba, where each patriarch made his home for a while. Beersheba was at the southern end of the land, while Dan was at the northern end. Thus the saying arose "from Dan to Beersheba." Elijah escaped to Beersheba when he ran away from the wicked Queen Jezebel. (Gen. 21:31, 32; 22:19; I Kings 19:3.)

Beggar

There were no beggars during the time of Moses, for the law of Moses had rules about taking care of the poor. Later, it became difficult for the blind, the sick, or the lame to earn a living. If there was no one to care for them, they had to beg for food or money. Beggars sat near the homes of the rich, along the roadside, or by the Temple gates. (Mark 10:46–52; John 9:8, 9; Acts 3:1–11.)

Bellows

When a metalworker wanted more heat in his furnace, he blew air into it from bellows. This made the fire hotter. Bellows were leather bags which a man squeezed by standing on them, one bag under each foot. After each bag was empty, the man pulled it up with a string attached to a pole. This refilled the bag with air. (Jer. 6:29.)

Belial

To call someone a "son of Belial" or "man of Belial" was the same as calling him a fool, a wicked man, or a scoundrel. The word means "worthless," but was also used for Satan. That was about the worst name a Bible-time person could call another. Abigail called her husband Nabal such a name. Paul spoke of those who oppose Christ as Belial. (I Sam. 25:25; II Cor. 6:15.)

Belshazzar

King Belshazzar sat with a thousand guests, eating and drinking from gold and silver vessels. But as the King of Babylon and his guests feasted, they saw a great hand writing on the wall. No one knew what the strange words meant until Daniel told the king that he was "weighed and found wanting" and that God would remove his kingdom. (Daniel 5.)

Benaiah

One snowy day a lion was trapped in a pit. Benaiah jumped into the pit and killed the lion. On another occasion, he killed two great men of Moab. Although he was the son of a priest, Benaiah became a great warrior as captain of King David's bodyguard. Later he replaced Joab as commander-in-chief of the whole army. (II Sam. 23:20; I Kings 1:38, 44; 2:35.)

Benhadad

As many Egyptian kings had the title pharaoh, so many Syrian kings had the title Benhadad, which meant "son of Hadad." These kings were thought to be the descendants of the god of storm and thunder whose name was Hadad. One king by this name attacked Israel and was captured. But Ahab disobeyed God and set him free. (I Kings 20:26ff.)

Benjamin

Traveling to a new home, Jacob's beloved wife Rachel gave birth to Benjamin and then she died. The twelfth and last son of Jacob, Benjamin became the head of one of the twelve tribes of Israel. When Joseph was sold into Egypt, Benjamin became the favorite son. At first Jacob refused to let him go to Egypt for food, fearing that some harm would come to him. (Gen. 35:17ff; 44:18–34.)

Beracah

When Jehoshaphat, King of Judah, faced a huge army of Moabites and Ammonites, he prayed for God to help. God answered that He would win the battle for Jehoshaphat. Then God caused the enemy soldiers to turn and fight one another. Jehoshaphat and all the people praised God for His deliverance. They called the place where this happened Beracah, meaning "blessing." (II Chron. 20:26.)

Berea

Stirred by jealousy, some men of Thessalonica forced Paul and Silas to leave town at night. But the people of Berea, a city in Macedonia, received the two missionaries and their message, and studied the Scriptures daily. Many at Berea believed in Christ. Then troublemakers followed from Thessalonica, forcing Paul to leave Berea while Silas and Timothy stayed behind. (Acts 17:10–14.)

Bernice

When only a girl of 13, Bernice married her uncle, Herod of Chalcis. When he died seven years later, she lived with her brother, Herod Agrippa II, as though he were her husband. Paul defended himself before Festus and Agrippa while Bernice listened. In his defense, Paul tried to persuade his listeners to become Christians. (Acts 25:13, 23; 26:30.)

Bethany

On the eastern slope of the Mount of Olives lay the little village of Bethany, which Jesus visited often. Some call it His Judean home, for He stayed there with Mary and Martha and Lazarus. One day Jesus raised Lazarus from the dead at Bethany. During the last week before His crucifixion, Jesus lived at Bethany with His friends. (Matt. 26:6–13; John 11:18.)

Bethel

In a dream one night, Jacob saw angels going up and down on a ladder reaching to heaven. Jacob named the place Bethel, which means "House of God." When the kingdom divided, Jeroboam set up a temple at Bethel with a golden calf so that the people could worship there instead of Jerusalem. Bethel was about 12 miles or 19 kilometers north of Jerusalem. (Gen. 28: 10–22.)

Bethesda

It was said that the waters of the Pool of Bethesda had special healing powers. Thus, many sick people lay around this pool waiting for an angel to stir the waters. They believed that the first person into the pool after the waters were stirred would be healed. It was here that Jesus healed a man who had been lame for 38 years. (John 5:1–16.)

Bethlehem

Nestled in the hills southwest of Jerusalem, the village of Bethlehem was first known as Ephrath or Ephratah, meaning fruitful. Rachel died near Bethlehem giving birth to Benjamin. There Ruth and Boaz met in the fields which became the shepherd's fields in the time of Jesus. Bethlehem was David's childhood home and Jesus' birthplace. (Ruth 2—4; I Sam. 17:12, 15; Luke 2:1–7.)

Bethphage

On the old road that led east from Jerusalem to Jericho lay a little village called Bethphage. It was on the Mount of Olives, not far from Bethany. The colt that Jesus rode into Jerusalem came from Bethphage. From there Jesus began this ride, often called The Triumphal Entry, when the people of Jerusalem welcomed Him as a king. (Matt. 21:1–20; Mark 11:1–14, 20, 21.)

Bethsaida

On the shore of the Sea of Galilee lay a little fishing village called Bethsaida. Some say there were two different villages in Galilee with that name. Peter, Andrew, and Philip had all lived in Bethsaida at some time. Near there was another village named Capernaum, where Jesus made His home after He left Nazareth. Jesus healed a blind man of Bethsaida. (John 1:44; 12:21.)

Bethshan

When Saul and his three sons were killed in the battle of Gilboa, the Philistines took their bodies to Bethshan and fastened them to the city walls. Saul's armor was hung in the temple of Ashtaroth, a trophy of victory. But brave men of Jabesh-gilead remembered how Saul had once helped them. They rescued the bodies by night and buried them with honor. (I Sam. 31:8–12; II Sam. 21:12–14.)

Bethshemesh

In a great battle with Israel, the Philistines captured the Ark of the Covenant and took it to their land. But it brought trouble to their cities. At last they realized they must send it back to Israel. The Philistines made a new cart for the Ark and hitched two cows to pull it. Then they sent it to Bethshemesh, a town on the northern border of Judah's territory. (I Sam. 6.)

Bezaleel

The Spirit of the Lord gave special skills to Bezaleel to work in wood, metals, and stone for the Tabernacle. He was put in charge of making the Tabernacle. He trained a band of workmen to help, including Aholiab, or Oholiab, who worked with textiles. Bezaleel's grandson, Boaz, was an ancestor of King David. (Exod. 31:2; 35:30.)

Bible

The Bible is God's way of telling men about Himself. It is His Word, speaking to us of the Person of God, His Son Jesus, the Holy Spirit, and God's home in heaven. Its great message is that God loves us and wants to bring us to Himself so that we might live with Him forever. The Bible tells of our sin and need for God and of His salvation which He provides through His Son Jesus Christ. The word Bible means
(Continued on next page)

"the books." It is a collection of books in two parts, called the Old and New Testaments. The Old Testament is God's covenant with His people through Abraham and his family. The New Testament is His covenant with the Christians, or believers, through Jesus Christ. The Old Testament was written over a period of 1,500 years, while the New Testament was written in less than 100 years. The major divisions of the Old Testament are The Pentateuch, the Books of the beginnings and The Law; History, a record of Israel as a nation; Major Prophets; and Minor Prophets. The major divisions of the New Testament are The Gospels, a record of the life and works of the Lord Jesus on earth; The Acts of the Apostles, a record of the work of the Holy Spirit among the people of the early church; and The Epistles, letters which Paul and others wrote.

Bitter Herbs

A salad of bitter herbs was eaten at the Passover meal after the lamb. These herbs included lettuce, endive, parsley, watercress, cucumber, and horseradish. The Passover herbs were easy to prepare quickly and their bitterness reminded the Israelites of the bitter and sorrowful time they spent as slaves in Egypt. (Exod. 12:8; Num. 9:11.)

Birthright

A firstborn son in Bible times was set apart from his younger brothers and his sisters. He inherited twice as much as any other son and usually became head of the family. These privileges were his birthright, what he was to receive because he was born first. Esau son of Isaac, son of Abraham, sold his birthright to his brother Jacob for some pottage. (Gen. 25:27–34; Deut. 21:15–17.)

Blasphemy

The purpose for which God made man was to glorify Him. To insult or dishonor God is to blaspheme Him and was punished with stoning. The one who accused the man threw the first stone. Naboth was accused of blasphemy and stoned. So was Stephen. Jesus was also accused of blasphemy when He said He was God's Son. (I Kings 21:10–13; Matt. 9:3; Acts 6:11.)

Blessing

"The Lord bless you and keep you," a priest pronounced after every morning and evening sacrifice. It was the blessing which the Lord had given for Aaron as High Priest to say to his people. We are also to bless God by praising Him and pleasing Him. Men often blessed their sons by telling of good things to come through God's help. (Gen. 1:28; 49; Num. 6:23–26; Deut. 33; Ps. 33:12; I Cor. 10:16.)

Blood

In the Old Testament the blood of an animal offered for the sins of the people was sprinkled on the altar. This showed that the animal's blood was offered for sin instead of the sinner's life or blood. Jesus gave His blood as a sacrifice for our sins. Thus, God accepts the sacrifice of Jesus instead of ours forgiving the sins of those who believe on Him. (Lev. 1:5; Heb. 9:22, 28.)

Blindness

There were many blind people in Bible times, because they lacked the care and cleanliness we know today. Jesus healed some blind men. But Elisha asked God to strike Syrian soldiers with blindness when they came against Israel. It was against the law to put a stumbling block before a blind person or to cause a blind person to wander out of the way. (Lev. 19:14; Deut. 27:18; Acts 9:8.)

Boanerges

When a Samaritan village refused to welcome Jesus as He was going to Jerusalem, James and John wanted to call down fire from heaven and destroy it. The two apostles, sons of Zebedee the fisherman, must have had quite a temper. Jesus gave them the nickname Boanerges, which means "sons of thunder." (Mark 3:17; Luke 9:54–56.)

43

Boaz

When Ruth went into the fields of Boaz, a wealthy man of Bethlehem, he took special care of her. He told the reapers to give her food and drop extra stalks of grain for her to glean, or gather. Ruth and Boaz were distant relatives through Ruth's first husband. Boaz married Ruth and became the great-grandfather of King David. (Ruth 2—4.)

Booth

When the hot sun beat down upon the open fields, people often built booths to shade themselves. Farmers, soldiers, and even the cattle enjoyed the shade of these rough temporary shelters, made of leafy boughs woven together. All Israelite families celebrated the joyful annual Feast of Booths, or Feast of Tabernacles, by living in booths for seven days. (Lev. 23:39–41; Isa. 1:8.)

Bottle

Some bottles were made of glass, especially in Egypt. But most of the bottles in Israel were made from the skins of goats or sheep. The skins were tanned and sewn into shape. Skin bottles often hardened and stretched with age, so Jesus said that people did not usually refill these old skins. Sometimes pottery was also used for bottles. (Luke 5:37, 38.)

Brazen Serpent

Once when the people of Israel grumbled about God and Moses, God sent deadly snakes to punish them. The people begged for help, so God told Moses to make a bronze or brazen serpent and put it on a pole. Whoever looked at it would not die of snakebite. This was a symbol of Jesus "lifted up" on the cross. Those who look to Him will live forever. (Num. 21:4–9; John 3:14–16.)

Bread

Jesus called Himself "the Bread of Life." Bread in Bible times was the most widely used food and perhaps the most important. It was made from the flour of wheat or barley mixed with water and leaven. The leaven was fermented dough which helped the bread to rise. After the dough was kneaded, it was baked over hot stones, a griddle, or in an oven. (Exod. 12; Judg. 8:5; John 6:48.)

Breastplate

The well-equipped soldier wore protective metal armor over his chest. This was called the breastplate or heart protector. Paul told the Ephesians that the breastplate was like righteousness, protecting us from evil attacks of Satan. He also spoke of other pieces of ancient armor, such as shield, helmet, and sword. (Eph. 6:13–17.)

Brick

The cheapest and most common building material in Bible times was the sun-dried brick. Mud was mixed with sand and straw or stubble and then dried under the hot sun. In some places, such as Babylon, bricks were fired in a brick kiln, making them very hard. These lasted much longer than the sun-dried bricks. Hebrew slaves made bricks for Pharaoh in Egypt. (Exod. 5:17–19; Nah. 3:14.)

Bride

On her wedding day, a bride was dressed in beautiful embroidered white robes, complete with veil and jewels. The bridegroom dressed in his best clothes and went with friends and musicians to the bride's house. After he received his bride from her parents, the groom led the wedding procession back to his home. (Gen. 24:65; Judg. 14:1–10; Isa. 61:10.)

Bridle

The part of a harness which went over an animal's head and connected to the bit was called the bridle. With the bridle the driver controlled and guided an ass, donkey, or horse. The Assyrians were fond of decorating the bridles on their animals. Sometimes Assyrians even bridled their prisoners. James says we should bridle our tongues, meaning we should control them. (Ps. 32:9; Isa. 30:28.; James 1:26.)

Burning Bush

While Moses watched Jethro's sheep near Horeb, the mountain of God, he saw a desert bush burning. But the bush never burned up. As Moses stepped closer, God told him he was on holy ground. He told Moses to speak to Pharoah in Egypt to free the Hebrew people. This was God's special call to Moses to be the leader of His people. (Exod. 3:1–6.)

Burnt Offering

A living animal, such as a sheep, goat, bull, pigeon, or dove was brought to the altar. There an Israelite placed his hands on it, a sign that the animal would take the person's place in giving his all. The sacrificial animal was then killed and its flesh burned on the altar. This burnt offering was a symbol of the offering Christ would make on the cross for us. (Lev. 1; I Kings 3:4.)

Bushel

Jesus told His disciples that they must let their light shine for Him in the world. By this He meant that they must let other people know that they are Christians. People light a lamp to put on a lampstand, not under a bushel where the light is hid. The bushel was a container used to measure grain. It held about two gallons. (Matt. 5:15.)

C

Caesar

At first the name Caesar was a family name. Later it became the title for the Roman emperor. Christians today remember Augustus Caesar best, for it was he who ordered the census that sent Mary and Joseph to Bethlehem, where Jesus was born. Paul was judged by Nero, who was a Caesar. (Luke 2:1; 3:1; Acts 11:28; 18:2.)

Caesarea

On the shores of the Mediterranean Sea, south of Mt. Carmel, Herod the Great built a beautiful city with palaces, an amphitheater, and a great temple dedicated to Rome and Caesar. To honor Augustus Caesar, he named the city Caesarea. It became the official residence for the Herods and the Roman governors. (Acts 8:40; 10; 21:8; 23:31—26:32.)

Caesarea Philippi

"Who am I?" Jesus asked Peter. Jesus was with His disciples at Caesarea Philippi, a little village in the foothills of Mt. Hermon, where the Jordan River begins. Philip the tetrarch rebuilt the ancient town of Paneas and named it "the Caesarea of Philip" to honor himself and Augustus Caesar. There Peter answered, "You are God's Son!" (Matt. 16:13–17; Mark 8:27—9:8.)

Caiaphas

"Are you really God's Son?" Caiaphas asked Jesus. Caiaphas, High Priest of Israel, had plotted Jesus' arrest. He had been the son-in-law of Annas, former High Priest, since 18 A.D. He would remain High Priest until 36 A.D. and continue persecuting the Christians as described in the early chapters of Acts. "You have said that I am!" Jesus replied. (Matt. 26:57–68.)

Cain

Cain was violently angry because the Lord had received his brother Abel's offering but not his own. Cain, a farmer, was the oldest son of Adam and Eve. One day when he was alone with his younger brother Abel, Cain killed him. But God punished Cain by driving him from his home. Cain fled to the land of Nod and built a city. (Gen. 4:1–17; Heb. 11:4.)

Calah

The Assyrian king Shalmaneser III marched forth from Calah to attack Syria and Israel. After his victories, he set up a black stone monument in Calah's main square. The city was on the east bank of the Tigris River. Built originally by Nimrod, grandson of Ham, who was Noah's son, and later rebuilt by Assyrians, it is today known as Nimrud. (Gen. 10:6–12.)

Caleb

Of all the twelve spies who visited the Promised Land, only Caleb and Joshua trusted God enough to advise attack. Caleb was 40 years old then. At 85, he was still a mighty warrior and led an attack on Hebron, the Canaanites' greatest fortress, and won. His son-in-law Othniel became Israel's first judge. (Num. 13:6; Josh. 14:6, 7; Judg. 1:12–15, 20.)

Calendar

The ancient Hebrew calendar began the year with autumn. Each new month began when the thin crescent of the new moon was first seen at sunset. The twelve months of the year were alternately 29 and 30 days long. An extra month was included seven years out of every 19. Each new week began with the Sabbath at sundown on Friday. (Exod. 20:8; 23:16.)

Call

When we call upon the Lord, we pray to Him and believe that He will answer us, as He has promised. But the Lord also calls people to do special work for Him. Jesus called some of those who gathered around Him to remain and work with Him as His disciples. He still calls people today to special tasks in His service. (Rom. 10:13; Heb. 5:4.)

Calvary

Just outside the walls of Jerusalem, there was a low hill called Calvary or Golgotha. The name Calvary comes from the Latin word for a skull. Golgotha is the same word in Aramaic. Near the Damascus Gate of Jerusalem, there is still a rocky hill that looks like a skull. Many think this is Calvary. Jesus was crucified on Calvary, giving His life to bring us to God. (Luke 23:33.)

Camel

What strange, humpy animal is called "the ship of the desert?" The camel. No other animal can walk across a hot desert, carrying within itself enough water for several days. Abraham, Jacob, and Job all measured their wealth by the number of camels they owned. Jacob and his family fled from Laban on camels. Eliezer went to Mesopotamia on a camel. (Gen. 24; 31:17; Job 1:3.)

Camel's Hair

Camel's hair was clipped from the animal's neck, back, and hump and woven into a rough but hard-wearing garment. A camel hair cloak lasted a lifetime. It protected the wearer against heat, cold, and rain and could also be used to lie on or propped up as an extra tent. John the Baptist wore a camel-hair garment. (Matt. 3:4; Mark 1:6.)

Canaan, Canaanites

The borders of Canaan stretched from Egypt to Syria and from the Jordan River to the Mediterranean Sea. God made a covenant with Abraham and his people, promising this land to them as an inheritance. Thus, it became known as "The Promised Land." When the people of Israel left Egypt, they set out for Canaan. Later they conquered it under Joshua. (Josh. 3:10; Judg. 1:9, 10.)

Cana

Jesus and several disciples arrived in Cana, a village near Capernaum, during a wedding feast. Mary, Jesus' mother, was already there as a guest, and so Jesus and His friends were invited to join the party. But the extra guests caused a shortage of wine. Mary told Jesus the problem and He performed His first miracle by turning water into wine. (John 2:1–11; 4:36–54; 21:2.)

Candle, Candlestick

A Bible-time candle was not a wax stick like ours, but an oil lamp. Thus, the candlestick was a lampstand which held oil lamps. Beside the Holy Place in the Tabernacle stood a seven-branched candlestick or lampstand. It was made of pure gold. The lamps were lit at the time of the evening sacrifice. (Exod. 25:31–40; I Kings 7:49.)

Capernaum

After the people of Nazareth tried to kill Jesus, He moved to Capernaum, a city on the northwest shore of the Sea of Galilee. There he called Matthew to become a disciple and healed the servant of a Roman centurion. Capernaum remained Jesus' headquarters throughout His earthly ministry. He often visited the synagogue at Capernaum. (Matt. 8:8, 9; 9:9–13; 11:23, 24.)

Cappadocia

On the Day of Pentecost the Holy Spirit came upon the disciples, giving them power to serve Jesus. Many of the Jews who were in Jerusalem on that day came from Cappadocia, a Roman province in Asia Minor, which is Turkey today. The first epistle which Peter wrote was addressed to the believers of the Diaspora, which included Cappadocia. (Acts 2:9; I Pet. 1:1.)

Captivity

A victorious army often took conquered people away from their homes into captivity, frequently to work as slaves. Not only soldiers were taken, but ordinary men and women too. Sometimes this was done to punish a rebellious people. Over a period of years, many Israelites, including Daniel and his friends, were taken into captivity by Assyria and Babylon. (Dan. 1:1–4.)

Caravan

Young Joseph was sold to a caravan of traders headed for Egypt. Later, he helped his father and brothers organize a caravan to bring their families to Egypt. Groups of traders banded together to form a caravan for safety. These traders carried goods for great distances along the caravan routes. Caravan cities such as Damascus, grew rich by supplying the caravans. (Gen. 37:25; 46:1–7.)

Carchemish

On his way to Canaan, Abraham may have stopped at the city of Carchemish. The city was located on the west bank of the Euphrates River overlooking an important ford of the river. King Sargon II of Assyria conquered the city and ended the Hittite empire. Nebuchadnezzar defeated Pharaoh Necho there in 605 B.C. (II Chron. 35:20; Isa. 10:9; Jer. 48:2.)

Carmel

The lovely green slopes of Mt. Carmel were a welcome change from the low flat lands that surrounded it. Here Elijah challenged the priests of Baal and showed that the Lord was the true God. Mt. Carmel is a range of mountains which sticks out of a somewhat straight coastline along the Mediterranean Sea. (I Kings 18; II Kings 2:25; 4:25.)

Carpenter

Most Jewish boys learned a trade, usually the same work as their fathers. Jesus became a carpenter, the same trade as that of His earthly father Joseph. A carpenter made carts, wagons, chairs, beds, tables, doors, and other objects of wood. His tools included a saw, drill, plane, hammer, square, and adze. King David hired foreign carpenters to build his palace. (II Sam. 5:11; Matt. 13:55; Mark 6:3.)

Cassia

Both men and women perfumed their clothes with cassia. In Jerusalem, brides could spend as much as one-tenth of their dowry on this fragrant perfume. The holy oil used in the Tabernacle included some cassia. The perfume was obtained from the inner bark of the fragrant cassia tree, which was similar to the cinnamon tree. (Exod. 30:22–25; Ps. 45:8; Ezek. 27:19.)

Cauda, Clauda

When Paul was on his way to Rome as a prisoner, his ship was caught in a storm. Sailing near the little island of Cauda, the crew found shelter from the storm. Here they prepared the ship for the storm by throwing cargo overboard before they were blown farther to sea. Cauda was about 25 miles, or 42 kilometers, south of Crete. (Acts 27:16.)

Cedars of Lebanon

The great cedar trees from the mountains of Lebanon were an important source of lumber in Bible times. The beautiful red cedar wood was prized for ships, houses, palaces, and temples. David used cedar for his royal house and Solomon included it in his great Temple. The cedars of Lebanon often grew 120 feet, or 36 meters, high. (II Sam. 5:11; I Kings 7:2, 3.)

Cenchrea

On his way to Ephesus from Corinth, Paul stopped at a little town called Cenchrea. There he made a vow and shaved his head as a sign of that vow. Cenchrea was on the sea to the east of Corinth and served as its port. Phoebe, whom Paul mentions in his letter to the Romans, was a member of the Christian church there. (Acts 18:18; Rom. 16:1.)

Censer

In the worship at the Tabernacle or Temple, incense was ignited with live coals from the altar. The coals and the incense were carried in a bronze or gold vessel. It was shaped like a small shovel and was called a censer. Only the High Priest could carry incense into the Holy of Holies on the Day of Atonement. King Uzziah tried, but priests stopped him. (Lev. 10:1; 16:12; II Chron. 4:22.)

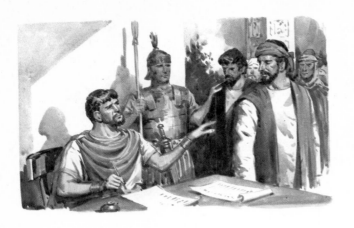

Census

From time to time the Romans took a census in their empire. This was to find out how many people there were in each province so they could be taxed. Sometimes people had to go back to the town where they were born in order to register. Because of a census Joseph and Mary returned to Bethlehem, where Jesus was born. (Num. 1:1–49; II Sam. 24:1–10; Luke 2:1–5.)

Centurion

In the Roman army, a centurion commanded a hundred soldiers. There were 60 centurions in a Roman legion. A centurion's duties included drilling his men, inspecting their armor, food, and dress, and commanding them in camp and in battle. Five centurions are mentioned in the New Testament, all of them kind men. (Matt. 8:5–13; Acts 10; 27:1–43.)

Chaff

At a threshing floor, grain was separated from the useless husks and broken pieces of straw, called chaff. It was done by throwing the mixture into the air. The chaff blew aside, leaving the grain in a heap on the ground. This was called winnowing. Chaff was usually burned to keep it from blowing back into the grain. Chaff was also a symbol for godless people. (Isa. 17:13; Luke 3:17.)

Chains

Romans sometimes bound a prisoner to his guard with a chain. Paul was bound with chains at least twice. Peter was bound to his guards in prison. But chains were also used as ornaments. When Joseph was governor of Egypt, he wore a golden chain around his neck. The priests of Israel wore two golden chains. (Gen. 41:42; Exod. 28:14; Acts 12:6, 7; 21:33; 28:20.)

Chamber, Chamberlain

Daniel was in trouble. The Babylonian king had signed an order forbidding special requests from anyone but the king. Thus, praying was outlawed. But Daniel went to his chamber and prayed as usual. A chamber was a private room in the home. In the royal palace, chambers were under the charge of an officer called a chamberlain. (Gen. 43:30; Esther 1:10; Dan. 6:10; Acts 12:20.)

Chariot

Pharaoh, King of Egypt, was pleased that God had told Joseph of a coming famine. So Pharaoh appointed Joseph governor and gave him a chariot. The chariot was a fast two-wheeled cart pulled by two horses. It was used for battle, for transportation, and to carry important people about. Philip talked with an Ethiopian official in a chariot. (Gen. 41:43; Acts 8:28–31.)

Chebar

Many of the Israelites had been brought to Babylon to live in exile. Some set up a community by the banks of the Chebar, a river or canal of Babylon. Ezekiel the prophet lived in this community. While he was by the river, God gave him a number of visions which Ezekiel describes in his book. He prophesied for more than 22 years. (Ezek. 1:1; 3:23; 10:15.)

Chedorlaomer

After serving Chedorlaomer, King of Elam, for twelve years, the people of Sodom and Gomorrah rebelled. But the king led an army against the two cities and took away goods and captives. Among the captives was Lot, Abraham's nephew. Abraham and his men pursued Chedorlaomer, surprised him by night, and defeated him. (Gen. 14:1–17.)

Cherub, Cherubim

As they left the garden of Eden, Adam and Eve looked back to see it guarded by cherubs or cherubim. These were heavenly beings with wings. They appeared part human and part animal. The word cherub is singular; cherubim, cherubs, or cherubims is plural. Cherubim of beaten gold were placed on the mercy seat above the Ark of the Covenant. (Gen. 3:24; Exod. 25:18–22.)

Christian

Believers were first called Christians at Antioch. The name was given to those who believed in Christ as their Savior and Lord, as it is today. Herod Agrippa II told Paul that the apostle was trying to persuade him to become a Christian. In the early church, Christians were also called believers, brethren, disciples, or followers of The Way. (Acts 9:2; 11:26; 26:28.)

Chronicles

Two Old Testament books are named Chronicles. Originally they were one book. They tell of the work of God among His people from the time of King David until the time the Israelites were taken in captivity to Babylon. Much of the material in these two books is also included in the books of Samuel and Kings. (The Books of I and II Chronicles.)

Church

In the New Testament, church means a gathering of Christian people and never refers to a building. Christians met in private houses, for in the early days there were no church buildings. Christians came together as a church to pray, read the Scripture, and to share in breaking bread to remember the death of Jesus. The church was founded by Jesus Himself. (Matt. 16:18; Acts 5:11; 13:1.)

Cinnamon

Solomon cultivated cinnamon trees, which were highly valued for their spice. Cinnamon was used in the holy oil for the Tabernacle, as a perfume on beds, and to flavor food. The best cinnamon comes from the inner bark of the cinnamon tree, a kind of scented laurel that grows to about 20 feet, or six meters, high. (Exod. 30:23; Prov. 7:17.)

Citizenship

Roman citizenship brought certain privileges. A citizen could not be punished without a trial. This happened to Paul and on one occasion he made the magistrates at Philippi apologize for beating him. Citizenship could be bought or it could be given for a special reason. Paul was a citizen because one of his parents was a citizen. (Acts 22:25–29; 23:27.)

City

The difference between a village and a city in the Bible is that a city was fortified with a wall and citadel. If war broke out, villagers took refuge in a city. A city also had the right to conduct its own courts. Trading took place at the city gate, which was shut at sunset and guarded all night. Samson carried away the gate of the city of Gaza. (Lev. 25:29ff; Deut. 3:5; Josh. 2:5, 7; Judg. 16:3.)

City of Refuge

In the days when Israel first settled in Canaan, men were quick to get revenge for a relative who had been killed, even though it may have been an accident. So God told the Israelites to set up six cities of refuge where anyone who killed another person by accident could flee. There he could remain safely until he was given a fair trial. (Num. 35:6–14; Josh. 20:7ff; 21:13.)

Claudius

The Jews of Rome had been causing riots about "Chrestus," the Christians. So by 49 A.D. the Roman Emperor Claudius forced all Jews to leave. Among those who went to Corinth were Priscilla and Aquila, whom Paul led to Christ. Claudius ruled from 41 to 54 A.D. He was the nephew of Tiberius, who ordered the census when Jesus was born. (Acts 11:28; 18:2.)

Clay

One day a blind man begged Jesus to heal him. Jesus spread clay on the man's eyes and told him to wash it off in the Pool of Siloam. When he did, he could see again. Clay, a special dirt mixed with water, was used mostly for bricks. Many cities in Egypt, Babylon, and Assyria were made of clay bricks. Clay was also used to make pottery. (Exod. 5:7–19; Jer. 18:6; John 9:6–15.)

Clay Tablets

Bible-time people did not have paper, as we do today. So they wrote on papyrus, parchment, broken pottery, or clay tablets. These tablets were usually about the size of a box of cough drops. The writing was done by pressing a sharp stick into the clay before it dried. The people did not use the same letters we do today. Many of these clay tablets have been found.

Coat

Other names for a coat in Bible times were a cloak, or mantle, or a robe. It was a large garment which fit over the other clothing. Some coats were made of wool, goat hair, or camel hair. Others were made of linen, velvet, or silk. Often people wrapped themselves in their coats at night to keep warm. Jacob gave Joseph a coat of many colors because he loved him. (Exod. 22:26; I Sam. 2:18, 19.)

Cock Crowing

The Roman night was divided into four parts or "watches." The third of the four, from midnight to three A.M. was called the cock crowing. Roosters, or cocks, were alarm clocks for Bible-time people. Just before His arrest, Jesus warned Peter that by cock crowing he would deny Him. That could have meant the watch of the night or the time an actual rooster crowed. (Matt. 26:34; Mark 13:35.)

Cohort

A Roman legion consisted of 60 groups of 100 men, called centuries, each commanded by a centurion. Ten centuries made a cohort, which was under the orders of a tribune or prefect. The centurion Cornelius, whom Peter visited, belonged to the Italian Cohort serving in Caesarea. When arrested by the Romans, Paul was guarded by a centurion of the Augustan Cohort. (Acts 10:1; 27:1.)

Colossae, Colossians

The Christians in Colossae, who were a mixture of Greeks, Asians, and Jews, were talking about some strange ideas. From his prison in Rome, Paul wrote that they must love Christ and trust God's true wisdom. Philemon and Onesimus belonged to the church at Colossae. Colossae was in present-day Turkey. (The Epistles of Paul to Philemon and the Colossians.)

Comforter

One name for the Holy Spirit is "The Comforter." Jesus called Him that. However, the word does not really mean "to console" us but to come beside us. The Holy Spirit continues on earth the work Christ began, coming beside us to remind us of sin, God's righteousness, and God's judgment. He also leads us into God's truth through His Word. (John 14:16, 26; 16:8–11.)

Coney

It is not unusual to see a coney sitting at the mouth of a cave sunning himself. A coney is a grey-brown animal with a yellowish patch on its back. The coney is similar to a rabbit, but it has short sturdy legs, short ears, and no tail. The coney was listed among the animals that could not be eaten, because although it chewed its cud, it did not have a divided hoof. (Lev. 11:5; Deut. 14:7.)

Consecrate

To consecrate means to set apart or dedicate a person or thing to God's service. Aaron and his sons were set apart for God's service in the Tabernacle. The law spoke of setting people apart from unclean things. The word is used only in the Old Testament and in Hebrews. The word is not used in the Bible for Christians set apart for God's service. (Exod. 28:41; Lev. 8:33.)

Confession

Two men went into the Temple to pray. One boasted that he was not a sinner, while the other confessed that he was and asked God for forgiveness. To confess sin is to admit to God or others that we have sinned. To ask forgiveness is to ask God and others not to hold those sins against us. To confess Christ is to tell others we belong to Him. (Matt. 3:1–6; Luke 12:8; I John 1:9.)

Convert, Conversion

The person who repents from sin and turns to God is converted. The Christian has turned to God by recognizing his sin, turning from it, and trusting Christ as Lord and Savior. The Bible says that such a person is "a new creature: old things are passed away; behold, all things are become new." He has been converted. (Acts 3:19; II Cor. 5:17; James 5:20.)

Copper

During the time of Solomon, copper was used for vessels, cups, knives, and weapons. Bronze was a mixture of copper and other metals. In the wilderness, the Israelites looked at a bronze snake to show obedience to God. Solomon had copper mines and sold some of his copper to other countries. Copper was used in building the Temple. (Ezra 8:27; I Tim. 4:14.)

Corinth, Corinthians

In the time of Paul the city of Corinth was a beautiful seaport of Greece. But the people of Corinth loved a rich and easy way of life, spiced with many pleasures that were not considered good for Christians. Paul wrote two letters to the Corinthian Christians, reminding them that although they were Corinthians, they were Christians most of all. (The Epistles of Paul to the Corinthians.)

Cormorant

"You shall not eat of them for they are unclean." The Lord made a list of birds and animals which the Israelites were not permitted to eat. Among them was the cormorant, a large, glossy, black bird which lives on fish and builds its nest of seaweed. Young cormorants can be trained by fishermen to catch fish. (Lev. 11:17; Deut. 14:17.)

Cornelius

One day an angel spoke to a Roman centurion named Cornelius and told him to send for Peter. Cornelius was a good man, prayed to God, and gave his money to the poor. When Peter arrived, he talked with Cornelius, about Jesus. Cornelius, who was part of the Italian Cohort stationed at Caesarea, was the first Gentile to become a Christian. (Acts 10.)

Cornerstone

The most important stone in a building or city wall was called the cornerstone. It was laid at a corner and was usually known for its strength. The cornerstone helped to keep the surrounding walls level and straight. The rest of the building or walls depended on the cornerstone. Paul calls Jesus the Chief Cornerstone of His church. (Matt. 21:42; Acts 4:11; Eph. 2:20.)

Cos, Coos

After leaving the Ephesian elders, Paul began his last journey to Jerusalem. The first island he passed on his voyage was Cos. This was a massive and mountainous island off the southwest coast of Asia Minor. A famous medical school had been founded there by Hippocrates 500 years earlier. Cos was also noted for its fine weaving. (Acts 21:1.)

Cosmetics

When Jezebel heard that Jehu was coming to Jezreel, "she painted her face." Jezebel's cosmetics were not new, for Egyptian ladies had been using them for centuries. They stored their cosmetics in stone jars or boxes and used cosmetic spoons shaped like lotuses, ducks, or girls. Eye paint was put on with small bronze sticks. (II Kings 9:30; Ezek. 23:40.)

Couch

Most homes in Bible times had very little furniture. Only the well-to-do people had couches. Amos the Prophet complained about the rich who lived in luxury, lying on couches of ivory, while poor people could scarcely find enough to eat. People reclined on couches to eat or used them as beds. The mat on which a poor person slept was also called a couch. (Amos 6:4; Luke 5:24.)

Council

The Jews who ruled over their people met together as a group called the Council. In New Testament times, the Council was the Sanhedrin, a group of 70 rulers plus the High Priest. The Council members included elders, scribes, lawyers, and priests. When they were in session, the members sat in a half circle. Both Jesus and Stephen were tried before the Council. (Matt. 26:57–68; Acts 6:15—7:60.)

Courtyard

Houses in Bible times were often built around an open space called a courtyard. It frequently contained a well, or a cistern, which collected rainwater. In palaces and large houses the courtyard was paved with stone or even marble. A courtyard was often decorated with pots of flowers, fruit trees, or grapevines.

Covenant

"With thee will I establish my covenant." Thus God made His first covenant with a man. A covenant was an agreement. God agreed to be with Abraham and his family as long as they would serve and worship Him. The Old Testament is God's covenant with His people through Abraham. The New Testament is God's covenant with His people through Jesus Christ. (Gen. 6:18; Heb. 8:6–13.)

Covetousness

When Jericho fell, Achan desired some of the gold and silver and beautiful cloaks which the Israelites had captured. But his desire, or covetousness, led him to steal something God had forbidden. When he was discovered, he was stoned to death. Covetousness is a selfish desire for something that belongs to another person. (Exod. 20:17; Josh 7.)

Creation

In the beginning, God made the universe and all that is in it. He created it all from nothing. To care for His creation, God made a man and a woman and placed them in charge of it. After God finished His work of creation, He rested, a pattern He gave for us to follow. The Bible reminds us that God constantly cares for His creation and His creatures, including us, His people. (Gen. 1—2.)

Crete

On the way to Rome, Paul's ship stopped at Fair Havens on the southern coast of Crete. Later Paul visited Crete with Titus and left Titus in charge of the Christian work there. Crete is an island of mountains and fruitful valleys in the Mediterranean Sea south of Greece. It is about 155 miles or 250 kilometers long. (Acts 27:7–13; Titus 1:12.)

Cross

Crucifixion was one of the cruelest forms of Roman punishment. The victim was tied or nailed to an upright wooden beam called a cross and left to die in agony. "The Cross" has come to mean redemption or salvation. Through His death on a wooden cross, Jesus made it possible for us to be redeemed from our sins and to be saved. (Matt. 27:32; Mark 15:30; Gal. 6:14; Col. 1:20.)

Crown

There has always been great honor in wearing a crown on one's head. Usually a crown was for kings, high priests, or those who won a great battle or race. But Jesus was crowned with a circle of thorns to mock Him for his claim to be a king. Paul and John spoke of a crown as a symbol of victory in Christian living. (Matt. 27:29; II Tim. 4:8; Rev. 2:10.)

Crown of Thorns

Before they crucified Him, the Roman soldiers placed a crown of thorns on Jesus' head. Then they dressed Him in a royal robe and put a reed in His hand as a royal scepter. The soldiers pretended to pay homage to Jesus by kneeling down in front of Him and calling out, "Hail, King of the Jews!" (Matt. 27:29; Mark 15:17; John 19:2.)

Crucifixion

Rome's worst death penalty for slaves and criminals was crucifixion. A prisoner was nailed or tied to a cross to die slowly and cruelly. Some of the kind women of Jerusalem gave a drugged wine to crucified men to ease their pain, but Jesus refused to accept it when He was crucified. The Emperor Constantine finally abolished crucifixion in the Roman Empire in 315 A.D. (Luke 23:33; John 19:32.)

Cruse

"Take a cruse of honey," King Jeroboam told his wife. So the queen took a little jug of honey and some bread and went to see the prophet Abijah. The cruse was a little clay or stone jug about four or five inches tall. It was used for water, honey, or olive oil. Saul carried a cruse of water when he chased David in the wilderness of Ziph. (I Sam. 26:12; I Kings 14:3; 17:12.)

Cubit

Merchants in Bible times did not carry such things as tape measures, yardsticks, or rulers. Instead, they often measured by cubits, the distance from a man's elbow to the tip of his second finger. It was about 17 inches or 45 centimeters. Architects, builders, and engineers used a more accurate cubit, about 21 inches or 53.4 centimeters. (Gen. 6:15; Exod. 25:23; Matt. 6:27.)

Cucumber

"We remember the fish, which we did eat in Egypt freely; the cucumbers, and the melons" the people of Israel complained to Moses. Later, when Israel settled in Canaan, the people grew fields of cucumbers. But they had to build booths and guard the fields constantly because jackals also loved these green vegetables. Jeremiah spoke of scarecrows used as guards in the fields. (Num. 11:5; Isa. 1:8.)

Cup

"And all king Solomon's drinking vessels were of gold." The king could afford gold cups, but most people in the Bible drank from cups of pottery, copper, or bronze. Joseph had a silver cup from which he drank as Egypt's governor. Cups had various shapes and often had some design on them. At the Last Supper, Jesus and His disciples drank together from a cup. (Gen. 44:2; I Kings 10:21; Matt. 26:27.)

Cupbearer

How could a king know that his wine was not poisoned? By having his royal cupbearer sip some first. The cupbearer not only served his king, but protected him as well. He spent much time with the king and so he was often asked for advice. The cupbearer was a man of great influence, an important and highly trusted official. (Gen. 40:1ff; I Kings 10:5; Neh. 1:11.)

Curse

"I set before you this day a blessing and a curse," Moses told his people. The blessing would come by obeying God's commandments. The curse would come by disobeying them. A curse was some harm or punishment. Through His prophets, God warned His people that sin would bring a curse upon them. (Deut. 11:26–28; Acts 23:12; Gal. 3:13.)

Curtain

In the Temple between the Holy Place and the Holy of Holies, there was a great curtain called the veil. This curtain told the people that they could not come to God directly, but only through a priest and the sacrifices. But when Jesus died, the great curtain tore from top to bottom, telling the people they could now come to God through Jesus. (Mark 15:38; Luke 23:45; Heb. 6:19.)

Cymbals

"Praise him upon the loud cymbals: praise him upon the high-sounding cymbals," the Psalmist wrote. Musicians used cymbals in the services of the Tabernacle and Temple to praise God. One kind of cymbals looked like shallow plates, another looked like cups. Cymbals were struck together to make a musical sound. (I Chron. 13:8; Ps. 150:5.)

Cyprus

The first stop on Paul's first missionary journey was a beautiful island about 60 miles, or 96 kilometers, west of Antioch in the Mediterranean Sea. Barnabas had been born there and so he was returning to his homeland. The island, about 140 miles, or 225 kilometers long, was considered a choice post by the Roman officials. (Acts 13:4; 21:3.)

Cyrus

One night while the leaders of Babylon drank at a great party, a hand wrote on a wall. Daniel told the meaning of the writing, saying that Babylon would be captured. That night the army of Cyrus, King of Persia, captured Babylon. Cyrus let foreign captives go home, including many of the people of Israel. (II Chron. 36:22, 23; Ezra 1:1–6.)

D

Dagon

The Philistine god Dagon was like a mermaid, but he was half man and half fish. The Philistines built several temples for Dagon and put statues of the god in them. They brought the Ark of God which they had captured from Israel, into the temple at Gaza. But the statue of Dagon fell down before the Ark and broke. (Judg. 16:23–30; I Sam. 5:2–7; I Chron. 10:10.)

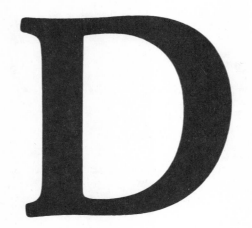

Damascus

On the way to Damascus, Saul was struck to the ground and blinded. Jesus talked with Saul and he was converted. Later Saul escaped from enemies in Damascus when friends let him over the wall in a basket. Damascus is the oldest city in the world that has always had people living in it. Abraham probably came through Damascus on his way to the Promised Land. (Gen. 15:2; Acts 9:3.)

Dan

"From Dan to Beersheba" was an old saying. It meant, "from the farthest north to the farthest south" in Israel. At first the city of Dan was called Leshem, but it was captured by the people of Dan for a home because the land given to them at first was too small. Dan was one of the 12 tribes of Israel. (Josh. 19:47; Judg. 18; I Sam. 3:20.)

Daniel

When Nebuchadnezzar took the Jews to Babylon, some of the younger men were trained for royal service. Daniel was one of these young Jewish men. His devotion to God set him apart. Even in the face of death, Daniel prayed daily to God and was therefore put into a den of lions. In Daniel's book, there are prophecies of the coming of Christ. (The Book of Daniel.)

Darius

At least two rulers of Bible times were named Darius. Darius the Mede captured Babylon and appointed Daniel one of the three presidents. He ruled the area under Cyrus. Later, Darius the Great, or Darius I, learned that the Jews had been mistreated and gave permission for them to continue rebuilding Jerusalem. (Ezra 6:1–15; Dan. 5:31.)

David

"The Spirit of the Lord came upon David from that day forward." When Samuel obeyed God and anointed David, the Lord was with the young shepherd boy. David became the greatest king of all Israel, a writer of psalms, a great warrior who killed Goliath, and a wise ruler. Jesus' human family descended from David. (I Sam. 16:13; II Sam. 5:1–10.)

Day's Journey

How far was a day's journey? It was the distance a traveler went in one day. But how far was that? It all depended on the type of transportation and the load that was carried. Couriers on horseback rode about 50 miles or 80 kilometers. Caravans could only travel about 19 miles or 30 kilometers in a day. (Num. 11:31; Luke 2:44.)

Deacon

The word *deacon* in Greek means someone who serves or ministers to the needs of others. When the apostles found that preaching and praying took too much of their time, they appointed seven disciples to look after the needs of poor Christians. These men became known as deacons of the church. Stephen, the first martyr, was one of them. (I Tim. 3:8–13; Phil. 1:1.)

Dead Sea

The lowest place on earth is a sea of water filled with salt and minerals. The Dead Sea, also called The Salt Sea, East Sea, or Sea of the Arabah, is 1,290 feet or 394 meters below sea level. The Jordan River flows into the sea, but there is no escape for the water. It evaporates leaving the salt and minerals behind. (Gen. 14:3; Deut. 3:17; Joel 2:20.)

Debir

What was it worth to capture a city? Caleb promised his daughter Achsah in marriage to anyone who would capture Debir, also known as Kirjath-sepher. The name meant "town of books" or "town of scribes," because it was a center of culture for the Canaanites. Othniel, Caleb's nephew, captured Debir and married Achsah. It became one of the cities of the Levites. (Josh. 15:15–17; 21:13–15.)

Deborah

Long before the kings ruled Israel, the land was governed by a wise woman named Deborah. Israel at that time was under the power of the Canaanites, who made life miserable for Deborah's people. But under her leadership, the army of Israel won a great victory. Deborah's victory song is a great chapter in the Book of Judges. (Judg. 4 and 5.)

Decapolis

"And he departed, and began to publish in Decapolis how great things Jesus had done for him." Decapolis was also known as "Ten Towns," a league of ten cities southeast of the Sea of Galilee. Jesus healed a demon-possessed man there sending the demons into a herd of pigs which drowned. The Decapolis was established shortly before the time of Christ. (Matt. 4:25; Mark 5:20; 7:31.)

Dedication

Many things were dedicated to God, that is, set apart for God's use. Temples, houses, children, and even loot from a battle were all dedicated to God. The Jews rededicated the Temple after it was defiled by Antiochus Epiphanes when he offered pagan sacrifices in it. Each year afterward the Feast of Dedication celebrated the event with music and lighting. (Deut. 20:5; John 10:22ff.)

Delilah

In the days of the judges, Samson was the strongest man alive. His enemies, the Philistines, wanted to learn why so that they could conquer him. When they found that he was in love with Delilah, a Philistine woman, they paid her to learn his secret. While he slept, they cut his hair which took away his strength. Then Samson was blinded and made a slave. (Judg. 16:15–22.)

Demas

"Demas hath forsaken me," Paul sadly wrote to Timothy from his prison in Rome. Paul often mentions friends in his letters. Once he had spoken of Demas as "my fellow worker," but something changed. Perhaps Demas grew tired of the difficult life surrounding Paul's ministry and longed to go back to the life he had enjoyed before. (Philem. 24; II Tim. 4:10.)

Demetrius

The silversmiths of Ephesus stirred up a riot. Paul had preached to the people of Ephesus, saying the little silver gods they made were not gods at all. "Our craft is in danger," Demetrius told his fellow silversmiths. If people believed Paul, they would stop buying the idols. But the Town Clerk quieted the riot and sent everyone home. (Acts 19:23–41.)

Denarius

Jesus held the coin in his hand and looked at it carefully. "Whose picture is on this coin?" He asked. The "penny" which He held was actually a denarius, a Roman silver coin with the emperor's picture on it. The denarius was pay for a day's work of a soldier or laborer, although it was worth only 16 cents in today's money. (Matt. 22:19; Luke 10:35.)

Demons

"Let us alone!" the demons cried out to Jesus. But Jesus commanded them to leave the man in whom they lived and they did. Jesus commanded demons to leave other men too. They recognized Him and knew Him by name. Jesus knew them too and knew that they were evil spirits. Demons usually hurt the people in whom they lived. (Matt. 8:16; Mark 1:24; Luke 8:26–36.)

Derbe

Paul had friends in many cities across the ancient world. One of his friends, Gaius, was from Derbe. Paul and Barnabas visited Derbe when they went across Asia Minor on their missionary journeys. Paul first visited Derbe after the people of Lystra stoned him. The city was part of the Roman province of Galatia. (Acts 14:20; 16:1.)

Deuteronomy

Looking across the Jordan Valley, Moses saw the Promised Land, a land he could not enter, although he had struggled for forty years to take his people there. The Book of Deuteronomy, the last of the five books of Moses in the Old Testament, records the final part of the journey through the wilderness as well as the law, God's rules for living. (The Book of Deuteronomy.)

Diana

"Great is Diana of the Ephesians!" the people of Ephesus cried out. Demetrius the silversmith had stirred up a riot against Paul. Paul had suggested that the people should worship God instead of the goddess Diana and her little silver statues. The silversmiths were angry, for this would ruin their business. Diana's temple at Ephesus was one of the most beautiful in the world. (Acts 19:28.)

Devil

The devil is another name for the evil person known as Satan. This person has great power in the world and is called "the prince of the power of the air." He tried once to tempt Jesus to sin so he could keep Jesus from doing the work God sent Him to do. The devil also tempts us to turn away from God and to sin. (Matt. 4:1–11; II Cor. 4:4.)

Dibon

"Let us pass through your country to the Promised Land," the people of Israel asked. King Sihon answered by attacking them. But God was with Israel and Sihon was defeated. Among the cities which they captured was Dibon. Many years later the King of Moab took it from Israel and told of his victory on a stone now known as the Moabite Stone. (Num. 21:21–31; II Kings 1:1; 3:4, 5.)

73

Dinah

While living with her father and mother, Jacob and Leah, near the city of Shechem, Dinah went to visit some local women. But the prince, who was also named Shechem, saw Dinah and fell in love with her. When he tried to force her to become his wife, Dinah's brothers became angry and killed Shechem and many of his people. (Gen. 30:21; 34.)

Disciple

"The disciples went and did as Jesus commanded them." There were many disciples in the ancient world, learning from and pleasing a master. Jesus had many disciples to do His work, but twelve were set apart for special work and called apostles. A disciple was a learner or follower. Those who follow Jesus today and learn from Him are also His disciples. (Matt. 5:1; John 13:35.)

Doctor, Physician

In the Bible the word *doctor* usually means a teacher. At that time medical doctors were called physicians. In his letter to the Colossians, Paul writes warmly of Luke as "the beloved physician." Jewish rabbis had a rule that each town must have a physician. One Temple official was a physician who cared for the priests. (Luke 2:46; 5:17; Acts 5:34.)

Doeg

When David was fleeing from King Saul, he received food and a sword from Ahimelech, one of the priests of Nob. Doeg the Edomite, one of Saul's servants, saw David and reported to Saul what had happened. Saul ordered the death of all the priests of Nob and their families. When Saul's men refused, Doeg seized his sword and killed 85 priests and their families. (I Sam. 21:1–9; 22:11–23.)

Dog

The Bible mentions dogs about 40 times, but not as pets. They were half-wild, half-starved, vicious animals. At night dogs prowled the streets in bands, devouring the garbage which had been thrown from houses. When dogs licked the sores of Lazarus at the rich man's gate, it only made the poor man's misery worse. (Matt. 15:21–28; Luke 16:21.)

Dorcas

No one in all of Joppa was loved more than Dorcas. That is because she was always on the run to help others. She was "full of good works" until the day she died. Then Peter brought Dorcas, whose other name was Tabitha, back to life again. Christians will always remember Dorcas as a woman who showed her love to God by doing good things for His people. (Acts 9:36–42.)

Dothan

Almost a thousand years after Joseph was sold as a slave at Dothan, Elisha moved there. God revealed the secret movements of the Syrians to Elisha, who reported them to his king. When the King of Syria learned this, he sent an army to capture Elisha. But Elisha struck them blind, led them to Israel's king, and then sent them home in peace. (Gen. 37:17; II Kings 6:8–23.)

Dove

Noah chose a dove to show him when the waters of the flood were gone. Three times he sent the dove out. When it did not return on the third trip, Noah realized that the waters were gone and it was time to leave the ark. At Jesus' baptism, the Holy Spirit came upon Him in the form of a dove. The dove and pigeon were probably the same bird in Bible times. (Gen. 8:8, 9; John 1:32.)

Dream

While he slept, young Joseph had a dream. He and his family were all sheaves of grain. But the sheaves of his family bowed before him. His parents were annoyed with the dream. Joseph's brothers were so angry that they sold Joseph as a slave. Later, the brothers did bow before Joseph, governor of Egypt. God spoke to other men of Bible times in dreams, too. (Gen. 20:3; 28:10–17; 37:9–11.)

Drusilla

Drusilla's father was the evil Herod Agrippa I who killed James and threw Peter into prison. When she was only 14 she married a Syrian king, but soon left him to marry the Roman procurator Felix. When Paul was a prisoner, Drusilla heard him speak in court before Felix. Some say that Drusilla often talked with Paul in prison and wanted to spare him. (Acts 24:24–26.)

Dumbness

Zacharias and his wife Elizabeth had grown old without having a child. One day an angel appeared to Zacharias in the Temple and told him that God would give them a son. Zacharias did not believe what the angel said and so he was not able to talk until the child was born. A dumb person is one who is not able to talk. (Luke 1:5–25.)

Dyeing

Colors were not easily found in Bible times. There were no stores with paints and dyes, so dyers had to find dyes for coloring cloth in other places. The murex shellfish gave a purple dye and almond leaves a yellow dye. Red was found in the roots of the madder plant and crimson in the eggs of a tiny insect that lived on oak trees. Pomegranate rind produced indigo. (Acts 16:14.)

E

Eagle

"They shall mount up with wings as eagles," Isaiah wrote. There are several kinds of eagles in Israel. The most common are the imperial and tawny eagles. Some of these birds live to be over 100 years old and are famous for their great size and powerful flight. God reminded the Israelites that He had cared for them as an eagle cares for its young. (Exod. 19:4; Isa. 40:31.)

Earring

In Bible times both men and women wore earrings. Rebekah wore earrings she received from Abraham's servant and Job was given earrings by his friends. Often the rings were made of gold. When the Bible mentions rings, it sometimes refers to nose rings instead of earrings. Egyptian women often wore very large rings of gold in their ears. (Gen. 24:47; 35:4; Exod. 32:2, 3; Job 42:11.)

Earthquake

When Jesus was crucified, the earth shook and the rocks split, for it was a time of great earthquake. There were other times of earthquake mentioned in the Bible, too. Elijah, Amos, and Zechariah all spoke of earthquakes. God used earthquakes in Bible times to show His presence and power. (I Kings 19:11; Amos 1:1; Zech. 14:1–11; Matt. 27:51–53.)

Ebal, Mount

Two mountains guarded the entrance to the valley of Shechem: Mt. Ebal and Mt. Gerizim. When the people of Israel arrived in the Promised Land, Joshua took them to Mt. Ebal. There he built an altar and wrote the words of the law on the stones. Blessings were recited on nearby Mt. Gerizim and curses on Mt. Ebal. Thus Mt. Ebal became known as the Mount of Cursing. (Deut. 27:4–26; Josh. 8:30–35.)

Ebenezer

After winning a great victory over the Philistines, Samuel set up a stone monument which he named Ebenezer. It was erected at the same place where some years before the Philistines had captured the Ark of the Covenant and killed the sons of Eli. Ebenezer, meaning "stone of help," encouraged the Israelites to trust God to help them overcome their enemies. (I Sam. 4:1; 5:1; 7:7–12.)

Ebed-melech

It was a sad day for a man put into an ancient prison, especially if he had no one to help him. Jeremiah's prison was a damp, muddy pit, without food and water. But Jeremiah had a friend named Ebed-melech who was a servant of the king. This friend went to the king and got permission to pull Jeremiah from prison with a rope made of old rags. (Jer. 38:6–13.)

Ecclesiastes

The Old Testament book with this name was written by someone known as The Preacher, or The Teacher. Many believe that the writer was Solomon. The book tells how money, power, possessions, and pleasure do not bring true happiness. It tells how we please God most by loving and serving Him. (The Book of Ecclesiastes.)

Edom

Edom, which means "red," was another name for Esau. He had been a red, hairy baby at birth. As a man, he sold his birthright for a bowl of red pottage, or soup. Later, he moved near Mt. Seir, a land of red rocks and mountains stretching toward the Red Sea. The Edomites refused to let the Israelites go through their land during the Exodus. (Gen. 25:20–34; Num. 20:14–21.)

Ehud

In the days of the Judges, the Moabites oppressed the people of Israel with heavy taxes. It was the Israelite Ehud's job to carry the taxes to Eglon, the Moabite king. On one trip, Ehud pretended to have a secret message for Eglon. Alone with the fat king, Ehud plunged a dagger into Eglon and then hurried home to rally the forces of Israel against Moab. (Judg. 3:15–30.)

Egypt

As a young man, Joseph was sold as a slave into Egypt, a country in the most northeastern part of Africa. But God helped him become governor. Later he brought his entire family there to live. Their descendants became slaves and later Moses led them to the Promised Land. Egypt was also a land of refuge, for here the infant Jesus was safe from Herod the Great. (Gen. 39:1; 41:41; Matt. 2:13–15.)

Ekron

About a thousand years before Christ, the people of Israel were oppressed by the Philistines. One of the five chief cities of the Philistines was Ekron, located near the boundary of Dan and Judah. When the Philistines captured the Ark of God, great trouble came to their cities. So the Philistines sent the Ark back to Israel from Ekron. (I Sam. 6; 7:14.)

Elam

North of Assyria and east of Persia lay a land known as Elam. In the days of Abraham, Elam's king, Chedorlaomer, made war in Canaan, far from his homeland. But Abraham and his forces defeated the king and returned the spoils of battle to the king of Salem. Later, the Elamites sided with Babylon in wars against Assyria, but Assyria defeated them. (Gen. 14; Acts 2:9.)

Eldad and Medad

Moses had summoned the elders of Israel to come to him so they might receive the gift of prophecy. As the elders gathered around the Tabernacle, Eldad and Medad remained in the camp. The elders received the gift of prophecy, but so did Eldad and Medad. Joshua suggested that Moses should stop them from prophesying, but Moses rejoiced that they too were prophets. (Num. 11:24–29.)

Elders

In ancient times the older men of the community, called the Elders, were respected for their wisdom. They often governed the community with authority. In the time of Samuel, the Elders of Israel put pressure on him for a king. This led to Saul becoming the first king. When the scribes and Pharisees turned against Jesus, the Elders joined them. (Exod. 3:16, 17; Num. 11:25; I Sam. 8:4, 5; Matt. 27:12.)

Eleazar

As the people of Israel made their way slowly toward the Promised Land, Moses' brother Aaron ministered as the High Priest. When Aaron died on Mt. Hor, his third son, Eleazar, became the High Priest. Eleazar went into the Promised Land with Joshua and helped him divide the land among the tribes. (Exod. 6:23; Num. 20:28; 34:17.)

Eli

For 40 years Eli was the priest at the Tabernacle in Shiloh. He was there at the time when Hannah prayed for a son and promised that her prayers would be answered. Hannah's young son, Samuel, went to live at the Tabernacle with Eli and help him with God's work there. God chose Samuel to take Eli's place, for Eli's sons were not fit for the job. (I Sam. 1—4.)

Eliakim

When Hezekiah was king of Judah, he put Eliakim in charge of his royal household. The Assyrian king Sennacherib sent a messenger one day to threaten Judah. Eliakim was sent to meet the Assyrian messenger. Eliakim then begged Isaiah to pray for God's help and when he did an angel of God struck 185,000 Assyrians dead. (II Kings 18—19.)

Eliezer

When it came time for Isaac to marry, he did not go out to find his own bride. Instead, his father Abraham sent Eliezer, a trusted servant, to find a bride for Isaac. Eliezer went to Abraham's relatives in Mesopotamia and asked God to guide him to the right girl. When Eliezer met Rebekah, God revealed that this was the right wife for Isaac. (Gen. 24.)

Elihu

When Job was in great suffering, three of his friends came to comfort him. But their long speeches did not help. They said that Job must have done something wrong. Then Elihu spoke up. He had kept quiet because he was much younger than they. Elihu said that Job's troubles were not a punishment, but were sent to strengthen him. (Job 32—36.)

Elijah

It was a time of hunger and drought in Israel. The land was ruled by wicked King Ahab and Queen Jezebel who tried to get Israel to worship the god Baal. But on Mt. Carmel, Elijah, the prophet of God, showed that God could send fire from heaven while Baal could not. Elijah did not die, but was taken to heaven in a fiery chariot. (I Kings 17—19; II Kings 2:1–15.)

Elim

After crossing the Red Sea on the Exodus from Egypt, the Israelites entered the Wilderness of Shur. At Marah, their first campground, they found the water bitter and unfit to drink. Then they moved to their second stop, a lovely oasis called Elim. At Elim there were twelve springs and seventy palm trees. (Exod. 15:27; 16:1; Num. 33:9.)

Elimelech

In the days of the judges, Elimelech of the tribe of Judah and his wife Naomi lived in Bethlehem. But famine swept over the land and Elimelech took his family to Moab in search of food. Later, Elimelech died in Moab, leaving Naomi with her two sons and their wives. The two sons then died and Naomi returned to Judah with Ruth, one of her daughters-in-law. (Ruth 1:2, 3; 2:1, 3.)

Elisha

One day God sent the prophet Elijah to see Elisha, who was plowing with a yoke of oxen. Elijah took off his cloak and put it around Elisha's shoulders. This was a sign that Elisha would join him and some day would carry on his work. Elisha did follow Elijah and became a great prophet when Elijah went to heaven. (I Kings 19:16; II Kings 4:1–7.)

Elizabeth

One day an angel of God announced to Zacharias that he and his wife Elizabeth would have a son, even though they were old. When Elizabeth's cousin Mary visited her, the two talked of the babies God had promised them. Elizabeth's son John grew up, and became known as John the Baptist for he baptized people who repented of their sins. (Luke 1:5–57.)

Elymas

Paul and Barnabas had arrived on Cyprus to tell about Jesus. Sergius Paulus, the Roman proconsul of Cyprus, brought the two before him. But a magician and false prophet named Elymas did not want Sergius Paulus to hear the Gospel and tried to speak against Paul and Barnabas. Paul scolded Elymas and struck him with blindness for a while for trying to stop God's work. (Acts 13:4–12.)

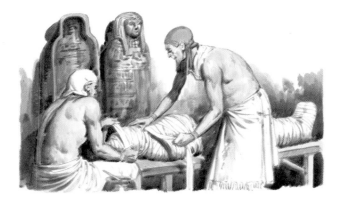

Embalming

When Jacob died in Egypt, his son Joseph ordered his body to be embalmed. This was a secret process that took about 40 days. Egyptians embalmed their dead to preserve them for a future life. But Joseph and Jacob were embalmed so their bodies could be taken to the Promised Land to be buried. Jacob was buried in a cave which Abraham had bought for a burying place. (Gen. 50:2, 3, 26.)

Emerald

One of the stones in the High Priest's breastplate was a rich green gem called the emerald. It was the hardest precious stone except for the diamond. The Hebrew name for the emerald comes from a word which means "to flash forth lightning." Merchants of Tyre and Edom were well known for trading in emeralds. (Exod. 28:18; Ezek. 27:16.)

Emmaus

Two of Jesus' disciples were on their way home to Emmaus, a little village west of Jerusalem. A stranger joined them as they talked sadly of the things that had happened to Jesus. The stranger shamed them for not believing what the Scriptures prophesied about Jesus dying and rising again. When they came to Emmaus, they realized that this stranger was Jesus Himself. (Luke 24:7–35.)

Endor

King Saul was frightened. He would soon go into battle with the Philistines and he wanted to know what would happen. So Saul disguised himself and went to Endor, a town in which lived people of the tribe of Manasseh, to see a witch. As she called back the spirit of Samuel from the dead, Saul learned that he would die in battle the next day. (I Sam. 28:7–25.)

En-gedi

In the barren hills west of the Dead Sea lay a beautiful green oasis named En-gedi with sparkling springs of water and rich plants. Here David hid in caves when Saul searched for him to kill him. En-gedi means "spring of the wild goat" probably because of the wild goats that roamed the hillsides. Its original name was Hazazon-tamar. (I Sam. 23:29; 24:1; II Chron. 20:2.)

Enoch

There was once a man named Enoch who never died. He was also the father of the man who lived longer than any other man on earth. Enoch lived to be 365 years old. But because he had lived so close to God, Enoch was taken into heaven without dying here on earth. Enoch's son Methuselah lived to be 969 years old. (Gen. 5:21, 22; Luke 3:37.)

Epaphras

Paul called him "my fellow slave" and "my fellow prisoner." Epaphras was certainly a faithful helper, for he visited Paul in his Roman prison and brought him the news of the churches. He was a missionary who taught the Christians in the church at Colossae. Because of his report on this church, Paul wrote the letter to the Colossians. (Col. 1:4–8; 4:12.)

Epaphroditus

Paul had many good friends who helped him while in prison at Rome. One of these was Epaphroditus. This friend brought a gift of money from the Christians at Philippi. Epaphroditus saw that Paul needed a friend to help him, so he stayed and worked so hard that he became sick. Later, Paul sent him home with the Epistle to the Philippians. (Phil. 2:25–30.)

Ephah

In one of his visions, the prophet Zechariah tells of an angel lifting the lid from a large vessel that would hold an ephah. Inside this large pot or basket a woman was sitting. An ephah was equal to ten omers. But no one is sure how much the ephah was. Some say it was about a bushel or a little less. Others say it was as much as four bushels. (Exod. 16:36; Zech. 5:6–10.)

Ephesus, Ephesians

For more than 18 months Paul lived at Ephesus, one of the most important cities in Asia Minor. It was a great seaport with many craftsmen. Many Ephesians worshiped the goddess Diana. Later, when Paul was in prison in Rome, he wrote to the Ephesian Christians. In this epistle, he compares the Christians to the parts of our body, working together in unity. (The Epistle of Paul to the Ephesians.)

Ephod

"They shall make the ephod of gold, of blue, and of purple, of scarlet, and fine twined linen, with cunning work." This beautiful garment, worn by the High Priest of early Israel, was something like an apron. It was worn over the robe, held in place by two shoulder straps. Later others including Samuel and David wore ephods. (Exod. 28:6–14, 31–35; 39:22–26.)

Ephphatha

It was spoken only once, but it changed the life of a deaf, speechless man. The poor man was brought to Jesus, who touched the man's tongue, put His fingers in his ears, and spoke the wonderful word *ephphatha,* an Aramaic word which means "be opened." At once the man's ears and tongue were well again. Many people heard about this miracle. (Mark 7:31–35.)

Ephraim

When Jacob was dying in Egypt, his son Joseph brought Ephraim and Manasseh for Jacob's blessing. These were Joseph's two oldest sons. To Joseph's surprise, Jacob blessed Ephraim above his older brother, Manasseh. But Jacob knew that some day Ephraim would be the greater of the two, and head of the half tribe of Israel that had his name. (Gen. 41:50–52; 48:13, 14.)

Ephron

Abraham's wife Sarah had just died and the old man went out to find a suitable cave for her grave. Ephron the Hittite owned a field with just the right cave in it and so Abraham bargained with Ephron and bought the Cave of Machpelah for 400 shekels of silver. Later, Abraham was buried there along with Isaac, Rebekah, Jacob, and Leah. (Gen. 23:8–20; 50:13.)

Epicureans

The Epicureans of Athens were always curious to hear a new speaker and so they listened to Paul. But they paid no attention to his teachings, for they did not believe in God or heaven or a life beyond this one. These people followed a Greek philosopher called Epicurus who taught that the chief purpose in life is pleasure. (Acts 17:16–32.)

Epistle

"When they had gathered the multitude together, they delivered the epistle." Thus Paul and his friends delivered a letter to the church at Antioch. These epistles, or letters, were written on scrolls. They often encouraged others to live for Christ. Many New Testament books are epistles, written by Paul and other early church leaders. (Acts 15:30; I Thess. 5:27.)

Erastus

Three times the name of Erastus is mentioned as a friend of Paul. These may have been three different men or the same man. No one knows for sure. One was the city treasurer of Corinth. He sent greetings to the Christians in Rome when Paul wrote his epistle to them. This man laid a pavement in Corinth at his own expense. (Acts 19:22; Rom. 16:23; II Tim. 4:20.)

Esar-haddon

After the murder of King Sennacherib of Assyria, his son Esar-haddon became king. From 681 to 669 B.C. Esar-haddon ruled over the Assyrian Empire, which included Palestine and Syria. He then conquered Edom, Moab, Ammon, and Egypt. But when his army returned home, Egypt rebelled. Esar-haddon returned to put down the rebellion, but died on the way. (II Kings 19:36–37.)

Esau

Esau was hairy and red when he was born. Although Esau was the firstborn son of Isaac and Rebekah, God had planned that Jacob, Esau's younger twin brother, would receive the birthright. Esau became the father of the Edomites who later troubled Jacob's descendants as they went toward the Promised Land. (Gen. 25:23–25, 30–34; 26:34.)

Esdraelon, Plain Of

South of Nazareth is a great plain shaped like a triangle. It has three names in the Bible—the Plain of Jezreel, the Plain of Esdraelon, and the Plain of Armageddon. The city Megiddo guarded the plain and the trade route that passed through it. The plain is important in a battle, for it controls the movement of troops from north to south. One of the last great battles will be fought here. (Rev. 16:16.)

Eshcol

To the north of Hebron there was a lovely valley of vineyards. Its name Eshcol means "a cluster of grapes." When Moses sent spies to survey the Promised Land, the men brought back from Eshcol a cluster of grapes so large that two men carried it on a pole between them. In spite of the richness of the land, most of the spies were afraid to fight the people who lived there. (Num. 13:23, 24.)

Esther

When King Ahasuerus of Persia looked for a queen, he searched his land for the most beautiful girl of all. That girl was young Esther, a cousin and foster daughter of Mordecai, a Jewish official of the palace. When the evil Haman plotted to kill the Jews, Queen Esther risked her life to save her people. Her story is told in the book bearing her name. (The Book of Esther.)

Ethiopia

Jeremiah was saved from death by an Ethiopian. Philip shared the Gospel with the Ethiopian treasurer. The Ethiopian king Tirhakah was an ally of King Hezekiah. Because of their tall, dark skinned, and handsome appearance, Ethiopians often attended royal courts. In the early Bible history, Ethiopia, which was south of Egypt, was also known as Cush. (Gen. 2:13; Acts 8:26–40.)

Ethiopian Eunuch

As his chariot rumbled across the dusty road from Jerusalem to Gaza, the royal treasurer of Queen Candace of Ethiopia read aloud from a scroll. The Holy Spirit had sent Philip to meet this man and share Christ with him. When Philip explained Isaiah's writings and how they told of the coming Christ, the Ethiopian believed and was baptized. (Acts 8:26–40.)

Eunice

"I call to remembrance," Paul wrote to his young friend Timothy. The young man had much to remember, for he had been blessed with a godly mother and grandmother. Eunice, Timothy's mother, was a Jewish Christian who was married to a Greek. She and Timothy's grandmother, Lois, lived at Lystra. (Acts 16:1; II Tim. 1:5.)

Euodias and Syntyche

In the church at Philippi two women named Euodias and Syntyche were quarreling. It seems that neither would forgive the other and this upset the other Christians in the church. The news of this quarrel reached Paul, far away in prison in Rome. When Paul wrote his epistle to the Philippians, he urged the two women to make up. (Phil. 4:2.)

Euphrates

In Old Testament times, the Euphrates River was so important that it was sometimes called "the river." It is the longest river in western Asia, stretching over 1,200 miles, or 1,900 kilometers, from eastern Turkey to the Persian Gulf. Many ancient cities including Babylon were built on its banks, but the course of the river has now moved to the west. (Gen. 15:18; Josh. 1:4.)

Eve

In God's wonderful plan for the world, He created a man and named him Adam. From one of Adam's ribs, He made a woman and Adam named her Eve. When Satan came to tempt, he began with Eve, who then persuaded Adam to eat forbidden fruit with her. Because they disobeyed God, He drove them both from the Garden of Eden. (Gen. 2:18–25; 3:20–24.)

Eutychus

Late one night Paul preached in a crowded upstairs room in Troas. Eutychus sat on a windowsill, listening to the apostle. But the crowded room and the warmth of the many lamps made Eutychus drowsy and he fell from the window to the ground and died. Paul hurried down to him and restored him to life. Eutychus' name means "fortunate." (Acts 20:7–12.)

Exile

Because Israel and Judah had sinned again and again, God permitted the people to be carried away to foreign lands. The time when they lived away from their homeland was called the Exile. Part of the people were carried away by Assyria and part of them by Babylon. A portion of the tribes of Judah returned to Jerusalem with Ezra and Nehemiah. (II Kings 25:21; Ps. 137:4.)

Exodus

For 400 years the Hebrews had lived in Egypt. But a new Pharaoh did not care that their ancestor Joseph had saved Egypt from starving. He made the Hebrews his slaves. Then God sent Moses to lead his people from their slavery. This going out is called The Exodus, and is described in the book of the Bible by that name. (The Book of Exodus.)

Ezion-geber

From Ezion-geber King Solomon sent a fleet of ships to trade with Ophir and Arabia. The city became a great seaport under Solomon. Nearby he mined copper and iron. Ezion-geber was on the northern tip of the Red Sea, today known as the Gulf of Aqabah. It was also a stopping place for the Israelites on their way to the Promised Land. (Num. 33:35, 36; I Kings 9:26–28.)

Ezekiel

When the Babylonians swept over the land of Judah in 597 B.C. and took the choicest people back to their homeland, a young priest named Ezekiel was taken with them. His message of hope from God helped his people endure their captivity. In his home by the river Chebar, Ezekiel received messages from God, including a vision of a valley of bones. (The Book of Ezekiel.)

Ezra

The Jews who were captives in Babylon were fortunate to have a leader named Ezra who was also an adviser to the king. When a large group of the Jews were permitted to return to their homeland, Ezra led them home and was appointed their governor by King Artaxerxes. Ezra worked hard to teach his people God's Word by reading the Scriptures in public. (The Book of Ezra.)

91

Fair Havens

On its way to Rome, Paul's ship had lingered too long at Fair Havens, a small bay on the southern coast of Crete. But although Paul warned the ship's officers that it was dangerous to sail on, they ignored him because Fair Havens was not a good place to spend the winter. A violent storm blew the ship out to sea and it was wrecked upon an island. (Acts 27:8–12.)

Faith

When God wanted to find how much Abraham trusted Him, He asked Abraham to sacrifice his beloved son Isaac. Today people show their faith or absolute trust in God by believing what He has said in His Word, the Bible. When they do, they accept Him as Lord of their lives. In Hebrews, God lists men and women who lived by faith. (Eph. 2:8; II Tim. 1:5; Heb. 11.)

Fall

In the Garden of Eden there was only one tree that was forbidden. God had told Adam and Eve to eat any fruit in the garden except from this tree. But Satan tempted Eve to eat from the forbidden tree and she persuaded Adam to eat too. Because Adam and Eve did not obey God, they sinned and God made them leave the lovely garden. This first sin is called "The Fall." (Gen. 3.)

Famine

There were many causes of famine, or lack of food, in ancient lands of the Bible. Sometimes the rains were not enough for crops to grow. At other times locusts invaded the land and ate the green crops. Hailstorms and wars destroyed many fields of grain. When famine came, many families moved to other lands, as Naomi's family did. (Gen. 12:10; 41:56; Ruth 1:1.)

Farthing

One of the smallest and least valuable of the Roman coins was a small copper one called the farthing. It took several farthings, perhaps 15 or 20, to equal a denarius, which was a day's wage for a soldier or a laborer. Jesus said that two sparrows were sold for a farthing. The farthing was also called a lepton. (Matt. 10:29; Mark 12:42.)

Fast

Fasting means to do without food for some reason. Usually it was an act of worship to God, often with prayer. Nehemiah fasted to show his grief when Jerusalem was ruined. The Jews fasted on the Day of Atonement as they confessed their sins. Jesus told his followers to fast in secret, for God would see them. They did not need to show others that they were fasting. (Neh. 9:1; Esther 4:3; Matt. 6:16–18.)

Fat

The law of Moses said that the fat of an animal which had been sacrificed was to be given to God by being burned on the altar. This fat was considered to be the richest part of the animal. Thus the Israelites learned that they should offer the best that they had to God. The rest of the animal's flesh was eaten by the priests and the worshipers. (Lev. 7:3, 31.)

Father

The father of a family had the duty of bringing up his children to love and serve God by teaching them God's laws. While a father was alive, all property was held in his name and was under his control. On the father's death, the oldest son inherited a double share of his father's goods and became head of the family. Jesus said believers should call God "our Father." (Exod. 20:12; Matt. 6:9.)

Feasts

Each year the Jews held several special feasts or festivals to celebrate important events, such as the new year, the end of harvest, and the Exodus from Egypt. Feasts were more than times for enjoyment, for many friendships were built as people ate together. Early Christians learned this too as they ate a love feast, remembering what Christ had done for them. (Deut. 16:9–13; I Cor. 11:26, 33.)

Felix

Marcus Antonius Felix was appointed procurator of Judea by the Roman emperor Claudius in 52 A.D. He was a cruel ruler, crushing opponents without mercy. It was said of him that he used the power of a king with the mind of a slave. Felix lived in Caesarea and kept Paul in prison there for two years, hoping for a bribe. (Acts 23:24—25:14.)

Festival

Feasts or festivals were times of rejoicing and thanksgiving. The Jews had several important festivals or feasts including the Feast of Unleavened Bread (Passover), the Feast of Harvest (Pentecost), the Feast of Tabernacles, the weekly Sabbath, the Feast of Trumpets, the Day of Atonement, the Feast of Purim, and the Feast of Dedication. (Lev. 23:34; 25:5–8; Deut. 16:9–13.)

Festus

Porcius Festus succeeded Felix as Roman procurator of Judea in 59 A.D. Felix told Festus about an unusual Jewish prisoner he was leaving behind in prison. Festus investigated Paul's case and soon recognized that Paul was innocent. But he, like Felix, did not free Paul and so Paul claimed his right as a Roman citizen to appeal to Caesar. (Acts 24:27—26:32.)

Fetters

Blind and weak, the great Samson was taken by the Philistines to Gaza and bound in bronze fetters. Fetters were shackles or clamps placed around the arms or legs. Chains were fastened between the fetters to keep the prisoner from moving freely. Jesus healed a demon-possessed man who had been bound in fetters. (Judg. 16:21; Luke 8:29.)

Fever

One Sabbath day Jesus went to Peter's house for a visit. But Peter's mother-in-law was sick with a fever. When Jesus heard about this, He touched her hand and the fever left. The Hebrew word for fever means "a burning heat." Fevers were common in ancient Israel, especially in late summer and early autumn. (Matt. 8:14, 15; Acts 28:8.)

Fiery Furnace

"Our God whom we serve is able to deliver us from the burning fiery furnace." When Daniel's three friends said that, King Nebuchadnezzar had them thrown in. But God protected Shadrach, Meshach, and Abednego, for they had been faithful to Him and had refused to bow to the king's golden statue. They walked unharmed from the fire. (Dan. 3.)

Figs

It was not easy to carry food on a long trip through the hot climate of Bible lands and so dried figs became an important food for people on the move. These fruits were carried on trips, to fields, and stored for use in the home. Fresh figs were also eaten and sometimes used for healing. Isaiah advised Hezekiah to put figs on his boil to help heal it. (I Sam. 30:12; Isa. 38:21.)

Fig Tree

For ten months of the year, a healthy fig tree can delight its owner or hungry travelers. Even the small green winter figs, which may never ripen before they are blown off by the wind, may be a treat to the hungry. One day Jesus looked for figs among the green leaves, but found none. To show the power of God, He commanded the tree to wither and it did. (Mark 11:12–14.)

Fir

"All manner of instruments made of fir wood." When David and his people brought the Ark of God to Jerusalem, they played music on these instruments. The fir was an evergreen tree, found on the hills of Israel and Lebanon. It was used in Solomon's Temple, for the musical instruments, and for decks of ships. (II Sam. 6:5; II Kings 19:23.)

Fire

Fire was used in homes for cooking and heating. Cooking was often done in the open air. Most of the time, the warm air of Bible lands made it unnecessary to heat the home. One night Peter warmed himself by a charcoal fire as he waited for Jesus to be tried. Fire was used also for burnt offerings. God spoke of fire as a symbol of testing and judgment. (Lev. 1:6, 7; I Cor. 3:12–15.)

Firstborn

In a Jewish family the first son to be born belonged especially to the Lord. So did every firstborn animal. When eight days old, the animal was given back to God by being sacrificed. When the son was a month old, five shekels of silver had to be paid to the priests. To convince the Egyptians to free the Hebrew slaves, God took the lives of all Egyptian firstborn children and animals. (Exod. 11:5; Num. 3:13.)

Firstfruits

Each year the first crops of barley, wheat, grapes, and olives to be harvested were offered to God in thanksgiving. So were the first loaves baked from the new corn, and the first fleeces which had been shorn from the flocks. These firstfruits were brought to the Temple and left there for the priests to use. (Exod. 23:19; Lev. 23:17.)

Fish

In all of the Bible, not one fish is named, not even the great fish that swallowed Jonah. The Bible does not call it a whale, as some people think. The Hebrews ate fish when they lived in Egypt. In Israel, the home of Peter, Andrew, James, and John was Bethsaida, which means "house of fish." Jesus fed 5,000 with five loaves and two fish. (Num. 11:5; Jon. 1:17; Matt. 14:17–20.)

Fisherman

Several of Jesus' disciples were fishermen who caught fish from their boats on the Sea of Galilee. Some fishermen used a hook and line or a barbed spear. In deeper water a long net was let out from two boats. The top of the net was held up with floats. The bottom sank with weights. When the two boats came together, the fish were trapped in the net. (Mark 1:16; Luke 5:6.)

Fish Gate

From the seaport of Tyre the fish merchants came, bringing their dried and salted fish to the markets of Jerusalem. But Nehemiah was angry because these merchants sold their fish on the Sabbath day. The Fish Gate was part of the wall of Jerusalem rebuilt by Nehemiah. It probably got its name from the fish market. (Neh. 3:3; 12:39; 13:16.)

Flax

Long before the Promised Land was settled by the Israelites, flax was grown there. Rahab hid two spies under some flax that was drying on her roof. Solomon said that a good wife is one who makes fine linen from flax. Linen clothes, ropes, and lampwicks were made from flax. The stalks were dried and beaten to loosen the fibers for spinning and weaving. (Josh. 2:6; Prov. 31:13.)

Fleece

In the late spring or early summer, as soon as the lambing season was over, the sheep were ready for shearing. This time of sheep shearing was a great day for the shepherd. A freshly sheared coat of wool is called fleece. Gideon used a fleece to learn God's will for him. He asked first that the dew wet only a fleece and not the ground and then only the ground and not the fleece. (Judg. 6:36–40.)

Fleshhook

"All that the fleshhook brought up the priest took for himself." In Samuel's time, a priest got his meat with a fleshhook. When someone boiled meat at a sacrifice, the priest sent a servant with a three-pronged brass hook. The servant plunged the hook into the boiling meat in the pot. Whatever clung to the hook belonged to the priest. (I Sam. 2:13, 14.)

Flood

In the days of Noah, people had grown more and more wicked. At last, God decided to destroy His world with a flood, covering the whole earth with water. Only Noah and his family would be saved because Noah obeyed God. For 150 days the flood was upon the earth. But Noah and his family were safe in a great ark, or boat, that God had told him to build. (Gen. 6:11–22.)

Flowers

More than 400 flowers bloomed in ancient Israel including tulips, irises, hyacinths, anemones, and the Rose of Sharon. On the night of the Passover in Egypt, hyssop was used to sprinkle blood on door posts. The dried bulbs of the Star of Bethlehem were ground and mixed with meal to make one type of bread. (Song of Sol. 2:1, 2; Matt. 6:28, 29.)

Flute

At weddings and parties, the cheerful musical notes of flutes helped in the merrymaking. But at funerals, flutes played sorrowful sounds for the mourners. Flutes of many sizes were popular in every Jewish family. The simplest flutes were made from reeds. Others were carved from wood, bone, ivory, or made of bronze. (Dan. 3:5–15.)

Food

Since there were no grocery stores in Bible times, people had to raise their own food. Fruit, vegetables, and bread were the most common foods. Grapes and figs were eaten fresh or dried to eat at a later time. Beans and lentils were boiled for pottage. Cucumbers, onions, garlic, and leeks were eaten raw. Meat was kept for special occasions. (I Sam. 25:18; 30:12.)

Fool

"The way of a fool is right in his own eyes." This is how God describes a fool. The wise person trusts in God. The fool trusts in himself or his riches or something else instead of God. The Bible says much about fools, including the rich fool in Jesus' parable. But Jesus warned us not to call another person a fool. (Prov. 12:15; Matt. 5:22; Luke 12:20.)

Foot

It was a sign of humility to fall down before another person's feet. Feet were considered a lowly part of the body. A captured enemy was often forced to put his neck under the victor's feet to show that he had been defeated. During the long journey through the harsh wilderness, God gave special protection to the Israelites' feet so that they would not swell. (Josh. 10:24.)

Footwashing

Who could keep clean when they traveled? The roads and paths were dusty. Instead of shoes, people wore sandals. So the traveler often arrived hot and dirty. When he did, the lowliest servant was sent to wash his feet. During the Last Supper, Jesus quietly washed the feet of His disciples, reminding them to serve one another. (John 13:5–14.)

Fords

It was not until after New Testament times that the first bridges were built by the Romans in ancient Israel. Therefore, travelers would cross a river at a shallow place called a ford. Jacob, Gideon, David, and Absalom all crossed the fords of rivers. John was probably baptizing at a ford of the Jordan near Jericho when Jesus came to be baptized. (Gen. 32:22; Josh. 2:7.)

Forest

Forests covered wide areas of the Holy Land. Bashan was famous for its oaks and Lebanon for its cedars. Olive groves grew on Mt. Carmel as well as on the Mount of Olives. The jungle of the Jordan Valley was filled in places with tamarisks and willows. Many of these places were haunts for wild animals and were thus places to be feared. (II Kings 19:23; II Chron. 9:16.)

Forgiveness

"Is seven times enough?" Peter asked Jesus. "Not seven times, but seventy times seven," Jesus replied. They were talking about forgiving others, no longer holding their wrongs or sins against them. Jesus said that we must forgive others if we want God to forgive us. God never stops forgiving us if we are truly sorry. We must do the same for others who wrong us. (Matt. 5:23, 24; 18:21, 22.)

Fortifications

"The cities are walled and very great," the spies of Israel reported when they returned from the Promised Land. So the people of Israel feared the walled cities or fortifications. Many cities were not very large, but they had built great walls around them. Usually the city was built on a hill near a spring of water and had stone walls circling the hill. (Num. 13:28; Heb. 11:30.)

Fountain

In a dry and thirsty land, springs of water called fountains were of great importance. Towns were built near them for a water supply, needed especially during the months without much rainfall. Many towns were named for these fountains. *En* means fountain, so *En-gedi* and *En-dor* mean fountain of Gedi and of Dor. (Ps. 68:26; Prov. 8:24.)

Fox

Three kinds of fox are found in Israel and Egypt. The red fox lives in hills and woods. The desert fox prefers the drier, hotter places. So does the fennee fox, which is a small animal with huge ears. Samson burned Philistine grainfields by tying firebrands to foxes, who ran through the fields. Jesus called Herod "that fox" because he was cunning. (Judg. 15:4, 5; Luke 13:32.)

Friend

Did anyone ever love God so much and trust Him so completely that he was called a "Friend of God?" Yes, Abraham did. Many years later, Peter, James, and John were the special friends of Jesus, for they followed Him and pleased Him with their lives. Jesus said that we are His friends too if we please Him with our lives. (John 15:14; James 2:23.)

Frankincense

From the East they came with gifts for the newborn King. Among the gifts the Wise Men brought to the Baby Jesus was frankincense, a milky gum resin. This popular but precious gift was obtained from certain trees which grew in South Arabia. When dried and ground, it was burned as incense in worship. (Lev. 2:1, 15, 16; Matt. 2:11.)

Fringes

From ancient times Jewish men were expected to wear fringes or tassels at the four corners of their outer garments. These fringes were to remind them to keep God's laws. Like other Jews, Jesus wore a cloak with fringes, which sick people often tried to touch. The Pharisees wore long fringes to impress people that they obeyed God's laws more than others. (Num. 15:38; Matt. 9:20.)

Frog

At God's direction, frogs came up from the marshes of the Nile and invaded Egypt. They got in the Egyptians' beds and ovens and food. This was one of ten plagues that caused Pharaoh to let the people of Israel leave their slavery in Egypt. There were also frogs throughout the Promised Land. The pale green tree frog lived only in the Jordan Valley. (Exod. 8:1–15.)

Frontlet

People today do not usually wear Bible verses on their foreheads. But men in ancient Israel did. Passages from the Law were written on parchment or hardened calf's skin and worn on the forehead. These were called frontlets or phylacteries. They reminded the wearer and others to keep God's laws or commandments. (Exod. 13:1–10; Deut. 6:4–9.)

Fuller

Before cloth was dyed, a fuller cleaned or bleached it as white as possible. He worked outside the village because of his large vats of foul-smelling soaps. The cloth was rinsed in the running water of a stream and spread in a fuller's field to dry. When Jesus was transfigured, His clothes became whiter than any fuller could bleach them. (II Kings 18:17; Mark 9:3.)

Funeral

When a person died, his body was wrapped in a linen cloth and sprinkled with spices. Around the head, hands, and feet a napkin was tied and bound with little bands. Friends carried the body to the grave on a stretcher, followed by mourners and flute players. This preparation for burial is called a funeral. Jesus stopped a funeral at Nain and raised a young man from the dead. (Luke 7:11–17; John 19:39, 40.)

G

Gabbatha

Near the Tower of Antonia, the Roman fortress built along the northwest corner of the Temple, was a place called "The Pavement," or Gabbatha. Here the public trial of Jesus took place before Pilate. The Jews were there and demanded that Jesus be crucified. Part of the pavement is still there today, with marks in the stone where Roman soldiers played games. (John 19:13.)

Gabriel

Of all the hosts of angels, only two had major roles in the Bible, Michael and Gabriel. Michael is the archangel. Gabriel is God's messenger. Gabriel explained visions to Daniel. It was Gabriel who brought the news of John's birth to Zacharias. He also brought to Mary the news that she would be the mother of Jesus. (Dan. 8:16; 9:21; Luke 1:11–38.)

Gad

Jacob and Zilpah named their first son Gad, which means "good fortune." His descendants, one of the tribes of Israel, became shepherds and settled in the rich pastureland east of the Jordan River. There was another important man named Gad, a prophet who helped King David and kept an account of his reign. (Gen. 30:9–11; Josh. 18:7; I Sam. 22:5.)

Gadara

The city of Gadara, one of the Ten Towns or Decapolis, lay a short distance southeast of the Sea of Galilee. It was famous for its hot springs. Not far from the city Jesus met a man possessed by demons. The demons had driven the man crazy and had forced him to live among the tombs. But Jesus commanded the demons to leave and the man was cured. (Luke 8:26–36.)

Gaius

At least four men named Gaius are mentioned in the New Testament. One was a Macedonian who went with Paul to Jerusalem. Another was a Corinthian who was baptized by Paul. The Apostle John wrote his Third Epistle to a man named Gaius. He spoke of Gaius as "well-beloved" and praised him for his love and hospitality to traveling believers. (Acts 19:29; I Cor. 1:14; III John 1.)

Galatia, Galatians

In the heart of ancient Asia Minor, which is Turkey today, lay the province of Galatia. It was named for the Gauls who came there from Europe about 300 years before Christ. Paul wrote to the Christians of Galatia, urging them to be free from old Jewish customs, free to follow Christ as they should. (Acts 18:23; The Epistle of Paul to the Galatians.)

Galeed

Jacob was running away from his Uncle Laban. Tired of the way Laban had been treating him, Jacob was heading to his childhood home with his family. But Laban caught up and he and Jacob agreed to live in peace. To mark their promise to be friends, they built a great pile of stones and called it Galeed, which means "a heap of witnesses." (Gen. 31:47, 48.)

Galilee

In the days when Jesus was a boy, Galilee was a province of northern Palestine. It stretched from the Jordan Valley on the east to the Mediterranean Sea on the west. The Sea of Galilee is really a lake. Much of Jesus' early ministry was on or around this sea. There He lived with His family and shared the Good News. (Luke 4:31; John 7:1.)

Gallio

When Paul arrived in Corinth for his first visit, Gallio was the Roman proconsul in charge of Achaia, the province in which Corinth was situated. Some Jews attacked Paul and his preaching and tried to get Gallio to punish Paul. But Gallio sent them away, giving Paul the right to preach Christ to the people of Corinth because he was not violating Roman law. (Acts 18:12–17.)

Gamaliel

The Jewish Council wanted to put Peter and John to death for preaching about Christ. But one member of the Council, a Pharisee named Gamaliel, warned the rest to be careful. He was a respected teacher of the Jewish law in Jerusalem, so the others listened. He warned that if the Christians were really doing God's work, the Council would be fighting God. (Acts 5:34–39.)

Garden of Eden

The first home was a garden planted by God and given to Adam to care for. The Garden of Eden contained beautiful fruit trees of every kind. There was also a tree of life and a tree of knowledge of good and evil. When Adam and Eve sinned, God drove them from their garden home and placed cherubim and a flaming sword there to keep them from returning. (Gen. 2:8–15.)

Gates

The gates of an ancient city were huge double doors, covered with metal to keep the enemy from setting them on fire. Nearby, people gathered to do business. Markets were often found near the gates and even the king held public meetings there. The enemy usually tried to enter through the gates because they were the weakest part of a wall. (Josh. 2:5–7; Ps. 107:16.)

Gath

To the Valley of Elah he came, a giant nine feet or almost three meters tall. Goliath's home was a Philistine city called Gath, one of their five chief cities. Men of Gath were known as Gittites. Later some of them became part of David's loyal bodyguard. Ittai the Gittite, their leader, was one of David's three top commanders. (I Sam. 17:4; II Sam. 15:18–22.)

Gaza

Near the sea, on the busy trade route between Egypt and Syria, lay Gaza, the oldest of the five great Philistine cities. Samson visited Gaza one night and the Philistine leaders tried to capture him. But he carried away the city gates on his shoulders and left them on a hill. Later Samson was blinded and put in prison at Gaza. (Judg. 16:1, 21.)

Gebal

When Solomon built the beautiful Temple in Jerusalem, he hired stonemasons from Gebal, a Phoenician seaport. The Greeks called the city Byblos, which means "papyrus." This was because Egyptian papyrus reeds were brought here to make scrolls. Gebal was famous for its trading ships, known as Byblos travelers. Gebalites were also called Giblites. (Josh. 13:5, 6; Ezek. 27:9.)

Gedaliah

Many of the leading Jews were carried by King Nebuchadnezzar to Babylon. Gedaliah remained as governor of Judah, ruling over the Jews who still lived in the land. Jeremiah was permitted to stay under the care of Gedaliah. A Jewish prince named Ishmael killed Gedaliah when visiting him at his home in Mizpah. (II Kings 25:22–25; Jer. 39:14.)

Gehazi

When a Shunamite woman gave Elisha a room, it was his servant Gehazi who mentioned that she had no children. So Elisha promised her a son as a reward for her kindness. Later, Gehazi pretended to the Syrian general Naaman that Elisha wanted a reward for curing him of his leprosy. As a punishment for his greed, Gehazi himself was made a leper. (II Kings 4:8–37; 5:15–27.)

Genesis

The first book of the Bible is a story of beginnings. In Genesis we read how the world began. It tells of the beginning of man and woman and all the animals and plants of the world. The beginning of sin and of God's plan to save mankind from sin are both in Genesis. It also tells how God began His work through Abraham, Isaac, Jacob, and Joseph. (The Book of Genesis.)

Gentiles

The people of the nations of the world are called Gentiles. To the Jew, this was anyone who did not belong to his race. In the Temple in Jerusalem, no Gentile was allowed to go beyond a low wall which marked the end of the Court of the Gentiles. A notice said that a Gentile caught further inside the Temple would be put to death at once. (Acts 9:15; Rom. 15:16.)

108

Gerar

For a time, Abraham lived at Gerar, a Philistine city, with Abimelech, the king. Later Isaac made Gerar his home too. The city was located near the Mediterranean Sea on the caravan route from Palestine to Egypt. Both Abraham and Isaac dug wells near Gerar. Some of the people of Gerar took Isaac's wells from him. (Gen. 20; 26:17–33.)

Gerizim, Mount

"Stand upon Mt. Gerizim to bless the people," Moses said. "And upon Mt. Ebal to curse." So the people were to recite the Law to one another when they arrived in the Promised Land. Many years later Jesus sat beside a well near Mt. Gerizim and talked with a woman of Samaria. "Worship the Father in spirit and truth," Jesus told her. (Deut. 27:12, 13; John 4:23.)

Gershon

The family of Gershon, the oldest of Levi's three sons, had a special work in the wilderness. It was their job to carry the curtains of the Tabernacle as the people of Israel traveled. They were given two wagons and four oxen for their work. Later, when David was king, the Gershonites became famous for their singing. (Num. 3:23–26; I Chron. 16:4, 5.)

Gethsemane

Across the Kidron Valley from Jerusalem there was a grove of olive trees where Jesus liked to visit. Its name, Gethsemane, means "oil press." The night of the Last Supper, Jesus went there with His disciples to pray. He prayed alone, knowing that he would be crucified. He was there when Judas Iscariot arrived to betray Him to the chief priests. (Matt. 26:36–56.)

Giant

Goliath was not the only giant in Canaan. Ten of the spies sent by Moses to view the Promised Land told of giants there. They even compared themselves to grasshoppers beside them. Og, King of Bashan, must have been a very large man. His iron bed was almost 14 feet or 4.2 meters long and six feet or 1.8 meters wide. (Num. 13:33; Deut. 3:11.)

Gibeah

Saul built his palace and set up the first capital of Israel at Gibeah. It was located on a hilltop about three to four miles, or five to six kilometers, north of Jerusalem. Gibeah was Saul's hometown. It was from Gibeah that Saul summoned Israel to help the people of Jabesh-gilead. It is often called "Gibeah of Saul" or "Gibeah of Benjamin" because it was in the territory of Benjamin. (I Sam. 10:26; 11:4.)

Gibeon

On the road from Jerusalem to Joppa there was a royal city of the Hivites called Gibeon. It was a great city with mighty men. The city was famous for a great water pool with steps cut from top to bottom. By the edge of the pool Abner and Joab met one day and their men fought a bloody battle. Later Joab killed Amasa at Gibeon. (Josh. 10:22; II Sam. 2:1–28; 3:30.)

Gibeonites

Joshua forgot to ask the Lord about some strangers who came to see him. The visiting Gibeonites tricked Joshua into signing an agreement that he would help them. They pretended to come from a far-off land, dressed in worn-out clothing and carrying stale food. But Joshua punished the Gibeonites for their trickery by making them slaves. (Josh. 9.)

Gideon

In the dead of night, Gideon, a judge of Israel, and his 300 faithful men crept up to the Midianite camp. There were thousands of the enemy. But Gideon and his men, following God's orders, frightened the Midianites with trumpet blasts and blazing torches. Gideon won a great victory but he refused to become king and went home to Ophrah. (Judg. 7.)

Gihon

"God save the king!" the people shouted. Solomon had just been anointed by Zadok the priest to rule in place of his father David. They stood by the Gihon spring in the Kidron Valley. It was one of the sources for Jerusalem's water. Gihon was also the name of one of the four rivers in the Garden of Eden. (Gen. 2:13; I Kings 1:32–40.)

Gilboa

Many great battles were fought near the mountains of Gilboa, a mountain range east of the plain of Esdraelon. Gideon, Deborah and Barak, and Jehu are names of mighty warriors who won great victories there. But Gilboa was also a place of defeat, for King Saul and his son Jonathan died on Mt. Gilboa as they fought the Philistines. (I Sam. 31:1–8.)

Gilead

East of the Jordan River lay a rugged and beautiful hilly land known as Gilead. The river Jabbok cut deep valleys through Gilead. It was a land with plenty of water, good for grazing flocks and growing grain. Moses allowed the tribes of Gad and Reuben to settle there on the way to the Promised Land. Gilead was also famous for its balm and its sturdy trees. (Gen. 37:25; Num. 32.)

Gilgal

When the people of Israel crossed into the Promised Land, their first camp was at Gilgal. It was not far from Jericho, the city where the Lord would give them their first great victory. At Gilgal the Israelites built a monument of 12 stones to remind people that the Lord had brought them across the river to a new land. They then held the first Passover celebration in the Promised Land. (Josh. 4:19, 20.)

Glean

The poor had no fields of grain and so the law said they could gather the grain or fruit that reapers left behind. In the time of harvest, the poor would follow the reapers, gathering their food. This was called gleaning. Ruth gleaned in the fields of Boaz near Bethlehem for herself and her mother-in-law Naomi. (Deut. 24:19–22; Ruth 2.)

Goad

Shamgar, a warrior of Israel, killed 600 Philistines with a goad. It was not easy, for the Philistines had swords and spears. The goad was a large wooden pole, sharpened at one end to prod oxen when plowing. The other end was flattened to scrape mud from the plow. Sometimes the two ends were made of iron. (Judg. 3:31; I Sam. 13:21.)

Goat

Rich men knew how rich they were by the number of goats, sheep, cattle, and camels they had. Nabal had 1,000 goats. But even the poorest family had at least one goat. Goats were important because they gave their owners meat, milk, hair for clothing and tents, and skin for leather. Goats were also used as an offering for sin. (Exod. 35:26; Lev. 16:15.)

112

God

All life and creation began with God. He has other names. The Hebrews called Him Yahweh or Jehovah. God is a perfect person, without sin. All that was made, the world, the universe about us, and man himself, was made by God. God is a spirit. That is, He has no physical body. When God looked for a way to tell men about Himself, He chose some to write the Bible. In it, God tells of His work with people from the earliest days. God also tells us much about Himself in His Book. He tells us that He is everywhere, that He can do anything, and that He knows all things. God never began and He never ends. He is forever. When God made man and woman, He made them something like Himself. Like God, people can love and hate, express their thoughts in words, and show goodness in their lives. But people can also sin, doing things that hurt God and displease Him. God loves people very much and wants them to live in His home, a place called heaven, forever. But it is impossible for anyone who keeps his sins to live with a perfect God in a perfect place. So God made a way for people to have their sin taken away. He sent His Son, Jesus, to die as a sacrifice for sin. God is a loving God who wants all people to find salvation and forgiveness of sin. It is available through His Son, Jesus.

Gold

There was no gold mined in Palestine, so this precious metal was brought from Arabia, Sheba, and Ophir. Jewels, idols, and royal shields were made of gold. It was also used as money. The mercy seat and the two cherubim in the Tabernacle were made of pure gold. Later, Wise Men brought a gift of gold to the Baby Jesus. (Exod. 25:18; Matt. 2:11.)

Golden Calf

While Moses was away on Mt. Sinai, his brother Aaron made a golden calf for the Israelites to worship. But when Moses returned with the Ten Commandments, he destroyed the calf. King Jeroboam later set up golden calves at Bethel and Dan. Golden calves were idols and God had warned against worshiping idols. (Exod. 32:1–4; I Kings 12:26–29.)

Golgotha

Outside the Damascus gate of Jerusalem stands a hill that looks like the face of a skull. Many think this was Golgotha, the "place of a skull" where Jesus was crucified. Golgotha was a Hebrew word, while Calvary was taken from the Latin word for skull. Some think the hill was a place of execution and received its name from the skulls that remained. (Matt. 27:33; John 19:17.)

Goliath

From the town of Gath came the Philistine giant Goliath, almost ten feet, or three meters, tall. As the armies of Israel and the Philistines faced each other in the Valley of Elah, Goliath challenged Israel to send a warrior to fight him. David was only a young man, but he trusted in God and killed the giant with a stone from his sling. (I Sam. 17.)

Goshen

During seven years of famine in Canaan, Joseph invited his father Israel (Jacob) to bring his family to live in Egypt. There Joseph would care for them as long as he lived. They were given lands in the district of Goshen in the east Nile delta. Goshen was a pleasant area, well suited to flocks and herds. The Hebrews lived there until the Exodus. (Gen. 47:1–11.)

Gospel

There wasn't much good news for the people of Israel before Jesus came. They had been captured by one nation after another. But one night some angels announced Good News. A Savior had been born. Gospel means "Good News." The four Gospels written by Matthew, Mark, Luke, and John tell the Good News of Jesus' coming, His life among us, and His death for us. (Luke 2:10.)

Gourd

While Jonah waited to see what would happen to the city of Nineveh after he preached there, he made a shelter of branches and leaves. This would protect him from the hot sun. God caused a gourd, a fruit that grows on a vine, to grow nearby. Its broad leaves gave Jonah some shade until it died. God used this gourd to teach Jonah a lesson of love. (Jon. 4:6–11.)

Granary

Wheat, barley, and other grains were stored in a granary. This could be a large earthenware jar, a dry pit or cave, or a building made for that purpose. The granary must keep out the dampness so the grain would stay dry. Other words for granary were garner, barn, and storehouse. Jesus told a parable about a rich fool who tore down his barns to build bigger ones. (Gen. 41:56; Luke 3:17; 12:16–24.)

Grace

Again and again God talks about grace in His Book, the Bible. People usually give others no more than they deserve. But God gives us more than we deserve. This is the meaning of grace. God's grace offers us forgiveness for our sins as a free gift through Jesus Christ. This grace is illustrated in the story of the Prodigal Son. (Luke 15:11–32; Rom. 3:21–26.)

Greece, Greek

When Paul set out across the Roman Empire, he went to many places where the Greek language was spoken. The New Testament was originally written in the Greek language. Jesus probably spoke Greek, as well as Hebrew and Aramaic. Macedonia and Achaia were the same lands as Greece today. This included the cities of Corinth, Athens, Berea, Thessalonica, and Philippi. (Acts 17:4; 20:1, 2.)

Grinding

When a family needed flour, it had to grind its own. Wheat or barley was ground between two round stones until it was fine enough for flour. The lower stone did not move while the upper one turned. Grinding was a lowly job, often done by two women who sat opposite each other. The Philistines made Samson grind flour to disgrace him. (Judg. 16:21; Matt. 24:41.)

Guard

The Temple in Jerusalem had its own police known as the Temple Guard. Most of these men were Levites, standing on duty at 24 places in the Temple. One important task was to keep Gentiles from parts of the Temple reserved for Jews only. Members of the Temple Guard were among those who arrested Jesus in Gethsemane. (Luke 22:52; Acts 4:1.)

Guest

When a guest arrived at a home, he was honored by the host in certain ways. He was welcomed with a kiss. Water was given to wash his hot and dusty feet. Often a lowly servant washed his feet for him. The guest's head was anointed or perfumed with oil. It was a special honor for the guest to be placed at his host's right hand at the meal. (Luke 7:44–46.)

Guest Room

There were no hotels or motels in Bible times. Inns were little more than campgrounds or stone buildings with few things to make the traveler's stay comfortable. Most travelers stayed in homes and so many homes had a guest room. Jesus and His disciples ate the Last Supper in a guest room in Jerusalem. Some think it was the home of Mark's mother. (Mark 14:22–26.)

H

Habakkuk

About 600 years before Christ, the prophet Habakkuk stood in his watchtower and saw the wicked Chaldeans punishing the people of God. In three short chapters Habakkuk asks why God would permit this and then realizes how sinful his people have been and how the Chaldeans themselves will face God's greater judgment. Habakkuk's name means "warm embrace." (The Book of Habakkuk.)

Hadad

To the Canaanites the god of storms was known as Baal. To the Syrians he was Hadad or Thunderer. He was pictured on monuments as a king on a bull's back, carrying forked lightning in his hands. They said his home was in a high mountain in the north sky. Two kings of Damascus, Hadadezer and Benhadad, were named for him. (II Sam. 8:10; I Kings 15:18.)

Hagar

God had promised Abraham a son, someone who would become the father of a great nation. But Abraham and his wife Sarah were growing old and they still had no son. At last Sarah gave Hagar, her Egyptian maid, to Abraham as a second wife. When Ishmael, the son of Hagar and Abraham, was born, Sarah grew jealous and Hagar ran away with her son to the desert. (Gen. 16.)

Haggai

"Consider your ways," Haggai the prophet told his people. For 16 years they had been back in their homeland. God had let them return from captivity in a foreign land. But they still had not rebuilt God's house. Instead they were building beautiful homes for themselves. Since they had put themselves before God, He gave them poor harvests. (The Book of Haggai.)

Hail

When Moses lifted his shepherd's rod, the Lord sent a great hailstorm across Egypt. The hail, small round pieces of ice, destroyed the crops of the Egyptians, but not the crops of the Israelites. Hail often caused great damage to crops and fruit and injury to men and animals. When the Amorites fled from Joshua at Gibeon, God sent great hailstones upon them. (Exod. 9:22–26; Josh. 10:11.)

Hair

The Jews expressed many things with their hair. On festive occasions, they anointed their hair with oil and perfume. To show sorrow, they left their hair in disorder. In a time of mourning, the head was often partly or completely shaved. Dark hair was admired and gray hair honored, but baldness was hated. Some children mocked Elisha's bald head. (II Kings 2:23.)

Hallelujah

"Hallelujah!" the people sang. It was a Hebrew word which meant "Praise the Lord!" In the Psalms the word appears 24 times as a call to worship. Hallelujah Psalms have a special part in synagogue services. Some are sung at the great feasts of Passover, Pentecost, Tabernacles, and Dedication. Hallelujah is in its Greek form "Alleluia" in the Book of Revelation. (Pss. 106:1; 111:1.)

Ham

While the rain poured down upon the ark, Noah's second son Ham was safe inside. His older and younger brothers Shem and Japheth, were also safe, for their father Noah had pleased God. Ham's descendants included the Ethiopians, Canaanites, Egyptians, and Libyans. Some psalms speak of Egypt as the land of Ham. (Gen. 9:18; 10:6–20; Ps. 78:51.)

Haman

Haman, chief minister of King Ahasuerus of Persia, was furious because Esther's cousin Mordecai refused to bow before him. So Haman planned a way to kill all the Jews, Mordecai's people. But Queen Esther bravely stopped the plot and the king ordered Haman to be hung on the gallows he had built for Mordecai. (The Book of Esther.)

Hamath

One of the oldest cities in the world is Hamath, located on the banks of the Orontes River in northern Syria. When the Israelites came from Egypt, the Lord named Hamath as the northern part of their new land. Hamath was famous for its huge water wheels which brought water from the river to the houses and gardens above. Solomon made Hamath a store city. (Num. 34:8; II Chron. 8:4.)

Hananiah

For many centuries the name Hananiah, which means "The Lord has been gracious," was common in Israel. Ten men of the Bible were named Hananiah. The best known was a false prophet denounced by Jeremiah. He wrongly predicted that the Jews would be freed from the yoke of Babylonian slavery in two years. Jeremiah warned it would take seventy. (Jer. 28.)

Hannah

Hannah made a vow to the Lord. "Give me a son, and I will give him to the Lord for his lifetime," she promised. So the Lord gave Hannah a son. She named him Samuel. As she had promised, Hannah gave Samuel to the Lord to help Eli the priest take care of the Tabernacle. Later Hannah had three more sons and daughters. (I Sam. 1:1—2:10.)

Haran

When Abram left Ur, his first home was in Haran. But when he moved to Canaan, some of his relatives remained there. When Eliezer looked for a bride for Isaac, he found Rebekah at Haran. Later Jacob fled to Haran and stayed with Laban. Jacob married Laban's daughters Leah and Rachel. All Jacob's children except Benjamin were born in Haran. (Gen. 11:31; 24:10; 28:10.)

Harod

Before he went to battle with the Midianites, Gideon pitched his camp by a spring named Harod, which means "trembling." God said Gideon had too many soldiers and told him to send home all who drank the water by lapping it like a dog. The spring is on the northwest side of Mt. Gilboa. It rises up in a cave and rushes into a valley. It provides so much water that it was an important prize in war. (Judg. 7:1.)

Harp

There was only one way to cheer King Saul. Whenever the evil spirit troubled him, David played the harp and Saul was calmed. The harp is the first and last musical instrument mentioned in the Bible. It was smaller than a modern harp and was usually carried. Harps were made from the wood of cypress or almug trees. (Gen. 4:21; I Sam. 16:23.)

Hart and Hind

Three kinds of deer were found in Palestine: the red deer deep in the forest, the fallow deer in open parkland, and the small roe deer in woodland. The hart was the male red deer and the hind was the female. They were very fast, as David and Habakkuk both mentioned. The hart was part of Solomon's food each day. (I Kings 4:22, 23; Ps. 18:33; Hab. 3:19.)

Hazael

When Benhadad, King of Damascus, became ill he sent a high official named Hazael to ask Elisha the prophet if he would get well. Elisha wept as he told Hazael his answer. The king would die and Hazael himself would become king. But Hazael would invade Israel and treat Elisha's people cruelly. (II Kings 8:7–15; 13:3.)

Harvest

The harvest, or gathering of food, continued through most of the year from March to November. March was the time of flax harvest. Barley was harvested in April, and wheat seven weeks later in June and July. Summer fruits included grapes and pomegranates and in the autumn the figs were gathered. Olives were harvested from mid-September to mid-November. (Ruth 2:23.)

Hazor

Hazor, the royal city of King Jabin, was in the northern part of the Promised Land. It was captured by Joshua and was the only city he destroyed by fire. The city was rebuilt, fortified, and allotted to the tribe of Naphtali. In the time of the Judges, Deborah and Barak defeated its army under Sisera. Later Solomon rebuilt the city, but it was captured by Assyria. (Josh. 11:1–15.)

121

Healing

There were not many doctors in Jesus' time and little was known about medicine. So when Jesus touched sick people and healed them, He caused a lot of excitement. More than 50 different times of healing by Jesus and His disciples are mentioned in the Bible. Jesus showed through His healing that He had special power from God. He then gave this special power to certain disciples. (Matt. 9:2–7.)

Heart

"Let not your heart be troubled," Jesus told His disciples. The Bible talks about the heart almost a thousand times, but it almost never means the organ that pumps blood through the body. The heart usually means the real person inside us or life itself. With the heart we accept Jesus into our lives and become Christians. (John 14:1; Rom. 10:9, 10.)

Heaven

"In My Father's house are many mansions," Jesus told His disciples. "I go to prepare a place for you." Jesus was speaking of heaven, God's beautiful home. In the Book of Revelation, John tries to describe it, but words are not enough. It is also the home of the angels and of those who accept the Lord into their lives. (Job 22:12; John 14:2; Rev. 21.)

Hebrew, Hebrews

There are three words that name Abraham and his descendants through Jacob—Jews, Israelites, and Hebrews. The writers of the Old Testament used the Hebrew language, which is written from right to left. The Book of Hebrews was written to Jewish Christians who put Jewish customs above their new faith in Christ. (The Epistle to the Hebrews.)

Hebron

When the Israelite spies went into the Promised Land, they were frightened by the Sons of Anak, giants who lived at the city of Hebron. Centuries before, Abraham had lived nearby at Mamre and was buried in a cave at Hebron. David became king at Hebron. Later, Absalom rebelled against his father David and was crowned king at Hebron. (Gen. 23:2; II Sam. 5:3.)

Heir

When a father died, his sons each had a share of his household goods, cattle, wells, and slaves. Each person who was entitled to receive some of the father's property was called an heir. The oldest son received a double share of the property, which helped him meet the expense of looking after the family's guests. He also had to pay for the family sacrifices. (Gen. 15:3, 4.)

Hell

Somewhere there is a place of torment that never ends, for it is everlasting. It is called hell, a place where the evil, the unbelieving, are punished for their sins on earth. The Bible speaks of hell as a place of fire, a place of a never-ending death. Jesus spoke of a man who died and was tormented in hell with flames. (Ps. 139:8; Matt. 18:9; Luke 16:19–31.)

Helmet

The Elamites were the first to make metal helmets, coverings to protect a soldier's head in battle. The Babylonians added flaps to cover ears and cheeks. The Assyrians put a point in the center to turn aside blows by attackers. Hebrew soldiers wore helmets of leather or bronze. A leather, felt, or woolen bonnet was worn underneath a metal helmet. (I Sam. 17:5; Ezek. 23:24.)

Herald

Royal announcements were made by heralds, who called messages to the people. Haman was shamed by his king because he had to walk through the streets shouting out the glory of his enemy, Mordecai. Jesus preached at Nazareth as one who announced good news from God. Preachers of the gospel are called heralds in the New Testament. (Esther 6:11; Dan. 3:4.)

Hermon

One of the few snowcapped mountains in the Bible world, Mt. Hermon rises up almost 9,000 feet or 2,743 meters above sea level. Its snows give water to the Jordan River and its cool heights bring refreshing breezes to the plains around it. Jesus was transfigured on a high mountain, probably either Mt. Hermon or Mt. Tabor. (Josh. 11:17; Ps. 89:12.)

Herod The Great

Even though Herod the Great rebuilt the Temple at great cost, the Jews hated him, for he brought in heathen customs and supported the Roman captors. Herod was born in 73 B.C. and ruled as King of the Jews from 40 to 4 B.C. When he was old, Herod became cruel and suspicious. The message of the Wise Men made him afraid and he tried to kill the Baby Jesus as a rival king. (Matt. 2:1–19.)

Herod The Tetrarch

"That fox," Jesus called him. He was speaking of Herod Antipas, or Herod the Tetrarch, son of Herod the Great. It was this Herod, the ruler of the Jews, who put John the Baptist in prison and had him beheaded. It was this same Herod who judged Jesus before He was crucified. Later Herod was banished and his territory given to Agrippa I. (Luke 13:32; 23:7–12.)

Herodias

Herodias deserted her first husband to marry Herod Antipas, the king of the Jews. One day her daughter Salome pleased Herod by dancing at his birthday party. When Herod promised a gift, Herodias told Salome to ask for the head of John the Baptist. Herod was exiled in 39 A.D., but Herodias chose to go with him, even though the Emperor Gaius was willing to show her favor. (Mark 6:19–22.)

Heshbon

When the Israelites came from Egypt, they asked King Sihon of the Amorites for permission to pass through his land. He refused, and so the Israelites captured Sihon's lands. Heshbon was Sihon's capital. Later the city was given to the Levites. Heshbon was an ancient city situated near the point where the Jordan empties into the Dead Sea. (Num. 21:25–30.)

Hezekiah

Of all the kings of Judah, Hezekiah was the best. He was the son of Ahaz and the father of Manasseh. Hezekiah banished idols from the land and encouraged his people to worship the Lord. Under his rule the land prospered. When the Assyrians threatened Jerusalem, Hezekiah and Isaiah prayed to the Lord and the enemy army was destroyed. (II Kings 18—20; II Chron. 29—32.)

High Place

Bible-time people often located their places of worship on a high hill, called the high place. If there were no trees, stone pillars or wooden piles were erected. People used these pillars as altars, where they burned incense and offered sacrifices. The high place was used by idol worshipers as well as those who worshiped God. (I Sam. 9:12–25.)

High Priest

The religious leader of Israel was called the High Priest. He was the only priest to be anointed with a special oil and to wear special clothing edged with red and blue pomegranates and golden bells. The breastplate of the High Priest had twelve precious stones and the names of the twelve tribes of Israel. Caiaphas was High Priest when Jesus was crucified. (Matt. 26:57.)

Hilkiah

Several men in the Old Testament were called Hilkiah. One of the best known was the son of Shallum. He was High Priest in the reign of King Josiah. Hilkiah found the lost Book of the Law in the Temple while repairs were being made. The discovery led to the destruction of idols in the land and a turning to the Lord. (II Chron. 34:14–33.)

Hinnom

The Valley of Hinnom was a dumping ground for trash which was usually burning. Human sacrifices to Molech, a pagan god were made there and so it became known as the valley of slaughter. Hinnom was the Hebrew name. When changed to Greek, *gehenna,* the word meant "hell" and was used by Jesus several times. (Josh. 15:8; II Kings 23:10; Matt. 5:22.)

Hiram

The name Hiram was given to several kings of Tyre, a merchant city between present-day Haifa and Beirut. The most famous of these kings was the son of Aribaal. He was a devoted friend and ally of King David. When Solomon built the Temple, Hiram provided the cedar wood and many of the craftsmen. (II Sam. 5:11; I Kings 5:1.)

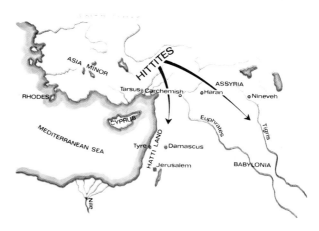

Hireling

A laborer or servant who was hired to do lowly work for a certain wage was called a hireling. Often his term of work was for three years. Malachi said that God would judge those who did not pay hirelings enough wages. But the father of the Prodigal Son had many hired servants who had more than enough food. (Mal. 3:5; Luke 15:17; John 10:12.)

Hittites

When Sarah died, Abraham bought her burial cave from Ephron the Hittite. Hittites were listed among the people of Canaan. Esau married a Hittite and after the Israelites came to the Promised Land, many of them married Hittites. The Hittite Empire began in Asia Minor and spread into Assyria and Palestine. Ancient records suggest that Palestine was called Hatti Land by some. (Gen. 23; 26:34.)

Hivites

When the Israelites came into the Promised Land, there were seven nations occupying it. One of them was the nation of the Hivites. The name Hivite means "villager." The people of Gibeon, who tricked Joshua into making peace with them, were Hivites. The people of Shechem in the time of Jacob also were Hivites. Solomon used Hivites as laborers for his building programs. (Gen. 34:2; Josh. 24:11.)

Hoarfrost

When the dew comes on cold, clear, still nights, it may freeze into hoarfrost, covering rocks and leaves with a white film. In one of the psalms the writer speaks of God scattering the hoarfrost like ashes. The Israelites said that the manna which fell in the wilderness was like a small round thing, small as the hoarfrost. (Exod. 16:14, 15; Ps. 147:16.)

Hobah

While Abraham's nephew Lot lived at Sodom, four kings and their armies attacked from the north and took Lot prisoner. But the news reached Abraham and he pursued with a band of trained fighters, chasing the kings all the way to Hobah, near Damascus. Abraham and his men surprised the enemy by night and defeated them. (Gen. 14.)

Holy of Holies

The most holy place in the Tabernacle and Temple was the inner sanctuary called the Holy of Holies. The Ark of the Covenant, with its solid gold lid known as the Mercy Seat, was the only thing that stood in the Holy of Holies. Only the High Priest could go inside the Holy of Holies and only once a year on the Day of Atonement. (Exod. 26:33–35.)

Holy Place

In the Tabernacle and the Temple the Holy of Holies was separated from the Holy Place by a great curtain or veil. Only priests could go into the Holy Place and only on certain occasions. The Holy Place contained the altar of incense, a golden candlestick, and a table of showbread. Zacharias was in the Holy Place when an angel told him that he would have a son, John the Baptist. (Luke 1:5–23.)

Holy Spirit

God has appeared to people in three different ways, each time as a different Person. He spoke to the patriarchs as God, He came to earth as Jesus, and He lives within His people today as the Holy Spirit. The Holy Spirit came at Pentecost and has dwelled with Christians since, giving help and comfort in living the Christian life. (Acts 1:8; 2:1–4.)

Honey

The Lord described the Promised Land as a land flowing with milk and honey. Even the Assyrians called it that. Honey was a common, plentiful food in the land. It was found wild in the cracks of rocks, in combs on the ground, or under stones. Samson found a honeycomb in the dead body of a lion. Honey was valued as a sweetener for foods. (Exod. 3:8; II Kings 18:32.)

Hophni and Phinehas

While Eli served as the chief priest at Shiloh, his sons Hophni and Phinehas also served with him as priests. But Eli was warned twice about his sons' evil ways. God's third warning came through the boy Samuel who lived at the Tabernacle with Eli. In a battle at Aphek, the two brothers were killed and the Ark of God was captured. (I Sam. 1:3; 2:34; 4:4, 17.)

Hor

On their way to the Promised Land through the wilderness, the Israelites had reached Mt. Hor after a long detour around Edom. Moses had asked permission to go through Edom, but was refused. When the Israelites arrived at Mt. Hor, Aaron, Moses' brother, died there and was buried on the mountain. All the Israelites mourned Aaron's death for 30 days. (Num. 20:14–29.)

Horeb

"The Lord our God spoke to us in Horeb," Moses told his people. It was at Horeb, or Mt. Sinai, that God gave Moses the laws to govern the people of Israel including the Ten Commandments. Earlier, God had spoken to Moses nearby from a burning bush. It was at Horeb that Moses struck a rock to give his people water. (Exod. 3:1; Deut. 1:6.)

Hormah

The Israelites had disobeyed God and so Moses warned that they would be defeated in battle. But the people insisted on fighting the Amalekites and Canaanites anyway. The Israelites were defeated and chased all the way to Hormah, a place east of Beersheba. Later, the Israelites killed many Canaanites and destroyed Hormah. (Num. 14:45; 21:3; Deut. 1:44.)

Horn

The hollowed-out horns of animals were used in Bible times for two main purposes: as musical instruments and a container to carry oil. At the fall of Jericho, rams' horns were blown as trumpets. The orchestras of David and Nebuchadnezzar played horns. David was anointed king with oil from a horn. So was King Solomon. (Josh. 6:8; I Sam. 16:1, 13.)

Horns of The Altar

In the Tabernacle and Temple there was an altar for burnt offerings. Each of the four corners had horn-like points called horns of the Altar. These horns were considered to be sacred because blood from the sacrifices was smeared on them by the priests. While a person clung to one of these horns, he was safe from punishment. (Lev. 4:30; I Kings 1:50.)

Hornet

"I will send hornets before thee," God told His people. With these fierce bees which lived in large nests, He helped the Israelites drive out the people who occupied the Promised Land. There were large numbers of hornets in the Promised Land. One town was named for them, for Zorah means "town of hornets." (Exod. 23:28; Deut. 7:20.)

Horse

The Israelites did not have many horses until the time of Solomon. Then Solomon equipped his army with thousands of horses and chariots. He built stables at Megiddo and Gezer with quarters for his horsemen. Solomon also exported and imported horses. The psalmist mentions the great strength of the horse as a reminder of the greater strength of God. (I Kings 4:26; Ps. 147:10, 11.)

Hosanna

At first, the word "Hosanna" was a prayer meaning "Save, now, we pray." But more and more it became a shout of praise. "Hosanna," the crowds cried out when Jesus rode into Jerusalem on a colt. At the Feast of Tabernacles, worshipers in the joyful processions waved palm branches and shouted "Hosanna." This was done especially on the seventh day. (Ps. 118:25.)

Hosea

One of the greatest love stories of the Bible is found in the little book of Hosea. The love of the man Hosea for a runaway wife was a shining example of God's great love for His sinful people. Hosea was a prophet who wrote about 700 years before Christ. It was a time when the rich grew richer while the poor grew poorer. (The Book of Hosea.)

Hoshea

Hoshea murdered Pekah, king of Israel, and took over as king. But Hoshea was an evil king and so God was not with him. Before long Shalmanezer, king of Assyria, came into the land and put Hoshea into prison. Then Shalmanezer took the people of Israel into his land as captives. Hoshea was the last king over Israel before this captivity. (II Kings 17:1–6; 18:1–10.)

Hospitality

A traveler in Bible times had the right to ask anyone for hospitality, even if he was a complete stranger. The host not only looked after his guest by giving him food and shelter, but as long as the traveler was in his home, he protected him. The early Christians made a special point of providing hospitality to other Christians. (Heb. 13:2.)

Host of Heaven

In the Old Testament the host of heaven meant either the angels or the stars. Sometimes people worshiped the stars instead of God. This happened especially during the reign of Manasseh, king of Judah, in the seventh century B.C. He built altars for all the host of heaven in the courts of the Temple in Jerusalem. (II Kings 17:16.)

Hour

There were no watches or clocks in Bible times, only a few sundials and water-clocks. Thus a person in Bible times could not tell time exactly. An hour was not measured by minutes or seconds, but as a twelfth part of daylight, the time from sunrise to sunset. The night was divided into three watches by the Jews and into four watches by the Romans. (John 1:39; 4:6.)

House

Many of the people in Old Testament times lived in tents, often moving from place to place with their animals. There were more houses in New Testament times. They were usually made of stone or sun-baked brick. The simplest house had a living room, a guest chamber, and an open courtyard where animals were kept. Stone steps led from the courtyard to the roof. (Luke 5:18, 19.)

Huldah

While repairing the Temple in Josiah's reign, the workmen found the Book of the Law. At the command of Josiah the king, Hilkiah the priest asked the prophetess Huldah, wife of Shallum, the keeper of the wardrobe, about it. Huldah sent word to King Josiah that God's judgment on Judah would not come until after Josiah's death. (II Kings 22:14–20.)

Hunter

Nimrod is the first man in the Bible to be described as a mighty hunter. The nobles of Egypt and Assyria enjoyed hunting and killing animals as a sport but the kings of Israel did not. Esau was a hunter, but Jacob was not. In New Testament times, Herod the Great became famous for his skill in hunting boars, stags, wild asses, and bears. (Gen. 10:8, 9; Lev. 17:13.)

Humility

"Humble yourselves therefore under the mighty hand of God," Peter wrote. Jesus had told Peter and the other disciples that they must humble themselves as little children to enter His kingdom. Jesus showed humility by coming as a baby, by washing His disciples' feet, and by other acts. We must humble ourselves before Him to receive Him as Savior. (I Pet. 5:5, 6.)

Hur

Not long after the people of Israel had escaped from Egypt, the Amalekites attacked them in the desert. As long as Moses held up his hands, the Israelites had victory. But when he let his hands go down, the Amalekites had the victory. When Moses grew too tired to hold up his hands, Aaron and Hur lifted them up for him. (Exod. 17:12.)

Hushai

David's son Absalom rebelled, and tried to take the kingdom from his father. David had to run away for his life. But Hushai, one of David's advisers, remained in Jerusalem. He pretended to give good advice to Absalom, but actually gave bad advice. Then he sent secret messages to David to tell him what was happening. (II Sam. 16:15–18.)

Husk

The Prodigal Son had spent all of his money and there was no friend to help him. Alone in a strange land, he took a job feeding pigs. But famine was in the land and the young man grew so hungry that he wanted to eat the husks, the sweet pods of the carob or locust tree, that he was feeding to the pigs. The pods were sold as cattle feed but poor people boiled them for food. (Luke 15:16.)

Hymn

On the night of the Last Supper, Jesus and His disciples sang a hymn or song in the upper room. The hymn was one of the psalms sung by Jews at Passover. Early Christians also sang hymns when they gathered. There are other songs recorded in Scripture—the song of Mary, Deborah, Zechariah, and Simeon. (Matt. 26:30; Rev. 15:3, 4.)

Hyssop

There may have been two different plants known as hyssop in the Bible. The hyssop of the Old Testament was used to sprinkle the blood of the sacrificed lamb on the doorposts the night of the Passover. In the New Testament, hyssop was used to carry a sponge full of vinegar to Jesus' mouth at the crucifixion. (Exod. 12:21, 22; Ps. 51:7; John 19:29.)

Ichabod

A great tragedy had happened in Israel. The chief priest Eli had died and his two sons, Hophni and Phinehas, had been killed. But a son was born at this time to Phinehas' wife. She named her son Ichabod, which means "Where is the glory?" because of the death of the priests and because the Ark of God had been captured by the Philistines. (I Sam. 4:19–22.)

Iconium

In the days of St. Paul, Iconium was a prosperous town in Asia Minor on the main trading road between Ephesus and Syria. When Paul visited there on his first missionary journey, a great many Jews and Greeks became Christians. He encouraged them on other visits. Today the city is Konya in central Turkey. (Acts 13:51; II Tim. 3:11.)

Idolatry

There were two kinds of idolatry mentioned in the Bible. Some people tried to worship false gods, either with images or without them. Others tried to worship God through images, or idols. But God did not want people to do either. Idols were images, often shaped like humans or animals. God's people were constantly warned against idolatry. (Exod. 20:4, 5.)

Image

"Thou shalt not make any graven images," God warned. But there were dozens of these images, statues or pictures of people or things, which people worshiped. Nebuchadnezzar set up an image of gold for people to worship. When Shadrach, Meshach, and Abednego refused to bow down to it, he threw them into a furnace. But God protected them and brought honor to His name. (Dan. 3.)

Immanuel

More than 700 years before Jesus was born, Isaiah said, "A virgin shall conceive, and bear a son, and shall call his name Immanuel." The name meant "God is with us" and foretold of the birth of Jesus. At the time, it was a sign to King Ahaz and his court to trust God to deliver them from the kings of Israel and Syria. (Isa. 7:14; Matt. 1:23.)

Incense

Among the Israelites, only the priests were permitted to offer incense, a mixture of certain gums and spices, in worship. There were strict rules for them to follow, which God had given to Moses. Aaron was the first priest to follow these rules and burn incense on the altar in the Holy Place. Once each year the High Priest carried burning incense into the Holy of Holies. (Lev. 16:12, 13.)

Inn

"There was no room for them in the inn." So Jesus was born in the stable nearby. Early inns were not buildings, but campgrounds by a well. Later, simple buildings were made with an open courtyard around the well. Most travelers stayed in homes, for people welcomed guests in those days. The Good Samaritan brought a traveler to an inn for care. (Luke 2:7; 10:34.)

Iron

Almost 3,000 years before Christ, some of the ancient peoples had learned to make and use iron. But it was almost 2,000 years later before the people of Israel learned its secret, when King David conquered the Philistines with their iron chariots. A forge where iron was worked has been found at Megiddo complete with iron slag. (II Sam. 12:31.)

Isaac

When Isaac was born, Abraham and Sarah named him "laughter," which is the meaning of his name. Isaac's parents were very old at this time and he was their first son, a promise from God. Sarah had laughed when she heard this promise. When he grew up, Isaac married Rebekah and they had twin sons, Jacob and Esau. Isaac lived until he was 180 years old. (Gen. 21:5.)

Isaiah

About 700 years before Christ, the prophet Isaiah told of a king who would come, a Messiah who would save His people through His own death. Isaiah was a member of a royal family. He spoke boldly of the people's sin and God's anger at that sin. He told of a holy God who wants His people to live holy lives. (The Book of Isaiah.)

Ish-bosheth

When King Saul died, his army chief Abner made Saul's youngest son, Ish-bosheth, king. But David had also been crowned king and it soon became clear that he would rule the land. One day while Ish-bosheth was resting, two of his own officers murdered him. David then became king over all Israel. David was angered by the death of Ish-bosheth and had the murderers executed. (II Sam. 2:8; 4:5–12.)

Ishmael

God had promised a son to Abraham, but he and his wife Sarah were both growing too old to have children. At last Sarah gave to Abraham her Egyptian maid Hagar as a second wife. Ishmael became their son. But Sarah became jealous and made Abraham send Hagar and Ishmael into the desert. Ishmael became an archer, married an Egyptian, and had twelve sons. (Gen. 16:15.)

Israel

Through the night Jacob wrestled with God, who visited him as a man. When morning came, God gave Jacob a new name "Israel," which means "he strives with God and prevails." Israel's twelve sons became the ancestors of the twelve tribes. For about 400 years they lived as slaves in Egypt, but God led them forth to a Promised Land. (Gen. 32:28.)

Issachar

One of Jacob's twelve sons was Issachar, who was the son of Leah, father of four sons, and the ancestor of one of the twelve tribes of Israel. Issachar's share of the Promised Land lay in the central part of the pleasant and fertile plain of Jezreel. Deborah and Barak were members of this tribe and their people helped them defeat Sisera. (Judg. 5:15.)

Italian Band

When Peter visited Cornelius, a Roman officer at Caesarea, he brought the message of Christ to a Gentile. Cornelius was a member of the Italian Band, a cohort of Roman soldiers made up of volunteer Roman citizens born in Italy. An inscription has been found which mentions that this cohort was in Caesarea in 69 A.D. (Acts 10:1.)

138

Italy

Italy is mentioned four times in the New Testament. In 49 A.D. the Emperor Claudius ordered all Jews to leave Italy. Aquila, a Jew from Pontus, and his wife Priscilla went to Corinth where they met Paul and helped him. Italy was named for King Italus. He ruled the southwest "toe" of the Italian "boot" about 1300 B.C. (Acts 18:2.)

Ituraea

Somewhere to the northeast of the Sea of Galilee, probably along the base of Mt. Hermon, lies the land known as Ituraea. Its people were descendants of Ishmael and were wild and lawless. They were known as skilled archers and fought against David. The Bible mentions Ituraea as part of the Tetrarchy of Philip. Today it is part of Syria. (Luke 3:1.)

Ittai

Goliath, the giant David killed, was a Philistine from Gath. So was Ittai, a loyal follower of David and one of his chief captains. When Absalom rebelled against David, Ittai helped Joab and Abishai command David's army. Ittai brought 600 of his warriors with him to fight for David. David urged Ittai to return to his own people, but Ittai remained loyal to David. (II Sam. 15:19–22.)

Ivory

It was a sign of wealth and luxury to own ivory. Until the time of David, most ivory used in Israel came from Syrian elephant tusks. Solomon's throne was made of ivory and overlaid with gold. King Ahab's house was paneled with ivory. Amos rebuked Ahab for this when his people were so poor. (I Kings 10:18; 22:39; Amos 3:15; 6:4; Rev. 18:22.)

J

Jabbok

Jacob was headed home from Haran with his wives and children. But Esau approached with 400 men. Jacob was afraid that Esau would kill him and his family because he had once stolen Esau's birthright. Jacob sent his family across the Jabbok River and remained alone to wrestle with God. The river is about halfway between the Dead Sea and the Sea of Galilee in ancient Gilead. (Gen. 32:22–24.)

Jabesh-gilead

When Nahash, king of Ammon, attacked Jabesh, a city in Gilead, the people appealed to Saul. They never forgot Saul's quick victory over Ammon. Years later, when they heard of the death of Saul and Jonathan in a battle with the Philistines, they crossed the Jordan and bravely recovered their bodies from the walls of Beth-shan. (I Sam. 31:8–13.)

Jachin and Boaz

Guarding the entrance to Solomon's Temple were two great pillars made of bronze. The one on the south was named Jachin, which meant "speed." The other was Boaz, which meant "power." Hiram of Tyre had designed them. When Jerusalem was captured in 597 B.C., the pillars were broken up and the metal carried away to Babylon. (I Kings 7:13–22.)

Jacinth

The eleventh jewel in the foundation of New Jerusalem, described in the Book of Revelation, was a precious stone known as jacinth. The color is uncertain. Some have described it as blue, others as amber or an orange-red color. The jacinth was one of the precious stones in the High Priest's breastplate. Sometimes it was called ligure. (Exod. 28:19; Rev. 21:20.)

Jacob

Jacob was the younger of twin sons of Isaac and Rebekah. Esau, the older, knew that Jacob was his mother's favorite. But God's covenant was through Jacob, the younger son. Jacob had twelve sons who became ancestors of the twelve tribes of Israel. Through the tribe of Judah, King David, and later Jesus the Messiah, was born. God changed Jacob's name to Israel. (Luke 3:23–38.)

Jacob's Ladder

Jacob had deceived his father and received the blessing intended for Esau. Esau was angry and Jacob ran away from home. On the way to Haran, Jacob stopped for the night at Luz and dreamed of a stairway to heaven with angels climbing up and down it. God promised Jacob that He would care for him. Jacob named the place Bethel, which means "House of God." (Gen. 28:10–19.)

Jacob's Well

Jacob had escaped from Laban and had won the friendship of his brother Esau again. At last he could settle in peace. So he bought a parcel of land at Shechem and dug a well on it. Hundreds of years later, Jesus talked with a Samaritan woman at this well, which was near the Samaritan city of Sychar, telling her that He is the water of Life. (Gen. 33:19; John 4:5–10.)

Jael

The Israelites under Deborah and Barak had won a great victory over the Canaanites and Sisera, their general. Sisera escaped and hid in the tent of Jael, wife of Heber the Kenite. Jael gave him milk to drink and covered him with a blanket so he would sleep. But while he was sleeping, she drove a wooden tent pin into his head and killed him. (Judg. 4:15–22.)

Jailer

The jailer in charge of the prison at Philippi, where Paul and Silas were arrested, was probably a retired Roman soldier. The city magistrates gave him strict orders to take special care of these two prisoners. To make sure that they did not escape, he put them into his deepest dungeon and clamped their feet in stocks. (Acts 16:22, 23.)

Jairus

Each synagogue had an official in charge. At Capernaum, the village where Jesus lived, the synagogue ruler, or official, was a man named Jairus. When Jairus' daughter became ill, he asked Jesus to come to help her. But the girl died before Jesus arrived. Jesus, however, took her by the hand and brought her to life again. (Mark 5:22–24, 35–43.)

James the Apostle

Two of Jesus' apostles were named James. The son of Alphaeus was called James the Less, for he was either shorter or younger than his namesake. James the son of Zebedee, was a fisherman like his brother John. Jesus nicknamed the brothers "boanerges" which meant "sons of thunder." They must have had fierce tempers, for they wanted to destroy an unfriendly village. (Luke 9:51–55.)

James the Greater

For a while, James did not believe that Jesus was the Messiah, God's Son. But after Jesus arose from the dead, James believed and became a leader in the church in Jerusalem. He led the first Council in Jerusalem, which let Gentiles join the church. In James' epistle, he urged Christians to show their faith by good works. (Acts 12:17; The Epistle from James.)

Jason

While Paul and Silas visited in Thessalonica, they stayed at the home of Jason. But the Jews of the city were envious of them and mobbed Jason's house, looking for Paul and Silas. When they could not find the two, they took Jason before the rulers of the city. Jason was freed only after he promised to keep peace. (Acts 17:5–9; Rom. 16:21.)

Japheth

The people of the earth had been destroyed by a great flood. But Noah and his family were safe in a great boat, including his three sons, Ham, Shem, and Japheth and their wives. All people are descended from these three families. Japheth had seven sons and became the ancestor of the fair-skinned tribes, most of whom lived in southeastern Europe. (Gen. 10:2–5.)

Javelin

"And he smote the javelin into the wall and David fled." Saul was jealous of David, for he was afraid that David would become king instead of him. So Saul threw his javelin at David. It was a short spear with a bronze tip designed to be thrown at the enemy. When not in use, it was carried slung across the warrior's back, held by a leather hoop. (I Sam. 18:10; 19:10.)

Jebusite

For many years the Jebusites kept their great walled city of Jebus until David captured it and made it his capital. He changed the name to Jerusalem. The Jebusites were a warlike tribe of Canaanites who were skilled mountaineers. One of the earliest Jebusite kings was Adonizedek, who died at Beth-horon fighting the Israelites who were entering the Promised Land. (Josh. 11:3; I Chron. 11:4.)

Jehoahaz of Israel

For 17 years Jehoahaz, son of Jehu, ruled in Samaria. But he continued the worship of the golden calf which King Jeroboam began at Bethel and Dan. God punished Jehoahaz by sending Syrian raiders into the land until he had almost no army left. Jehoahaz prayed to God and God freed the Israelites from the Syrians. Elisha prophesied during the reign of Jehoahaz, about 800 B.C., (II Kings 13:1–7.)

Jehoahaz of Judah

At the age of 23, Jehoahaz, who was also called Shallum, became king of Judah. He was a wicked king. His father, King Josiah, had been killed in a battle with Pharaoh Necho, king of Egypt. Three months later, the same pharaoh took Jehoahaz to Egypt as a prisoner. Then he made the brother of Jehoahaz king of Judah instead. (II Kings 23:30–45.)

Jehoiachin

Almost 600 years before Christ, Jehoiachin became king of Judah at the age of 18. His father Jehoiakim had been a wicked king and he was no better. After three months the Babylonian king Nebuchadnezzar took him away to Babylon and kept him prisoner for 37 years. He was finally released by a new Babylonian king, Evil-merodach. (II Chron. 36:9, 10.)

Jehoiada

Athaliah wanted to be queen so much that she killed all of the children who would rule the land. But the High Priest Jehoiada and his wife hid young Joash in the Temple until he was seven. Then they gathered the elders of Israel and proclaimed Joash king. Jehoiada helped Joash do many good things for God early in his reign. (II Kings 11.)

Jehoiakim

Although Jehoiakim was the son of good King Josiah, he was an evil man. At first his name was Eliakim. When the king of Egypt captured King Jehoahaz, he made his brother Eliakim king of Judah instead and changed his name to Jehoiakim. To pay tribute to pharaoh, Jehoiakim forced the people to pay heavy taxes and work without pay. (II Kings 23:34–37.)

Jehoram

When King Ahaziah died, his brother Jehoram, or Joram, became king in his place. Jehoram was a son of the evil King Ahab. During his reign, the king of Moab refused to pay tribute any longer so Jehoram went to fight him. When Jehoram's soldiers ran out of water, Elisha helped them get some. Jehoram was killed at Jezreel by Jehu. (II Kings 3:1–3.)

Jehoshaphat

There were only a few godly kings of Judah and Jehoshaphat was one of them. He ruled almost 900 years before Christ. Jehoshaphat was wise enough to know that His people needed religious education and so he sent out priests and Levites to train them. But he foolishly married his son Jehoram to Ahab's wicked daughter Athaliah. (I Kings 22.)

145

Jehu

Jehu was the commander of Jehoram's army at the battle of Ramoth-gilead. While the king of Israel was away recovering from wounds, Elisha sent a prophet to anoint Jehu as king. Jehu was at once supported by the army. Jehoram and the rest of the family of Ahab and Jezebel were killed and Baal worship in Israel was ended. (II Kings 9:24–26.)

Jephthah

More than 1,000 years before Jesus came, the Israelites were ruled by judges. Jephthah was one of these judges. When Israel had to defend itself against the Ammonites, the elders of Gilead begged Jephthah to be their leader. God gave him a great victory. But he foolishly vowed to sacrifice to God the first person he met when he returned from battle. His only daughter met him. (Judg. 11:29–40.)

Jeremiah

For 40 years Jeremiah was a prophet in Judah. Five kings of Judah reigned during this time. Jeremiah repeatedly warned Judah to return to God or God would punish them. Once he was thrown into a slimy pit because he advised his people to surrender to the Babylonian invaders. Jeremiah wrote of the coming of Christ and of the "new covenant" between God and Israel. (The Book of Jeremiah.)

Jericho

Jericho is probably the oldest city in the world, going back thousands of years before Christ. It is situated about 800 feet below sea level near the Dead Sea and its warm winter climate has attracted people for centuries. Joshua captured the city when God caused its walls to collapse. Jesus was baptized and tempted nearby. (Josh. 6; Matt. 3:13; 4:1.)

Jeroboam I

Because of Rehoboam's harsh rule, the ten northern tribes broke away from Judah and formed the separate state of Israel. Jeroboam had been Solomon's foreman in charge of fortifications, but the prophet Ahijah prophesied that he would become king instead of Solomon's son Rehoboam. When he became king of Israel, Jeroboam sinned by setting up golden calves at Bethel and Dan. (I Kings 12.)

Jeroboam II

During the 40 years that Jeroboam II ruled over Israel, he restored much of Israel's territory that it had lost. The land became prosperous and many of its people rich. But the rich lived in luxury while the poor were sold for a pair of shoes. The prophet Amos condemned this lack of concern for the poor and the worship of heathen gods. (II Kings 14:23–25; Amos 2:6.)

Jerusalem

The city was called Jebus when King David captured it and made it his capital. He renamed it Jerusalem. There Solomon built his great Temple, which was later rebuilt by Herod the Great. Jerusalem was often called the Holy City, Zion, and the City of God. Jesus visited Jerusalem many times and taught in the Temple. (Matt. 2:1; 20:17.)

Jesse

In the little village of Bethlehem there lived a man named Jesse. He was the grandson of Ruth and Boaz and, like them, kept a small piece of land outside the village. Jesse raised sheep on his land. They were cared for by the youngest of his eight sons, a lad named David. David later became the second king of Israel. (I Sam. 17:12–14; 22:3, 4.)

Jesus

The focal point of all the Bible is the coming of God's Son, Jesus Christ, and His death, burial, and resurrection. The Old Testament points to the coming of Jesus Christ. The prophets spoke of a Messiah who would come to save His people. Isaiah spoke of Him as "despised and rejected of men, a man of sorrows." He told how the Messiah would bear our griefs and carry our sorrows and how He would be "wounded for our transgressions," bruised for our iniquities, and that the punishment for our sins would be upon Him. Zechariah said that He would come riding on a colt and Micah said He would be born in Bethlehem. The mother of Jesus was Mary, a virgin, and God was His father. Jesus was God's Son who had come to save His people from their sins. When He was about 30, Jesus was baptized and began His public ministry, teaching and healing, and sometimes raising the dead. His ministry lasted about three years. At the appointed time Jesus was crucified, giving His life to pay for the penalty of our sins. Those who accept Jesus and what He did claim Him as Lord and Savior. They are called Christians because they follow Christ. Jesus ascended into heaven to be with God the Father, but He sent the Holy Spirit to be with us. (Isa. 55:3–5; Zech. 9:9; Micah 5:2; The Books of Matthew, Mark, Luke, and John.)

Jethro

Jethro was a man with two names. Reuel may have been his own name. Jethro may have been a title. When Moses ran away from Egypt, he went to live with Jethro in Midian, took care of his sheep, and married his daughter Zipporah. Years later, as Moses led his people from Egypt, Jethro met him and suggested he appoint judges to help him in his work. (Exod. 3:1; 18:1–7.)

Jezebel

Queen Jezebel was one of the most wicked women mentioned in the Bible. She was the daughter of Ethbaal, king of Tyre. When she married King Ahab of Israel, she persuaded the wicked king to set up the worship of Baal, build a temple for her god, and keep 450 priests of Baal who ate at her table. Her worst enemy was Elijah the prophet. (I Kings 21.)

Jezreel

King Ahab had a palace at the city of Jezreel. Nearby there was a vineyard owned by Naboth. When Naboth refused to give his vineyard to Ahab, he was stoned to death and Ahab took the vineyard anyway. At this palace, Jezebel, Ahab's wife, was thrown to her death and was eaten by dogs. The Valley of Jezreel is the plain stretching from Jezreel toward the Jordan River. (I Kings 21; II Kings 9:30–35.)

Joab

As the skilled commander of David's army, Joab won many great victories. He led the daring attack on Jebus, which became David's capital city of Jerusalem. When Absalom rebelled, Joab remained loyal to David and put Absalom to death. Joab was the oldest son of Zeruiah, David's sister. Joab was killed in the tabernacle where he held on to the horns of the altar. (II Sam. 10:1–14; 11:1; 12:26–29.)

Joanna

She had been healed "of evil spirits and infirmities." No wonder Joanna, the wife of Herod's steward Chuza, was so thankful. She and some other women ministered to Jesus and His 12 disciples. When Jesus was crucified, Joanna and her friends prepared spices and ointments to bury with Him. Joanna was one who came to Jesus' empty tomb. (Luke 8:2, 3; 23:55, 56; 24:10.)

Joash

When Athaliah seized the throne to Judah and killed all the heirs to the kingdom, only the baby Joash was saved. For six years the High Priest Jehoiada and his wife Jehosheba, who was Joash's aunt, hid Joash in the Temple. Joash was proclaimed king at the age of seven. During his reign of 40 years, he repaired the Temple in Jerusalem. (II Kings 12:20; II Chron. 24.)

Job

The Book of Job tells the story of a godly man with a large and happy family. Satan thought that Job lived a godly life only because God gave him wealth. So God allowed Satan to test Job by taking away his money, his children, and his health. But Job remained faithful to God despite his sufferings and the misleading things said to him by his friends. (The Book of Job.)

Jochebed

When Pharaoh, King of Egypt, gave orders that all Hebrew boys should be killed, Jochebed hid her baby boy in a basket made of bulrushes. But the princess found the baby and named him Moses, raising him as her own son. Jochebed's husband, Moses' father, was Amram. Both were descended from Levi. (Exod. 6:20; Num. 26:59.)

Joel

The Book of Joel tells of great swarms of locusts which devastated the land, stripping trees, vines, and fields. Even the Temple offerings were stopped because there was so little grain, wine, and oil. The prophet Joel called the priests to lead the people to fast and pray. He knew that the plague was God's judgment on the nation for neglecting Him. (The Book of Joel.)

Johanan

Johanan tried to warn Gedaliah, the new governor of Judah, of a plot to kill him. But Gedaliah would not listen and was murdered. Then Johanan tried to avenge his death. At last, this military captain led a group of his people to Egypt, even though Jeremiah the prophet advised him to remain in Judah. He forced Jeremiah to go with them. (Jer. 40:13, 14; 41:11–15.)

John the Apostle

John and his family had a prosperous fishing business on the Sea of Galilee. His brother was James, his father Zebedee, and his mother was probably Salome. John was one of the first disciples called by Jesus and became one of His closest friends and followers. John wrote a Gospel, three epistles, and Revelation. (The Gospel according to John; I, II, and III John; The Revelation of John.)

John the Baptist

He lived in the wild country and dressed in camel's hair with a great leather belt around his waist. But John the Baptist had a message to bring to all who listened. "Repent!" he cried out. He also told of Jesus who was going to come. Jesus went to hear His cousin John and was baptized by him in the Jordan River. John's head was cut off by Herod Antipas. (Mark 1: 4–11.)

Jonah

"Now the word of the Lord came to Jonah." Thus Jonah begins his book, written about 800 years before Jesus came. He tells of the time he tried to run away from God and the way God sent a great fish to save him from the sea. Through this, Jonah learned to obey God. Jonah went to Nineveh, as God directed, and preached, causing many to turn to God. (The Book of Jonah.)

Jonathan

Jonathan was the son of King Saul and was in line to become the next king of Israel. But he became David's best friend, even though he realized that the people might make David king instead of him. Jonathan did all he could to save David from his father's anger. He was a very brave young man. One time he and his armor-bearer attacked a Philistine garrison alone. (I Sam. 14:1–16.)

Joppa

Joppa, the seaport for Jerusalem, lay 32 miles or 52 kilometers to the west on the Mediterranean Sea coast. When Jonah tried to run from God, he boarded a ship at Joppa. Solomon brought the cedar logs of Lebanon to Joppa and carted them to Jerusalem for the Temple. Many years later, Peter brought Dorcas back from the dead at Joppa. (II Chron. 2:16; Acts 9:36–43.)

Jordan

The waters of the Jordan River begin in the sparkling streams that flow from the snow of Mt. Hermon. They end in the salty, murky lake known as the Dead Sea. Jesus was baptized in the Jordan River, not far from Jericho. Centuries earlier, the water of the Jordan parted so that the people of Israel could cross the river into the Promised Land. (Josh. 3:17; Matt. 3:13–17.)

Joseph of Arimathea

Although Arimathea was only a tiny village in the Judaean hills, Joseph became a respected member of the Sanhedrin Council in Jerusalem. He was a disciple of Jesus but kept it secret for fear of the other Jews. When Jesus was crucified, however, Joseph boldly asked Pilate for the body and buried it in a private rock tomb. (Matt. 27:57.)

Joseph of Nazareth

Although Joseph was not Jesus' real father, it was his job to care for him as a son. Jesus' true father was God, who caused Him to grow in the virgin Mary. When Herod tried to kill the Baby Jesus, Joseph fled with Him and Mary to Egypt. After Herod died, Joseph returned to Nazareth, began his work as carpenter again, and taught his trade to young Jesus. (Matt. 2:13–23.)

152

Joseph, Son of Jacob

While Joseph was still in his teens, God sent two dreams to hint of his future as a great leader. When he told his family about these dreams, his brothers were jealous and sold him as a slave in Egypt. But God was with him and helped him become governor of the land. God also helped him save Egypt and his own family from seven years of famine. (Gen. 37; 39—50.)

Joshua

When Moses sent 12 spies to enter the Promised Land, only Joshua and Caleb returned with a good report, urging their people to claim the land God had promised. At that time Joshua was Moses' chief assistant. When Moses died, Joshua was chosen to take his place. The Book of Joshua tells of the conquest of the land under Joshua's leadership. (The Book of Joshua.)

Josiah

Josiah was only eight years old when he became king of Judah. He destroyed the idols throughout the land and served God with all his heart. During his reign, the Book of the Law was found in the Temple and read to the people. The people of Judah then celebrated the Passover for the first time in many years. Josiah was only 39 when he was killed in a battle with the Egyptians. (II Chron. 34—35.)

Jotham, Gideon's Son

The first parable of the Bible was given by Jotham, the youngest of Gideon's 70 sons. All of Jotham's brothers were killed by Abimelech, whom the men of Shechem made their king. Jotham stood on a mountainside and shouted to them, telling them a parable of some trees who wanted a king. Then Jotham pronounced a curse on Abimelech and the men of Shechem. (Judg. 9.)

Jotham, King of Judah

After King Uzziah became ill with leprosy, his son Jotham ruled Judah for 13 years. When Uzziah died in 740 B.C., Jotham became the king. Isaiah probably influenced Jotham and helped him become a successful ruler. Jotham continued to fortify Jerusalem and built the Upper Gate of the Temple. He defeated the Ammonites who were forced to pay tribute of silver and grain. (II Kings 15:32–38.)

Judah

Judah's life was one of great blessing and shame. He was an ancestor of King David and, through Mary, the ancestor of Jesus. When Joseph's brothers plotted to kill him, Judah suggested they sell Joseph as a slave. Later, when Jacob agreed to let Benjamin go to Egypt, Judah promised to keep him safe. Judah was the fourth son of Jacob and Leah. (Gen. 29:35.)

Jubilee Year

Every fiftieth year was called the Jubilee Year. It was announced with a special ram's horn which the priests would blow. All Jewish slaves were freed by Jewish masters during this year. And all property which was sold because of poverty was returned to its original owners. Nothing was to be planted for harvest during the Jubilee Year. (Lev. 25:8–17.)

Judas Iscariot

Judas was treasurer for the 12 disciples, caring after their money. At the Last Supper, Jesus told Judas to hurry and do what he had planned. Judas rushed out to betray Jesus for 30 pieces of silver. In Gethsemane he betrayed Jesus with a kiss. In a fit of guilt, he threw the money before the chief priests and went out and hanged himself. (Matt. 27:3–10.)

Jude

The last epistle of the New Testament is called Jude, named for its author. Mark names Jude as a brother of Jesus. The Bible tells us that he did not believe in Jesus as Savior while Jesus was on earth. But after Jesus returned to heaven, Jude became a believer. His letter warns Christians about false teachers. (John 7:5; The Epistle from Jude.)

Judges

From the death of Joshua until Saul became king, the tribes of Israel were governed by judges. The Book of Judges tells how they delivered the people from their enemies in times of war and ruled the country in times of peace. Samuel was the last and the greatest of the judges. He anointed Saul as the first king. (The Book of Judges.)

Judgment Seat

When Jesus was placed on trial, He stood before the judgment seat of Pilate. Paul later went on trial because he worked for Jesus and he stood before the judgment seats of Felix, Festus, and Agrippa. A judgment seat is a place where a judge sits. The Bible speaks also of a judgment seat on which Jesus will sit to judge believers and their works. (Rom. 14:10; II Cor. 5:10.)

Julius

It was Julius' responsibility to take Paul to Rome. He was a kindly Roman centurion, a member of the Augustan band. Julius allowed Paul to visit Christian friends when the ship stopped at Sidon. Because he wanted to save Paul, Julius kept his soldiers from killing the prisoners when the ship ran aground off the coast of Malta. (Acts 27:1, 3, 43.)

K

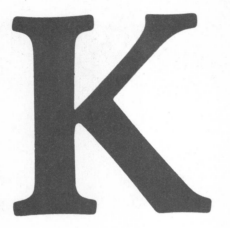

Kadesh-barnea

For two years the people of Israel had been on their way to the Promised Land. They stopped at Kadesh-barnea in the wilderness of Zin and waited while Moses sent 12 spies into the land to scout it. But when ten of the spies brought back a bad report, the people were afraid. So God made them live in the wilderness for another 38 years. (Num. 13:26.)

Kedesh

Ten thousand men gathered around Barak at the city of Kedesh, sometimes called Kedesh-naphtali. From there Deborah and Barak led their forces against the Canaanite forces under Sisera. God gave them a great victory and freed the people of Israel from Canaanite oppression in that area. Kedesh had been conquered earlier by Joshua and was given to the tribe of Naphtali. (Judg. 4:4–10.)

Keilah

Keilah will be remembered as the ungrateful city. When the Philistines raided it, stole its grain, and drove off its cattle, David and his men came to the rescue. Abiathar joined David at Keilah, bringing the sacred ephod with him. But the ungrateful people were going to betray David to King Saul and so David had to escape. (I Sam. 23:1–13.)

Kenites

As the people of Israel left Mt. Sinai, Moses' brother-in-law joined them and became their guide through the wilderness. His descendants were the Kenites. Most of them went with the tribe of Judah. Heber the Kenite moved northward to Kedesh. Heber's wife, Jael, killed Sisera by driving a tent peg through his head, giving the Israelites a great victory. (Judg. 4:16–24.)

Kidron

The bed of the brook Kidron runs from the north of Jerusalem past the Temple mount and the Mount of Olives, and at last reaches the Dead Sea. Only for short periods during the rainy season is it filled with water. Good kings of Judah like Asa, Hezekiah, and Josiah made bonfires of idols and threw the ashes into the Kidron. (I Kings 15:13.)

Kings, Kingdom

Two Old Testament books tell about the kings and the kingdoms of Judah and Israel for 400 years. They begin with the close of David's reign as king when there was only one kingdom and continue the story until about 500 years before Jesus came. The Books of Kings tell how God worked in the lives of His people during this time. (The Books of I and II Kings.)

Kinsman

"Naomi had a kinsman of her husband's." Boaz was a kinsman, or close relative, of Naomi. Therefore he could marry Naomi's daughter-in-law Ruth, who was a widow, and inherit her dead husband's property. Sometimes close friends or neighbors were called kinsmen. When a murder was to be avenged, it was a kinsman who had to do it. (Num. 5:5–8; Ruth 2:1.)

157

Kish

Kish was a wealthy man of the tribe of Benjamin who lived at Gibeah. One day some of his donkeys strayed away from home and so he asked his son Saul to look for them. Along the way, Saul met Samuel and was anointed by him as the first king of Israel. Kish was buried in Zelah in land belonging to Benjamites. Later, Saul and his son Jonathan were buried there, too. (I Sam. 9:1–3.)

Kishon

"And Elijah brought them down to the brook Kishon and slew them there." Elijah had called down fire from heaven. The prophets of Baal could not. Elijah had proven that God, not Baal, was the Lord of all. So he executed the prophets of Baal by the side of the brook which runs near Mt. Carmel. Deborah and Barak defeated Sisera and his men in chariots near there. (I Kings 18:40.)

Kohathites

When the Tabernacle was completed in the wilderness, the Kohathites were appointed to care for part of it. As the Israelites moved through the wilderness, it was their job to carry the Ark, table, lampstand, sacred vessels, and screen. The Kohathites were descendants of Kohath, Levi's second son and the grandfather of Aaron, Moses, and Miriam. (Num. 3:27–31; 7:9.)

Korah

Korah and his friends complained bitterly that Moses and Aaron had too much authority. "There are many holy people among us," they said. But the next day Moses led the people before Korah's tent. "If the Lord swallows them up, it will show they have provoked Him," Moses said. Immediately the earth opened and swallowed up Korah and his friends. (Num. 16.)

L

Laban

Although Laban was Jacob's uncle, he was not fair to Jacob. For 14 years, Jacob worked for Laban just so he could get married. Then Laban would not share his flocks with Jacob. Finally, Jacob took his family and possessions and ran away. Laban pursued him but God warned him in a dream not to harm Jacob. So Laban made a covenant with him. (Gen. 31.)

Lachish

Lachish was an old city by the time of Abraham. When Joshua invaded the Promised Land, he captured this Canaanite city and its king. King Rehoboam later fortified Lachish, but it was destroyed again and again as the Babylonians came against Judah. When the Jews returned from exile in Nehemiah's day, Lachish was rebuilt. (Josh. 10:31, 32.)

Lamb

"A lamb without blemish." Only the perfect lamb was to be sacrificed to God as an offering for sin. In the Passover, the blood of the sacrificed lamb was put on the door posts. When God provided the lamb as a sacrifice for the world's sin, He offered His only Son, Jesus Christ, as the perfect "Lamb of God," without sin. A lamb is a young sheep or goat. (Exod. 12:5; John 1:29; Heb. 9:14.)

Lamech

Long before the flood came upon the earth, Lamech became the first poet of the Bible. In his poetry he tells of killing a young man. Some believe he killed in self-defense and is claiming that he is innocent. Lamech had two wives, Adah and Zillah. One of his sons, Tubal-cain, invented metalworking and made weapons of war. Another was the "father of musicians." (Gen. 4:19–24.)

Lamp

There were no electric lights in Bible times and so the people had to use oil lamps. These were often like a saucer, sometimes with a top. The oil in the lamp was fed through a wick of flax, hemp, or peeled rush. Sometimes people left the lamp burning so that a fire could be lit at any time. The word *candle* in the Bible meant lamp. (Ps. 119:105; Matt. 25:1–9.)

Lamentations

In 586 B.C. the Babylonians captured Jerusalem and destroyed the Temple along with the city. The Book of Lamentations is a funeral poem written by the prophet Jeremiah, mourning this great loss. It consists of five sad poems, describing the suffering of the people, the destruction of the city, and the taunts of the enemy. (The Book of Lamentations.)

Laodicea

The people of Laodicea had too much wealth. This affected their attitude toward God. "You are lukewarm," was the way John wrote to them. "I wish you were either hot or cold toward God." Then he wrote God's view of them. "I will spit you out of My mouth," God said. Laodicea was a city in Asia Minor, which is in Turkey today. (Rev. 3:14–18.)

Laver

Between the altar and the door of the Tabernacle, there was a great bronze basin called a laver. It had been made from metal mirrors which women had given for the Tabernacle. The laver held water in which the priests washed their hands and feet before ministering. It showed daily purifying before the Lord and the need for cleansing from sin. (Exod. 30:17–22.)

Lazarus

Jesus often visited the little village of Bethany, just to the east of Jerusalem. While there, He always went to see Mary and Martha and Lazarus. When Lazarus became sick, the sisters sent Jesus an urgent message. But Lazarus died before Jesus came. Jesus raised Lazarus from his tomb, bringing him back to life again. (John 11:1–44.)

Law

"According to the law of Moses." Mary and Joseph offered a sacrifice in the Temple and presented the Baby Jesus, as the law commanded. All obedient Jews followed the commandments of the law, most of them found in the first five books of the Bible. The law told them how to worship and live. Jesus said He did not come to destroy the law but to fulfill it. (Matt. 5:17; Luke 2:21–24.)

Leah

Of the 12 tribes of Israel, six claimed Leah as their mother. Her father Laban tricked Jacob into marrying her. It was the custom in Laban's country to marry the older daughter first and Leah was older than Rachel, whom Jacob really wanted to marry. It was through Leah that the lineage of King David and Jesus came. (Gen. 29:21–30.)

Leather

The Israelites cured the skins of their animals and used the leather to make bottles. Travelers found leather bottles much more suitable for carrying than those made out of pottery, which were easily broken. A piece of leather spread on the ground served as a table. Leather was also made into sandals, girdles, tent coverings, quivers, and sword sheaths. (Matt. 3:4.)

Leaven

Today we call it yeast. But Bible-time people called it leaven. It was made by mixing flour and water and letting it stand until it soured. Leaven was mixed in with new dough to cause it to rise. The Jews ate unleavened bread the night of the Passover. Even today they continue to eat it as a reminder of their hurried flight from Egypt. (Exod. 12:15–20; Matt. 13:33.)

Lebanon

In the days of King Solomon, Lebanon was the land of great cedar trees. Solomon brought the cedars of Lebanon to Jerusalem for his Temple. The name Lebanon at first referred to the great mountain range stretching northward from Galilee. It means white, referring to the white snows that cover the mountains and the white limestone cliffs. (Pss. 92:12; 104:16.)

Legion

"My name is Legion," a demon-possessed man told Jesus. That was because there were so many demons in him. In the Roman army a legion numbered 6,000 men, divided into ten cohorts. The name became widely used for any large number. In Gethsemane, Jesus said that His Father would send twelve legions of angels if He asked. (Matt. 26:53; Luke 8:30.)

Lentil

Esau returned from the field one day to find his twin brother Jacob making a pot of lentil soup. Esau was so hungry that he traded his birthright for some of the soup. Lentils are the seeds of a small plant grown throughout Palestine for food. Lentils were brought to David when he hid from Saul east of the river Jordan. (Gen. 25:29–34.)

Leprosy

There was almost no disease more feared than leprosy. "Unclean! Unclean!" the leper cried as he went about. People shunned the leper and forced him to move away from his home and village. The disease began with white spots and sometimes caused fingers or other parts of the body to become deformed. Jesus healed ten lepers, but only one said "thank you." (II Kings 5; Luke 17:11–19.)

Letter

Until Roman times the postal service was only for government letters. Ordinary people sent their letters by friendly travelers or merchants. Many people could not write and so they hired scribes to write their letters. The 21 Epistles in the New Testament were letters from God's chosen men to others, often to churches. (II Thess. 3:17; II Pet. 3:1.)

Levi, Levite

All priests of Israel were Levites. But all Levites did not become priests. The Levites were descended from Jacob and Leah's third son, Levi. God gave them the special honor of priesthood, or helping the priests, partly because Moses and Aaron were also descended from Levi. The Levites helped the priests in the Tabernacle. (Num. 3:5–10.)

Leviticus

The third book of the Bible tells of the life and work of the Levites and priests. Leviticus also describes the sacrifices to God for forgiveness of sin and the way they were to be carried out. The book tells how God's people were to worship and obey Him and includes many special instructions to the priests of Israel. (The Book of Leviticus.)

Life

Life is a special gift of God. When God made man, He breathed the breath of life into Adam's nostrils. Jesus said, "I am the Way, the Truth, and the Life." He came that men might find a life that never ends and live with Him while on earth and later in heaven. The Lamb's Book of Life, mentioned in Revelation, is a list of those who belong to Jesus. (Gen. 2:7; John 14:6; Rev. 3:5.)

Lightning

"His countenance was like lightning." No wonder the guards at Jesus' tomb shook with fear. The Bible mentions lightning a number of times as a display of God's power. Jesus said that his Second Coming to earth would be as lightning. When the Lord appeared on Mt. Sinai to give Moses the Ten Commandments, lightning flashed around the mountain. (Exod. 19:16; Matt. 28:3.)

Lily

"Consider the lilies of the field," Jesus told His disciples. He pointed out that even the great King Solomon was never clothed so beautifully. Jesus was talking about the many flowers that color the springtime hills of Palestine. These include the scarlet anemonies, iris, saffron crocus, tulip, hyacinth, and star-of-Bethlehem. (Matt. 6:28, 29.)

Linen

Hebrew women became skilled in weaving fine linen cloth from flax. But some of the best linen came from ancient Egypt. Red linen was considered a luxury and was called royal linen. The coat, turban, and girdle of the priests were made of fine linen. When the Israelites escaped from Egypt, the fine linen they brought with them was used for the Tabernacle curtains. (Prov. 31:13, 19.)

Lintel

A doorway had two side posts and a beam across them. This beam, made of stone or wood, was called the lintel. In ancient Egypt it was often the custom to paint the name of the person who lived in the home on this lintel as well as the two side posts. On the night of the Passover, the Israelites were to sprinkle lamb's blood on the lintel and doorposts. (Exod. 12:21, 22, 23.)

Lion

When Samson killed a lion with his bare hands, he showed strength that only God could give. The lion was a strong, fierce animal. David also once killed a lion. Lions were common in Palestine in Bible times, but are not found there today. They often made their homes in the forests or brush or in mountain caves. (Judg. 14:5, 6; I Sam. 17:36.)

Locust

Swarms of locusts are driven along by the wind, invading Palestine from the Arabian desert to the south. The female locust lays her eggs in holes in the ground. The eggs of the insect hatch as wingless larvae which hop about, devouring all vegetation within reach. Then the locusts grow wings and swarm farther on to strip plants in another place. (Exod. 10:4–6.)

Lord's Supper

"As often as you do this, remember Me," Jesus told His disciples at the Passover feast before His crucifixion. It was at this meal, traditionally called the Last Supper, that Jesus delivered His farewell discourse. In the Lord's Supper Christians have celebrated this event, re-enacting it as the Eucharist or communion. (Mark 14:22–25; Luke 22:14–20; John 13–17; I Cor. 11:25, 26.)

Lots

While Jesus hung on the cross, Roman soldiers cast lots for his clothing. Bible-time people often cast lots to decide what they should do. Stones with certain marks were drawn from a jar. Each mark showed which person should make a choice or which choice was right. The Promised Land was divided among the tribes of Israel by lots. (Num. 26:55; I Sam. 14:42; Jon. 1:7; Matt. 27:35.)

Lot

When his father Haran died, Lot went to Canaan with his uncle Abraham. As Lot grew and had his own herds and flocks, his herdsmen quarreled with Abraham's. Abraham offered Lot his choice of land and so the selfish young man chose the best, the well-watered Jordan Valley. But living there meant living near Sodom. Before God destroyed the wicked city, He sent angels to warn Lot to leave. (Gen. 19.)

Luke

Only one writer in the New Testament was a Gentile. Luke, a Greek-speaking gentile physician, often traveled with Paul on his journeys. He was not one of the 12 apostles. Luke wrote the third Gospel and the Acts of the Apostles. He stayed with Paul while the apostle was in prison awaiting his death. Luke died in Greece at the age of 84. (The Gospel according to Luke and the Acts of the Apostles.)

Lycaonia

"Lystra and Derbe, cities of Lycaonia."
This is the way the Bible describes the two
cities to which Paul and Barnabas had to
flee when they were about to be stoned at
Iconium. Lycaonia was a division of a
Roman province in central Asia Minor,
which is Turkey today. It is not clear
where its boundaries lay, but it touched
Galatia, Cappadocia, Cilicia, and Pisidia.
(Acts 14:6.)

Lydda

Aeneas had been in bed with paralysis for
eight years. But one day Peter visited his
home town of Lydda and healed him.
Aeneas went about Lydda and the Plain of
Sharon telling of this miracle. In Old Testament times, the town was called Lod,
which is also its name today. It is about
ten miles or 16 kilometers east of Joppa.
(Acts 9:32–38.)

Lydia

Lydia was praying by the riverside when
Paul arrived to tell about Jesus. She was a
seller of purple dye and had come to
Philippi from Thyatira. The purple dye
was prized in those days and so Lydia had
become wealthy. When Lydia heard the
Gospel, she became the first European
Christian. Paul, Silas, and Luke stayed at
her home while in Philippi. (Acts 16:14,
15.)

Lystra

Paul and Barnabas were driven from
Iconium by jealous men and so they hurried on to Lystra. There Paul healed a man
who had never walked. This awed the
people of Lystra so much that they thought
Paul and Barnabas were gods. The people
quickly changed their minds and stoned
Paul. Timothy, Paul's devoted helper,
came from Lystra. (Acts 14:6–21.)

M

Macedonia

"Come over into Macedonia and help us," a man begged in Paul's vision. It was God's call for Paul to preach in Europe as he had done in Asia. Immediately Paul went to Macedonia and preached in Philipi, one of the important cities there. Macedonia is the northern part of Greece today but was part of the Roman Empire at that time. Thessalonica was also an important city in Macedonia. (Acts 16:9, 10.)

Machpelah

Abraham looked for a suitable place to bury his wife Sarah. There was such a place but it belonged to Ephron the Hittite. Abraham bought the cave and the field in which it was located for 400 shekels of silver. Later Abraham was buried there at Machpelah, which is at Hebron. Isaac, Rebekah, Jacob, and Leah were buried there, too. (Gen. 23:19, 20; 25:9; 50:13.)

Mahanaim

Mahanaim means "two camps." It was the place where Jacob was encouraged by seeing the angels of God before he reached Penuel and faced the dreaded meeting with his brother Esau. Later Mahanaim was for a short time the capital city of Ish-bosheth, the son of Saul. David took refuge there when he was being hunted by Absalom. (Gen. 32:2.)

Maher-shalal-hash-baz

Isaiah the prophet chose the strange name of Maher-shalal-hash-baz for his son. God told him first to write this name on a tablet and then to give his son the name. It means "speed the spoil, hasten the prey." The name was to be a special sign to the people of Judah. Before the child was old enough to talk, the Assyrians swept away Judah's enemies from her borders. (Isa. 8:1–4.)

Makkedah

After Joshua won a great victory over the Amorites, five of their kings hid themselves in a cave at Makkedah, a city in the plains of Judah. When Joshua heard about this, he ordered his men to block the entrance with huge stones until Israel had finished chasing the enemy. After the battle, the five kings were brought out and killed. (Josh. 10:16–27.)

Malachi

The name Malachi means "my messenger." It is the name of the last book of the Old Testament and the prophet who wrote it. The message that Malachi brings is that the people have been blessed because God has brought them back to their homeland, but that many have turned from Him. God will bless the faithful and judge the unfaithful. (The Book of Malachi.)

Malchus

Malchus, servant of the High Priest, had come to Gethsemane with the officers who arrested Jesus. While there, Peter chopped off one of his ears. John, who knew the High Priest and his household, mentions the name of Malchus in his Gospel. But Luke the physician tells how Jesus healed Malchus' ear again. (Luke 22:50, 51; John 18:10.)

Mammon

Mammon is a word that comes from the Aramaic language and means wealth or profit. Jesus told His disciples "Ye cannot serve God and mammon." He warned that one could not devote his life to God and money at the same time. Jesus never taught that it is wrong to have money, but that it is wrong to have money as a god. (Matt. 6:24.)

Mamre

For some time, Abraham lived by the oaks of Mamre, not far to the north of Hebron. He often stayed beneath a terebinth tree. At Mamre he built an altar to the Lord, entertained three angels, and received God's promise of a son. It was also at Mamre that Abraham saw the smoke of Sodom and Gomorrah when God destroyed those cities. (Gen. 13:18; 18:1.)

Manasseh

Joseph had only two sons and both were born in Egypt. The first was Manasseh. Joseph chose this name, which means "making to forget," because Joseph's new family in Egypt helped him forget the hardships he had suffered. Manasseh's descendants formed a half-tribe in Israel and were famous for their bravery. Gideon and Jephthah belonged to this tribe. (Gen. 41:51.)

Mandrakes

"Give me some of your son's mandrakes," Rachel asked her sister Leah. Rachel wanted the mandrakes because they were supposed to help women have children. The mandrake plant had plum-like berries and roots like carrots which the women ate. Perfume was also made from the mandrake plant. (Gen. 30:14; Song of Sol. 7:13.)

170

Manger

"She laid him in a manger." Mary had nowhere else to cradle the Baby Jesus. The delivery room was a stable and the crib was a stone box where animals were fed. A manger was a hollowed stone placed on the ground where the animals could reach it. Sometimes the manger was cut into a rock wall, which was probably the way it was in Bethlehem. (Luke 2:7.)

Manna

Manna came in time for the morning, a special gift of food from God. It looked like frost on the ground and tasted like honey wafers. The first time it appeared, everyone asked "Manna?" That really meant "What is it?" So manna became the name for the food that God gave the children of Israel throughout their wilderness journey. (Exod. 16:14–26.)

Manoah

Manoah and his wife had no children. But one day an angel revealed that they would have a son. He would save Israel from the hands of the Philistines. When Manoah prayed for help in bringing up the child, the angel reappeared. Then, as Manoah offered a sacrifice to God, the angel vanished in the altar fire. The child's name was Samson. (Judg. 14:1–11.)

Mantle

Clothing in Bible times was much different from ours today. Men and women wore garments like robes. Over these garments they wore a mantle. The ordinary mantle was a cloak, with openings for the arms at the sides. At night, people used mantles as a covering. Most mantles were made of camel's hair. Wealthier people could afford mantles of softer fabric. (I Kings 19:19.)

Marah

For three days the people of Israel marched through the wilderness without water. At last they came to a lovely oasis, but they could not drink the water because it was too bitter. They called the place "Marah," which means bitter. When the people complained, Moses cried to God. God told him to sweeten the water by throwing a tree into it. (Exod. 15:22–25.)

Mareshah

At Mareshah, King Asa met a large army from Ethiopia and with God's help chased it to Gerar and destroyed it. Rehoboam had considered this an important city and had fortified it years before. Mareshah was a city of Judah which lay at the foot of the hills southwest of Jerusalem, a few miles west of Hebron. (Josh. 15:44; II Chron. 11:5–12; 14:9–15.)

Mark

John Mark wrote the second Gospel, probably in Rome. Mark was a Roman name. John was Jewish. Mark's mother had a large home in Jerusalem, where some believe the Last Supper took place. It was used often by the Christians as a meeting place. Mark went with Paul and Barnabas on a missionary journey and then later cared for Paul while he was in prison. (The Gospel according to Mark.)

Market

The market was called by the Greeks the "agora," the place where people gathered for many purposes. Some came to buy, others to talk about business. Some merely gossiped or caught up on the news, while children played games in the streets. It was the place where laborers gathered to find jobs, and even the Pharisees walked by to receive the people's admiration. (Matt. 20:3–6.)

Marriage

An Israelite marriage was usually arranged by the father who chose a wife for his son. The girl's father decided whether she might leave home. If the marriage was agreed on, the bride's family was paid a dowry by the groom's father. This made the marriage legal. There was no religious ceremony. The celebrations lasted a week or more. (Matt. 25:1–13.)

Mars' Hill

While Paul waited at Athens for Silas and Timothy to join him, he spoke with a court made up of important men in the city. This Court met originally on Mars' Hill, also called Areopagus, a rocky hill near the Acropolis. Paul told his listeners that he had found an altar to the Unknown God. He then said that this God they did not know was the one who had raised Jesus from the dead. (Acts 17:22.)

Martha

Jesus often visited the little village of Bethany, just across the Kidron Valley to the east of Jerusalem. He stayed many times with His close friends Mary, Martha, and Lazarus. Once Martha, which means "lady," became angry as she hurried about doing kitchen chores while her sister Mary talked with Jesus. But Jesus said that talking to Him was more important. (Luke 10:38–42.)

Martyr

Paul spoke of "the blood of thy martyr Stephen." He should have known. Paul held the cloaks of those who killed Stephen, granting his consent to them. Usually we think of a martyr as someone who gives his life because of his devotion to Christ. Stephen was the first Christian martyr. Many have died for Christ since Stephen. (Acts 22:20.)

Mary Magdalene

Mary received her name from her birth-place, the little village of Magdala on the western shores of the Sea of Galilee. She was one of six New Testament women named Mary. Jesus had once cast seven demons from her and she followed Him gratefully. She stood beneath the cross, watched His burial, and came to His tomb on Sunday morning. (Matt. 28:1–8; Mark 16:9.)

Mary, the mother of Jesus

Of all women on earth, Mary was blessed with the greatest honor. God chose her to be the mother of His Son, the Lord Jesus. Mary was a virgin when Jesus was born, for He had no earthly father. Jesus per-formed His first miracle at the request of His mother. She was at the foot of His cross when He died and was present at the first Pentecost. (Luke 1:26–56; John 19:25–27; Acts 1:14.)

Mason

Ordinary houses in Palestine were simple in design and built by craftsmen who were equally clever as masons, working with stone, or as carpenters, working with wood. Specialist masons, who laid up brick or stone, were employed on great buildings like David's palace and Solomon's Temple. Masons also constructed waterworks such as the Siloam Tunnel for King Hezekiah and the immense walls of Jerusalem.

Matthew

The people hated tax collectors because they were Jews who collected money for the Romans. Matthew, one of these hated tax collectors, worked on the important cus-toms route between Damascus and the Mediterranean coast. He became rich in his tax booth, but when Jesus called him, he left all to follow Him. His Gospel gives a Jewish view of Jesus. (The Gospel accord-ing to Matthew.)

Matthias

Someone had to take the place of Judas, who had betrayed Jesus and then hanged himself. Matthias and Joseph Barsabbas were both nominated for the twelfth apostle's job. After the Christians prayed and asked God to guide them, Matthias was chosen by drawing lots. The name Matthias means "gift of the Lord." (Acts 1:15–26.)

Measures

Jewish measures of length were determined by the human body. The span is the distance from a man's thumb to the little finger extended, about nine inches or 23 centimeters. The cubit is the measure of a man's arm from the elbow to the end of the middle finger, about 18 inches or 46 centimeters. The fathom is the distance between the outstretched arms, about six feet or 1.8 meters. (Deut. 3:11.)

Media

For a time Media was the land now known as Iran. "The law of the Medes and the Persians, which altereth not" was mentioned in Daniel. This suggests the firm hard laws of the rulers. While the Jews were in exile, they were ruled by the Medes and Persians for many years. Their life is described in the Books of Esther and Daniel. (Dan. 6:8.)

Medicine

There were no drug stores in Bible times and so many medicines were homemade. Olive oil was widely used, sometimes mixed with wine. The Good Samaritan used this to help the injured man on the Jericho road. Honey was smeared over open wounds and swallowed for sore throats. Toothache was treated with garlic and pain in the gums with salt or yeast. (Luke 10:34.)

Mediterranean Sea

Many of the Bible lands bordered on the Mediterranean Sea, sometimes called the Great Sea. Egypt, Israel, ancient Syria, Asia Minor, Macedonia, Achaia, and Italy all touched this great inland sea. Winter storms made it dangerous to cross in the sailing ships of that time. The ship taking Paul to Rome to stand trial was blown off course and wrecked on Melita or Malta. (Acts 27:40–44.)

Melchizedek

When Abraham returned from his victory over Chedorlaomer and his allies, Melchizedek, king of Salem (Jerusalem), gave him bread and wine and blessed him in the name of the Lord. Abraham in return gave Melchizedek a tenth of the spoils of the battle. Melchizedek was not only a king but a priest also. His name meant "king of righteousness." (Gen. 14:18–20.)

Megiddo

Megiddo was a city located on the road from Gaza to Damascus. This road was both an important military road for armies marching north or south, as well as a commercial route for caravans. Deborah and Barak defeated the Canaanites near Megiddo. King Solomon built great stables and kept hundreds of horses and chariots there. Josiah died while fighting Egyptians near Megiddo. (I Kings 9:15–19.)

Melita

For days the storm battered Paul's ship as it was bound for Rome. At last the ship wrecked on Melita, which is today the island of Malta in the middle of the Mediterranean Sea. Many merchants called on Melita, making it famous and prosperous. There were safe harbors in Melita, but Paul's ship ran aground. He stayed on Melita for three months. (Acts 28:1.)

Memphis

The ancient capital of Egypt was Memphis, built on the west bank of the Nile River about 20 miles or 32 kilometers south of modern Cairo. Memphis is mentioned a number of times by the prophets including Hosea, Isaiah, and Jeremiah. Jeremiah and Isaiah referred to Memphis as Noph. The famous Sphinx is in Memphis. (Jer. 44:1.)

Mene, Mene, Tekel, Upharsin

During a great feast, for 1,000 guests given by Belshazzar, the ruler of Babylon, a man's hand appeared and wrote on the wall the words "Mene, Mene, Tekel, Upharsin." Only Daniel could explain their dreadful warning. That night the Persians surprised the city and killed the king. (Dan. 5.)

Mephibosheth

David and Jonathan had been very close friends. Before he died, Jonathan asked David to swear that he would harm none of Jonathan's children when he became king. So David took Mephibosheth, Jonathan's son, into his home and gave him a place of honor. Mephibosheth was lame because his nurse had tried to escape with him when Saul was killed. The child fell and was injured. (II Sam. 4:4; 9.)

Mesha

King Ahab had forced the people of Moab to pay tribute to him. But when Ahab died, the Moabites rebelled, led by their king Mesha. The combined armies of Israel, Judah, and Edom struck back. Mesha was so desperate that he sacrificed his oldest son to his god Chemosh. Mesha's account was written on a stone known as The Moabite Stone. (II Kings 3:4–27.)

Mesopotamia

When Abraham and his family left Ur of the Chaldees, they stayed for some time at Haran, a city of ancient Mesopotamia. When his father died, Abraham moved on to Canaan, leaving some of his family behind at Haran. Years later, Abraham sent his servant Eliezer back to Haran to find a bride for Isaac. Mesopotamia was the area that lay between the Tigris and Euphrates Rivers. (Gen. 24.)

Messenger

The Persians were the first to organize a regular messenger service, for which they used swift horses. The messenger's speed soon became famous and was referred to by Job when he complained that his days were swifter than a courier. Ordinary people sent their letters by friends. The Epistles of the New Testament were delivered in this way. (Esther 8:13, 14.)

Messiah

For centuries the prophets of Israel had told of the Messiah who would come to save His people. The people looked and longed for Him to come, for their lives were often filled with misery under foreign conquerors. Under Roman rule, the people of Israel were sure that the Messiah would come and restore the Kingdom of Israel. But when Jesus came he did not lead his people against the Romans. Instead, He told people about God and His home in

heaven and how people could follow Him. He spoke of freedom from sin through God's forgiveness. Many did not recognize Him as Messiah and refused to accept Him as God's Son. Some Jews accepted Jesus as the Messiah, God's Son, and later became known as Christians or believers. Gentiles also believed in Him as God's Son, the Messiah, and were accepted into the fellowship of believers. Messiah is a Hebrew word which means "anointed," someone specially appointed by God for His work. *Christos,* from which we get the word *Christ,* is the Greek word with the same meaning. Thus Jesus Christ means Jesus the Messiah. Those who accept Jesus as the Lord and Savior of their lives today accept Him as the Christ or the Messiah. "The Lord's anointed," which often referred to ancient kings and priests who were set apart for the Lord's service, could also be used to describe Jesus. (Dan. 9:25, 26; John 1:41; 4:25.)

Methuselah

In the days before the great flood, men lived much longer than they do today. Many lived to be several hundred years old. The oldest of all was Methuselah. He was the son of Enoch, who was a godly man, and grandfather of Noah. Methuselah was 187 when his son Lamech was born. He died in the year of the flood at the age of 969. (Gen. 5:22–27.)

Mezuzah

"Thou shalt write them upon the door posts of thine house, and upon thy gates." Thus the Lord commanded the people of Israel to put the Scriptures before them always. The Hebrew word for doorpost was *mezuzah*. Later mezuzah became the name for a little box in which the Israelites put Scripture verses, and attached it to their door post. (Deut. 11:20.)

Micah

About 700 years before Christ, a young prophet named Micah wrote a poem, warning his people of God's anger at their way of life. He spoke against the greed of the rich and how they oppressed the poor. Micah foretold the birthplace of the Messiah, the Lord Jesus, as Bethlehem (Mic. 5:2). Micah also told how God would punish the sin of his people. (The Book of Micah.)

Micaiah

Ahab wanted to recover the town of Ramoth-gilead, and so he summoned the prophet Micaiah. At first Micaiah mockingly echoed the words of the false prophets who had simply said what they thought the king wanted to hear. When Ahab insisted on knowing the truth, Micaiah sadly prophesied that the king would be killed and his army scattered. (I Kings 22:9–28.)

Michael

There are two main angels in the Bible, Gabriel and Michael. Both are probably archangels, although Michael is the only one named as an archangel. It was Michael's duty to guard the Jewish people, especially in times of trouble. Michael had a dispute with Satan. In a war in heaven, Michael and his angels defeated Satan and his angels and cast them upon the earth. (Jude 9; Rev. 12:7–9.)

Michal

Saul was jealous of David because he was afraid the people would make David king instead of him. So Saul married his younger daughter Michal to David with the hope of trapping him. One day Saul sent soldiers to David's home but Michal helped David escape and put an idol in David's bed. By the time the men discovered the trick, David was gone. (I Sam. 19:11–17.)

Michmash

The army of Israel was terrified. Philistine soldiers had gathered by the thousands to destroy them. There seemed to be no hope. Then Jonathan, Saul's son, and his armor-bearer climbed the steep canyon walls to Michmash, a village on the pass from Bethel to Jericho. They surprised the Philistines and caused such confusion that the Philistines fled. (I Sam. 13.)

Midianites

When Moses fled from Egypt, he went to Midian, probably the Sinai Peninsula, to live. There he worked for Jethro, priest of Midian, and married his daughter Zipporah. For a time, the Midianites were friendly to the Israelites in the wilderness. But near the end of Moses' life, God commanded Moses to fight them. By the time of Gideon, the Midianites had become the enemies of Israel. (Judg. 6:1–6.)

Miletus

By the time Paul visited Miletus, the city was no longer great as it had been 500 years earlier. The river that emptied into the harbor was bringing so much silt that ships could not come there as easily as they had. On one of his visits to Miletus, Paul had to leave his companion Trophimus behind because he had become sick. (Acts 20:15–17; II Tim. 4:20.)

Milk

There were no grocery stores in Bible times and so people had to raise most of their own food. Most people kept at least one animal for milk, either a sheep, goat, cow, or camel. The milk was stored in a bottle made from an animal skin, sewed around the edges. In the hot climate, milk quickly turned sour. From milk people also made cheese and butter. (Judg. 4:19; Isa. 7:22.)

Mill

Flour was ground at a mill from wheat, barley, rye, and sometimes oats. The grain was placed between two large round stones. One remained in its place while the other turned to grind the grain. Since a family depended on its mill, it could not be given as a pledge for a debt. Some mill stones were turned by hand. Large ones were turned by a donkey. (Deut. 24:6; Jer. 25:10.)

Millo

At a weak point in the walls of Jerusalem, King David built a fortress called Millo, a Hebrew word which means "to fill." It was intended to fill this weak point in the wall. David's Millo was later rebuilt by Solomon as part of his plan to make Jerusalem even stronger. Years later, King Joash was murdered at Millo by two of his own servants. (II Sam. 5:7–9.)

Miracle

In one sense, all of the great works in nature are miracles, for they show the power of God. But God sometimes does mighty things that cannot be explained by the laws of nature. These miracles show God's power and might in special ways. Jesus performed many miracles, healing sick people, and even raising the dead. These miracles showed that He was God's Son. (John 20:30, 31.)

Mite

The mite was the smallest bronze coin in Palestine and worth very little. Once when Jesus and His disciples were in the Temple, they watched as rich men put large gifts into the treasury. Then a poor woman came by and dropped in two mites. "She has given more than they," Jesus told his surprised disciples, "For she has given everything she has." (Luke 21:1–4.)

Miriam

Miriam's father Amram was a slave in Egypt. When her mother Jochebed had a baby boy, the family was frightened. Pharaoh had given orders for all Hebrew baby boys to be killed. Jochebed hid her baby in a basket by the Nile River and Miriam stayed nearby to watch. Later the Egyptian princess found him and named him Moses. (Exod. 2:1–10.)

Mitylene

The Aegean island of Lesbos lay off the southeastern coast of Asia Minor. Its chief city Mitylene became a popular holiday resort for many leading citizens of Rome. It had two harbors and strong fortresses. When Paul was returning to Jerusalem from his third missionary journey, his ship stopped overnight at Mitylene. (Acts 20:14.)

Mizpah, Mizpeh

There were at least five places named Mizpah in the Old Testament. The name means "watch tower." At one Mizpah, Jacob and Laban made a vow to end their quarrel. At another, Samuel judged his people from time to time. Here the Israelites repented and went out to win a great victory over the Philistines. (Gen. 31:43–55; I Sam. 7:5–16.)

Moab

Rising up from the eastern side of the Dead Sea is a high plateau cut by deep gorges. The Moabites lived here, making it difficult for enemy armies to attack. The Moabites descended from Lot's son Moab. Ruth was a Moabitess and so King David had Moabite blood in him. When David was in trouble with Saul, he took his parents to live in Moab. (I Sam. 22:3, 4.)

Mnason

Paul and his group stayed at Mnason's house when Paul made his last visit to Jerusalem in 57 A.D. Mnason, one of the very first Christians, came from the island of Cyprus. He was probably a friend of Barnabas, Paul's missionary companion, who also was a Cyprian. Mnason is a common Greek name and is the same as the Jewish name Jason. (Acts 21:16.)

Molech, Moloch

The worship of Molech was so wicked that any Israelite who did it was to be stoned to death. Molech was a heathen god of the Ammonites. Part of the worship of Molech was the sacrifice of children, which ended by placing their dead bodies in the burning arms of the idol. King Ahaz and King Manasseh both sacrificed their sons to Molech when danger threatened their country. (Lev. 18:21.)

183

Money

Abraham was rich "in cattle, in silver, and in gold." This was the money of Abraham's time. Even as late as 700 B.C. the silver and gold were not in the form of coins, because the Hebrews did not like the images. Bartering was the early way to buy and sell. Later, silver and gold were used, either as ornaments or as pieces of metal. By the time of Jesus, coins were widely used. (Gen. 13:2; Matt. 17:27.)

Money-changers

Only the sacred Jewish half-shekel was used for payments made in the Temple in Jerusalem. Since worshipers came not only from Palestine but from all over the world, money-changers were needed. They were unpopular because they overcharged for their services. Jesus drove out the money-changers who had brought their tables into the Temple itself. (Matt. 21:12.)

Moon

"Praise ye him, sun and moon," the psalmist wrote. Many ancient people worshiped the moon instead of the One who made it. The Bible tells how God made the moon and stars. But some of the priests in Judah offered incense to the moon and King Josiah had to stop them. The full moon set the date for the Passover and the Feast of Tabernacles. (II Kings 23:5; Ps. 148:3.)

Mordecai

Mordecai was a Jewish exile in the Persian capital of Susa. There he worked for King Xerxes (Ahasuerus) and helped his young cousin Esther to become the queen. Then Haman became the king's highest official and plotted to kill the Jews. Esther risked her life to tell the king. She saved her people and Haman was hanged. The king gave Mordecai Haman's job. (The Book of Esther.)

Moreh

When Abraham arrived in Canaan, he pitched his tent under an oak tree at the plain of Moreh, near Shechem. While there, God appeared to him and promised that the land of Canaan would be given to his descendants. Abraham built an altar at the place where God made His promise. Abraham did not settle at Moreh, but moved on to Beth-el and south. (Gen. 12:6, 7.)

Moriah

"Go to the land of Moriah," God told Abraham. There he would build an altar to sacrifice his son Isaac. God was testing Abraham's faith and obedience. But no matter how strange this seemed, Abraham obeyed. God saved Isaac by providing a ram for the sacrifice. Many years later Solomon built his Temple on a mountain named Moriah at the same place. (Gen. 22:2.)

Moses

Moses was born of Hebrew slaves but raised in the palace of an Egyptian princess. His life was divided into three equal parts. He spent one third as a prince in Egypt, one third as a shepherd in Midian, and one third as the leader of God's people in the wilderness. God sent His laws through Moses and used him to make a great nation from the descendants of Jacob. (The Book of Exodus.)

Mother

"Her children rise up and call her blessed." Many children learned about God from their mother. Young Timothy could certainly bless the name of his mother Eunice and even his grandmother Lois, for Paul praised their faith. There were several mothers such as Sarah, Elizabeth, and Mary who had miracle children, born by a special act of God. (II Tim. 1:5.)

Mount of Olives

Across the Kidron Valley, to the east of the Temple, the Mount of Olives rose up to a height of more than 2,700 feet or 830 meters. Gethsemane was on the Mount of Olives. From this mount Jesus ascended into heaven. It was also across this mount that He came in His Triumphal Entry into Jerusalem. Bethany lay just to the east of the mount. (Luke 19:29, 37.)

Mourning

When death or tragedy came, people mourned. But they did much more than cry. Mourners tore their clothes, put dust and ashes on their heads, and dressed in sackcloth, a crude cloth made from goat hair. A death was mourned for a week, although the body was buried immediately. Professional mourners were sometimes hired to cry and wail. (Josh. 7:6; II Sam. 1:2; Isa. 22:12.)

Mule

The mule was part horse and part donkey. It was a valuable animal because it had both the strength of a horse and the endurance and sure-footedness of a donkey. Mules were used for plowing and pack animals but they were also prized for riding. All of David's sons rode mules. Absalom met his death because his mule ran away and left him in a tree where Joab killed him. (II Sam. 18:9–14.)

Murder

Murder was punishable by death. Often a close relative of the murdered person would kill the murderer in revenge. But if a man killed someone accidentally, he could go to a city of refuge where he would be safe until he was tried. In the time of the kings, a murderer was often punished or set free by the king. A man was guilty of murder if his vicious animal killed someone. (Num. 35.)

Music

The day began with prayer and praise. The morning sacrifice closed with the singing of a psalm. The Psalms of the Bible were songs, many written by King David. Singing, playing, and dancing have always been enjoyed by the people of Bible lands. Some of the musical instruments of the time were harps or lyres, cymbals, trumpets, bells, and tambourines. (I Kings 10:12.)

Mustard

"Faith as a grain of mustard seed." Jesus used this phrase to tell people that a little faith can accomplish great things. He also told a short parable about a tiny mustard seed that became a tree where the birds came to roost. The mustard seed was like a speck of dust. But it grew quickly into a plant as large as a tree. (Matt. 13:31, 32; 17:20.)

Myrrh

Myrrh was given to Jesus at His birth and again at His death. The Wise Men brought a gift of myrrh to the Baby Jesus. Nicodemus brought myrrh to anoint Jesus' body after He was crucified. Myrrh was an expensive gift and was prized for use in perfumes. It came from a gum that oozed from a shrub-like tree. Condemned criminals were given wine drugged with myrrh to deaden pain. (Matt. 2:11.)

Myrtle

"Instead of the brier shall come up the myrtle tree," Isaiah wrote. It would be a sign of great joy when the Lord would be exalted. The myrtle is a large evergreen, almost 30 feet or 9 meters tall, with fragrant white flowers and scented leaves. Booths for the Feast of Tabernacles were made of myrtle, palm, pine, and olive branches. (Neh. 8:15; Isa. 55:13.)

N

Naaman

Although Naaman was an important Syrian general, he was a leper. But a slave girl, captured from Israel, told of a man who could heal him. Naaman went to see the prophet Elisha who ordered him to wash in the Jordan River seven times. Naaman was angry at first, but finally did what Elisha said and was healed. He tried to give Elisha gifts, but the prophet refused to take them. (II Kings 5:1–14.)

Nabal

David and his men were hiding from King Saul in the wilderness near Carmel. While there, they protected the nearby shepherds. But when David's men asked Nabal, a rich man who owned many sheep and goats, for some food, Nabal became rude and sent them away. Nabal's wife Abigail heard about this and brought food to David and his men. The name Nabal means fool. (I Sam. 25.)

Naboth

King Ahab wanted a vineyard near his palace belonging to Naboth, but Naboth refused to let him have it. The evil Queen Jezebel arranged for a false charge to be brought against Naboth. He was found guilty and stoned to death. The vineyard was taken over by the king. God sent Elijah to condemn Ahab and his family for this cruel deed. (I Kings 21.)

Nadab and Abihu

God had given specific commandments concerning His sacrifices. But Nadab and Abihu, the oldest of Aaron's four sons, decided to burn incense their own way. They should have known better because they went up Mt. Sinai with Moses to see God. Fire blazed from the altar and burned them to death. They were buried without mourning because they had disobeyed the Lord. (Lev. 10:1–7.)

Nahor

When Abraham's family moved from Ur, they settled in the city of Haran in Mesopotamia. Nahor, Abraham's brother, became a leading man of the city and it was later known as "the city of Nahor." Nahor's granddaughter Rebekah became the wife of Abraham's son Isaac. Nahor had 12 sons, the same number that Jacob had many years later. (Gen. 11:22–32; 24:10.)

Nahum

About 600 years before Christ, the prophet Nahum told how the destruction of Assyria would come some day. Assyria had been cruel with the people of Judah when they had captured them, torturing many to death. But God, who was hated by the Assyrians, would not permit this wicked empire to last. Nineveh, Assyria's capital, was destroyed in 612 B.C. as Nahum predicted. (The Book of Nahum.)

Nail

In the earliest days, nails were made of stone, wood, or bone. Later they were made of bronze or iron. Solomon used gold nails to fasten the plates of gold to the walls of the Holy of Holies in the Temple. The Romans nailed their victims to the cross with iron nails driven through their hands and feet. Jesus was nailed to the cross in this way. (John 20:25.)

Nain

Jesus approached the little village of Nain in Galilee one day just as a funeral procession was coming through the gate of the city. A young man, the only son of his mother, was about to be buried. Jesus raised the young man from the dead and gave him back to his mother. Nain is just a few miles south of Jesus' hometown of Nazareth. (Luke 7:11–17.)

Name

In the Bible every name has a special meaning. Sometimes a name was changed to mark a change in character. Jacob ("cheat") was called Israel ("a prince with God") after he turned to the Lord for help. An angel told Mary that her Baby was to be called Jesus, meaning "Savior," because He would save His people from their sins. (Matt. 1:21.)

Naomi

During the days of the judges, a famine caused Elimelech and his wife Naomi to leave Bethlehem and go to Moab with their two sons, who were married there. Then Elimelech and both sons died. When Naomi returned to Bethlehem, her daughter-in-law Ruth insisted on going with her. Naomi helped Ruth marry her relative Boaz. Naomi became an ancestor of King David. (The Book of Ruth.)

Naphtali

When the people of Nazareth tried to kill Jesus, He moved to Capernaum, a little village in the territory of Naphtali. Chorazin and Bethsaida were also in this land along the western shores of the Sea of Galilee. Naphtali, which means "wrestler," was Jacob's fifth son. His tribe inherited this land when they entered the Promised Land with Joshua. (Gen. 46:24; Josh. 19:32–39.)

Napkin

"His face was bound about with a napkin." Thus Lazarus came forth from the tomb when Jesus called, wrapped in grave-clothes. The napkin was a narrow piece of linen used as a scarf or handkerchief to wipe away perspiration. Also, a dead person's head was wrapped with a napkin. Jesus told a story about a servant who tied his master's money in a napkin, refusing to use it. (Luke 19:20; John 11:44.)

Nathan

At least 11 men in the Bible are called Nathan. The most famous was a prophet who was one of David's trusted advisers. When David planned the great Temple in Jerusalem, Nathan told the king that God wanted Solomon his son to build it. But Nathan encouraged David to get everything ready including the music for the Temple worship. (II Sam. 7:1–17.)

Nathanael

It was hard for Nathanael, who was also called Bartholomew, to believe that his friend Philip had met the Messiah, the Son of God. "Can any good thing come from Nazareth?" Nathanael asked. But Nathanael found that Jesus knew much about him and he believed. Nathanael then became one of the 12 disciples, who were later called The Twelve, or The Twelve Apostles. (John 1:45–49; 21:2.)

Nazarene

Nazarenes, people of Nazareth, were considered unimportant, for Nazareth was not even mentioned in the Old Testament and it was an obscure village. Some early Christians were mockingly called Nazarenes. Centuries before Jesus was born, prophets had said that Jesus would be called a Nazarene. (Matt. 2:23; John 1:45, 46; Acts 24:5.)

191

Nazareth

The carpenter's shop where Jesus spent His childhood was in the little village of Nazareth. Here Jesus learned the trade as a boy. Nazareth had been the home of Mary and Joseph before Jesus was born. Jesus preached his first sermon in Nazareth. It was a small village in Galilee, nestled in the hills that rise up to the north from the plain of Esdraelon. (Matt. 2:23; Luke 1:26; 4:16–30.)

Nazirite

The word Nazirite has nothing to do with Nazareth, but comes from a Hebrew verb meaning "to separate." A Nazirite was one who separated himself from others to serve God under a special vow. The vow could be for life or for a limited period of time. A Nazirite lived simply. He drank no wine and left his hair uncut. Samson was a Nazirite. (Num. 6:1–21; Judg. 13:5.)

Neapolis

"Come over to Macedonia and help us," the man in the vision begged. Paul left for Macedonia and landed at the seaport of Neapolis, which was about ten miles or 16 kilometers from Philippi. Two other cities also had this name. One is today known as Naples in Italy. The other is known as Nablus, near Mt. Gerizim in Israel. (Acts 16:9–12.)

Nebo

From the lonely plains of Moab Moses went into Mt. Nebo. There the Lord showed him the vast land that stretched from north to south across the Jordan River. For 40 years Moses had led his people to this land, The Promised Land. Now he must die in this mountain and let another take his people across the Jordan River to their inheritance. (Deut. 34.)

Nebuchadnezzar

Throughout the Books of Daniel, Jeremiah, and Ezekiel, there are many references to Nebuchadnezzar, king of Babylon. He was a great soldier and leader, increasing his empire and rebuilding his cities. When Nebuchadnezzar captured Jerusalem, he took many of the Jews, including Daniel, to Babylon. (II Kings 24—25.)

Nebuzaradan

After Jerusalem had been captured, Nebuchadnezzar ordered his captain of the guard, Nebuzaradan, to completely destroy the city and the Temple. Nebuzaradan took the Temple treasures back to Babylon along with Jewish captives. Then he freed Jeremiah from prison and let him choose to stay in Judah or go to Babylon. (II Kings 25:8–20.)

Needle's Eye

"It is easier for a camel to go through the eye of a needle, than for a rich man to enter into the kingdom of God," Jesus said. The needle's eye may have referred to a sewing needle. But many believe it was the small inner gate to a city. To enter, a camel must kneel and have all his burdens removed. Then he would struggle to go through. (Matt. 19:24.)

Negeb

The desert south of Judea was called the Negeb, which means "dry." People who lived in this dry land had to get water by digging wells. It is a rolling land, bounded on the east by the Dead Sea and on the west by the Mediterranean Sea. Hagar went into this wilderness country when she fled with her son from Sarah. (Gen. 13:1; 16:7; 21:14–21.)

Nehemiah

The king asked why his favorite cupbearer was sad. Then Nehemiah told the Persian king Artaxerxes I about his homeland. He told how the broken walls and destruction of Jerusalem made him feel sad. He asked the king to send him back to fix the city. When the king let him go, Nehemiah rebuilt the walls, even though some people were against him. (The Book of Nehemiah.)

Neighbor

"Who is my neighbor?" someone asked Jesus. So Jesus told him a story about a foreigner who helped a stranger who had been robbed and beaten. He told how priests and Levites had passed by the stranger when he was in need. The answer became clear. My neighbor is someone who needs me, or someone who helps me when I need him. (Luke 10: 29–37.)

Nero

"I appeal to Caesar," Paul said at his trial before Festus. Caesar at that time was Nero, a very cruel and strange man. He won literary prizes in Greece. But he was so suspicious of anyone who might take his throne from him that he had his own mother killed. Nero was the Roman Emperor, or Caesar, from 54 to 68 A.D. Both Paul and Peter became martyrs under Nero. (Acts 25:11, 12.)

Net

There were many different kinds of nets in Bible times, some for catching animals and birds and others for catching fish. Fishing nets were used often on the Sea of Galilee. The casting net was circular, thrown upon the water. Weights caused the edges to fall over the fish. The drag net had floats on top and weights on the bottom and was dragged behind boats. (Matt. 4:20, 21.)

New Moon

The first day of the new moon was kept as a holy day to mark the beginning of the Jewish month. In the Temple special sacrifices were made in addition to the daily offering and the trumpets were blown. Trading was not allowed on this day. Amos described how the merchants impatiently awaited the end of the new moon. (Num. 28:11–15; Amos 8:5.)

Nicodemus

Nicodemus was a member of the Sanhedrin, the council of religious leaders who ruled the Jews. Troubled by Jesus' words and miracles, he visited Jesus one night and learned that Jesus was God's Son. Nicodemus remained on the Sanhedrin, but when Jesus was crucified, he showed his devotion to Jesus by bringing expensive spices to anoint His body for burial. (John 3:1–21.)

New Testament

A testament is a covenant or sacred agreement. Through Abraham and his family, God made a covenant which we now call The Old Testament. God promised that He would go with His people and take care of them and bless them. His people should love Him, follow Him, and obey Him. They should accept Him as their only God, putting no other god ahead of Him. When Christ came, God made a new covenant, or sacred agreement, with His people which we now call The New Testament. God promised to be with those who accept Him by claiming Jesus as their Lord and Savior. Both covenants required the people to love the Lord, accept only Him as the Lord, and to obey Him completely. But the way to God was different. In the Old Testament, animal sacrifices atoned for the sins of the people. In the New Testament, the sacrifice of Jesus on the cross atoned for the sins of the people. The New Testament is composed of 27 books. These include the four Gospels, which tell of the Life of Christ; the Acts of the Apostles, which tells of the work of the Holy Spirit in the lives of the early believers; the 21 epistles, letters which Paul and others wrote to the believers; and Revelation, a book of prophecy. The Gospels tell of the life Jesus lived on earth while the epistles tell of the life we can live for Him on earth. (Hebrews 8:6–13; 13:20.)

195

Nicolaitans

"Christ set us free," the Nicolaitans said. "And if Christ set us free, we can do whatever we want." So those who said this ate things sacrificed to idols and committed evil acts while they still claimed to be Christians. God said that he hated the deeds of the Nicolaitans, and praised the church at Ephesus because it hated those deeds also. (Rev. 2:6, 15.)

Nicopolis

Nicopolis, which means "city of victory," was built in Macedonia by Augustus to mark his victory in the battle of Actium. Herod the Great was responsible for many beautiful additions to the city. When Paul wrote his Epistle to Titus, he was intending to spend the following winter in Nicopolis and he asked Titus, who was in Crete, to join him there. (Titus 3:12.)

Night

In the Old Testament the Israelites divided the night into three watches of four hours each—the first watch, the middle watch, and the morning watch. By New Testament times the Jews had adopted the Roman system of four watches of three hours each. They are referred to in Mark's Gospel as the evening, midnight, cockcrow, and morning watches. (Mark 6:48.)

Nile

For almost 3,000 miles or 4,800 kilometers, the Nile River stretches across Africa. Each year it brings rich muddy soil to Egypt, which the people use for farming. In Bible times Egypt often had food when other nations had famine because their crops were not dependent on rain. When Moses was a baby, he was hid among the reeds along the Nile. (Exod. 2:1–10.)

Nimrod

After the great flood in which Noah and his family were saved, Nimrod, the son of Cush and grandson of Ham, founded a mighty empire in the north. He started the great cities of Nineveh and Calah in Assyria. His name is given in Genesis as a mighty hunter. Centuries later, Micah refers to land near Assyria as the land of Nimrod. (Gen. 10:6–12; Micah 5:6.)

Nineveh

"Go to Nineveh," God commanded. But Jonah ran the other way. Nineveh was a wicked city, the capital of Assyria, the nation that would one day carry Jonah's people away into captivity. The city was one of the oldest in the world, dating back thousands of years before Jonah. At last Jonah preached, and the people repented. Later, in 612 B.C., the city was destroyed by an enemy army. (The Book of Jonah.)

Noah

"Noah walked with God." In a world filled with every form of wickedness, it was unusual to find such a man. So Noah lived in God's favor. When God decided to destroy the world with a flood, He told Noah to build an ark, a great boat where he and his family and certain animals could be safe. Noah obeyed and became the father of all mankind after the flood. (Gen. 6—9.)

Nob

David had to run away from Saul's palace in such a hurry that he had no time to get food or a sword. Immediately he went to Nob, where the Tabernacle stood, and asked the priest Ahimelech for these things. When Ahimelech helped David, Doeg reported it to Saul. Insane with jealousy, Saul ordered all the priests of Nob killed. Only one escaped. (I Sam. 21:1–9; 22:9–20.)

Nomad

The first nomad or wanderer was Cain, who was banished from his home for murdering his brother Abel. When Abraham left Ur he lived the life of a nomad, moving from place to place with his camels, sheep, and goats. After escaping from Egypt, the Israelites were nomads in the desert for 40 years, before entering Canaan and settling in towns. (Gen. 4:12, 16.)

Number

The Israelites used letters of the alphabet for numbers. The units 1 through 9 were represented by the first nine letters and tens were represented by the next nine. The last four of the 22 letters in the Hebrew alphabet stood for 100 to 400. For other hundreds double letters were used. Thousands were indicated by the unit letter with two dots above.

Numbering

Joab realized that it was wrong for David to number his people. If David learned that he had a vast army, he might rely upon his soldiers instead of God. But David went ahead with his plans for the census. Later he realized that God was not pleased and that he must choose one of three punishments God had for him. (II Sam. 24.)

Numbers

Most of the Book of Numbers tells about the 40 years of wandering in the wilderness. The Hebrew title for the Book is "In the Wilderness." Twice God commanded Moses to take a census of the Israelites. The lists of families are included in this Book, along with laws, stories, and poems about their stay in the wilderness. (The Book of Numbers.)

O

Oar

Ships were equipped with oars to help them along if there was no wind for the sails and during heavy storms. Sea-going ships had 60 double-banked oars and some warships were far larger. Rowers were kept in time by flute-music or hammer-blows. Oars were often made from the wood of the oaks of Bashan. (Isa. 33:21; Ezek. 27:6, 29.)

Oath

With an oath a person called upon God to witness his promise. It was a serious matter to break one's oath because it was binding. The person taking an oath often lifted his hand to heaven as a gesture of God's presence or witness. Sometimes an oath was taken before the altar, Jesus taught that the Christian's word was as important as his oath. (Gen. 21:23; Gal. 1:20; Heb. 6:16, 17.)

Obadiah the Prophet

The prophecy that Obadiah wrote is the shortest Book in the Old Testament. It tells of the misery of Jerusalem when captured by the Babylonians. It also tells about the coming destruction of Edom because the Edomites had done such evil to Jerusalem. Although Edom was like an eagle's nest, safe in the mountains, it was not enough to protect it. (The Book of Obadiah.)

199

Obadiah the Steward

When Queen Jezebel was persecuting the Lord's prophets, Ahab's steward Obadiah bravely hid 100 of them in two caves and sent them food. During a great drought, Obadiah was seeking grass for Ahab's animals when he met Elijah. Obadiah agreed to arrange a meeting between Elijah and Ahab. This led to the contest between Elijah and the prophets of Baal. (I Kings 18:3–16.)

Obed

Obed was the grandfather of King David and the son of Ruth and Boaz. His name means "the servant." Naomi had helped to arrange the marriage between Ruth and Boaz and she was especially happy when Obed was born. Her husband and two sons had died and there was no one else to carry on the family. (Ruth 4:17, 21, 22; Matt. 1:5; Luke 3:32.)

Oded

In the days when Israel and Judah were divided, King Pekah of Israel invaded Judah. He killed 120,000 men of Judah and took 200,000 back to Israel as captives. But when his officers came into Samaria, Oded the Prophet met them and warned that God would punish them for their cruelty. So they gave the prisoners food and clothing and sent them home. (II Chron. 28:9–15.)

Og

In the days of Og, many thought that he could never be defeated in battle because he was a giant. But the people of Israel with Moses as their leader defeated King Og of Bashan and conquered his land and its 60 cities. All of these cities had high walls and gates. Og had a great bed, more than 14 feet or 4.5 meters long and six feet or 1.8 meters wide. (Deut. 3:1–13.)

Oil

The oil mentioned in the Bible is usually olive oil. It was obtained by squeezing the ripe olives in presses and was stored in huge earthenware jars. Oil was used as money in early times, being bartered for something else. Solomon paid Hiram of Tyre in oil for the workmen and materials he sent for the Temple in Jerusalem. (Lev. 24:2; II Chron. 2:10.)

Ointment

While Jesus ate with Lazarus and Martha, Mary poured some ointment of spikenard on Jesus' feet and wiped them with her hair. It was a very expensive gift and showed her love and adoration of Jesus. Ointment was usually made from olive oil with perfumes added. Sometimes it was used for medicine and sometimes as a lotion for dry skin. (Matt. 26:6–13; John 12:1–8.)

Old Testament

When Jesus spoke of the Scriptures, He meant the part we now know as the Old Testament. The Bible is made up of two covenants, or testaments, between God and His people. In the Old Testament, God agreed to be with Abraham and his descendants as long as they obeyed His commandments. In the New Testament, God agreed to come into the lives of believers and live in them and care for them. This was made possible through the death and resurrection of His Son, Jesus Christ. The 39 books of the Old Testament are divided into groups of fives and twelves. There are five books of law (Genesis through Deuteronomy) followed by 12 books of history, from the time when Israel entered the land until its return from exile (Joshua through Esther). Five poetry books (Job through Song of Solomon), five major (long) prophecies, and 12 minor (short) prophecies (Isaiah through Malachi) complete the rest. In addition, Catholics accept seven deuterocanonical books as part of the Old Testament. Much of the Old Testament points to the coming of Christ, the focal point of the New Testament. The prophets told of His coming, the events of the kings prepared the way for His coming, and the law showed the impossibility of our being perfect without His coming.

Olive

The olive tree was prized in Palestine because its fruit and wood produced many good things. Olive oil was used in cooking and as lamp oil. Even kings were anointed with it and people used expensive ointments made from olive oil and perfumes. Olives were eaten fresh or pickled. The hard timber of the olive tree was polished or used as firewood. (Deut. 28:40; I Kings 6:32.)

Omer

The word omer meant "a sheaf of grain," and was a measure of the amount of grain produced by one sheaf. Each Israelite gathered an omer of manna daily in the wilderness, for that was the amount allotted to him. The omer was a dry measure sometimes called a tenth because it was a tenth of an ephah. It was about four liters, a little more than a gallon. (Exod. 16:16–18, 36.)

Omri

About 900 years before Christ, Omri reigned as the seventh king over Israel. He was an evil man who married his son Ahab to the Phoenician princess Jezebel, probably to build better trade with the land. It was this marriage that encouraged the worship of Baal in Israel. Omri built a new capital at Samaria and permitted people to worship golden calves. (I Kings 16:15–28.)

Onesimus

In Rome, Onesimus heard Paul preach about Christ and became a Christian. But he was a runaway slave from Colossae. Paul wanted to keep Onesimus with him, for he had been helpful. But he sent Onesimus back with a letter to his master, Philemon, one of Paul's friends. Paul asked Philemon to receive Onesimus as a brother, not as a slave. (The Book of Philemon.)

Onesiphorus

In the Second Epistle to Timothy, Paul sends greetings to Onesiphorus, who had proved a true Christian friend. Onesiphorus had gone to much trouble finding out where Paul was imprisoned in Rome. By contrast, Paul mentions other Christians who had deserted him in his hour of need. Onesiphorus had lived up to his name, which means "profit-bringer." (II Tim. 1:16–18; 4:19.)

Onyx

The eleventh stone in the High Priest's breastplate was onyx, a form of chalcedony. The High Priest also wore two onyx stones on his shoulders. Onyx was mentioned in the foundation of the Holy City. The stone has layers of color and is prized for its beauty. The name comes from the Greek for nail because its shades are like those of a fingernail. (Exod. 28:9, 12, 20; Job 28:16.)

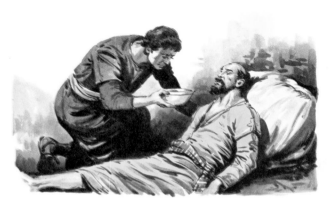

Ophir

Solomon's navy brought rich treasures from many places. From Ophir came silver, ivory, precious stones, two kinds of apes, and gold of particular fineness. With this gold from Ophir, Solomon made targets and shields and goblets and a throne. Nobody knows for sure where Ophir was, although some think it was in India and others believe it was in Arabia. (I Kings 9:28; 10:11.)

Ophrah

Gideon was threshing wheat at his home in Ophrah when the Angel of the Lord appeared. The angel sat beneath an oak tree, commanding Gideon to set Israel free from the Midianites who oppressed the people. Ophrah was Gideon's home. When Gideon had conquered the Midianites, he foolishly made a golden Ephod and put it at Ophrah and the people came to worship it. (Judg. 6:11; 8:27.)

Orpah

"Orpah kissed her mother-in-law, but Ruth clave unto her." With that, Orpah went back to her people in Moab, while Ruth went on to Bethlehem with Naomi. Orpah had married Chilion, Naomi's son. Ruth had married Mahlon, Naomi's other son. Both sons died and so Naomi returned to Bethlehem. Orpah went part of the way and then returned to Moab at Naomi's suggestion. (Ruth 1:11–18.)

Othniel

Caleb promised to give his daughter Achsah to the man who captured the city of Debir. Othniel won the prize and in addition to his new wife, he was given the springs in the neighborhood. After the death of Joshua, Othniel became the first judge of Israel. He rescued the Israelites from eight years of oppression by the king of Mesopotamia. (Josh. 15:13–19.)

Oven

Bread was the "staff of life" in Bible times, one of the most important of all foods. So the ovens, used for baking and roasting, were important parts of Bible-time homes. There were various kinds. Some were clay-lined holes. The dough was baked quickly on the heated clay sides. Others were stone ovens. The simplest was perhaps an inverted bowl over a fire. (Lev. 26:26.)

Ox

"They take the widow's ox for a pledge," complained Job when he thought God did not care about wickedness. This was something that should never be done because a family depended on its ox to plow, haul heavy loads, drag threshing boards across the grain at harvest time, or pull a cart. The ox cart was sometimes the family's transportation. An ox was often sacrificed to God. (Job 24:3.)

P

Padan-aram, Paddan-aram

Jacob had stolen his brother Esau's blessing from Isaac, his father. He could no longer live at home because Esau hated him. So Jacob ran away to Padan-aram where he married Rachel and Leah. The area, now in southeastern Turkey, was once part of Mesopotamia. (Gen. 25:20; 28:2–7; 31:18.)

Palace

Kings and high officials usually lived in large, beautiful homes called palaces. The Bible speaks of the palaces of many kings, including Saul, David, and Ahab. Solomon's palace was a beautiful building where he showed his wealth. Jesus was taken to both the palace of the High Priest as well as Herod's palace to be judged. (I Kings 21:1; John 18:15.)

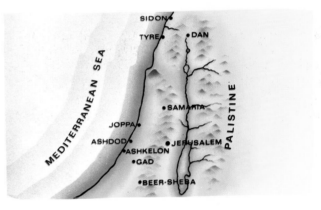

Palestine

The land known as Palestine has had many names. Abraham knew it as Canaan. Moses led his people to the Promised Land. It is often called "The Holy Land." The word Palestine came from Philistia, the land of the Philistines. They came to the land about the time the Israelites were slaves in Egypt. Today the land is known as Israel.

Palm

Jericho was known as the city of palms, for in its warm climate palm trees grew in abundance. The date palm was a welcome tree in the hot regions, providing shade and fruit. Mats were woven from the leaves and the fibers were used for thread and rope. Deborah held court beneath a palm tree. The people who welcomed Jesus into Jerusalem as king carried palm branches. (Deut. 34:3; Judg. 4:5.)

Paper

There was no paper like ours in Bible times. People wrote on broken bits of pottery, animal skin, and papyrus. The word paper comes from "papyrus." This was a tall plant that grew in swampy places. Strips from the papyrus stem were laid side by side, then a second layer of strips was laid across them. The strips were beaten together, forming a type of paper called papyrus. (II John 12.)

Pamphylia

During his first missionary journey, Paul visited Pamphylia, a coastal region in southern Asia Minor. To the west was Lycia and to the east Cilicia. In Paul's time, Pamphylia was controlled by the Romans. Paul preached at Perga, the chief city of Pamphylia. At Pentecost, some visitors to Jerusalem came from there. (Acts 13:13; 14:24, 25.)

Paphos

At the beginning of their first missionary journey, Paul and Barnabas visited the island of Cyprus. When they came to Paphos, the city at the far western end of the island, they shared the Gospel with Sergius Paulus, the Roman governor. A sorcerer named Elymas tried to stop them, but Paul caused him to be temporarily blinded for resisting God. (Acts 13:6–13.)

206

Parable

Jesus told many stories to His disciples so that they would understand more clearly the truths He wanted to teach. The story and the truth were side by side. That is the meaning of the word "parable." Jesus told parables about things his listeners would understand such as lost sheep and how they were like lost people, lost coins, and tiny mustard seeds. (Matt. 13:10, 11.)

Paradise

The word paradise comes from an old Persian word which means a royal garden or park. The Garden of Eden was a paradise on earth. Jesus told the thief on the cross that he would go with Him to paradise. The Bible also speaks of the paradise of God where the tree of life grows. This refers to heaven. (Luke 23:43; II Cor. 12:4; Rev. 2:7.)

Parchment

There was no writing paper like ours in Bible times. People wrote on papyrus, broken pieces of pottery, or parchment. Parchment was the dried skins of sheep, goats, or young calves. The word parchment comes from "Pergamum," the city in Asia Minor where some people think parchment was first used. In New Testament times parchment was used for scrolls and important documents. (II Tim. 4:13.)

Passover

Nine plagues had come to the land of Egypt and still Pharaoh would not let the Israelites go free. At last God sent the angel of death through the land. Every firstborn son died except in the families which sprinkled blood on their doorposts. The angel passed over those homes. This Passover was celebrated with a feast each year by the people of Israel. (Exod. 12.)

Patmos

Southwest of Asia Minor, which is Turkey today, there is a tiny island named Patmos only eight miles or 13 kilometers long and four miles or 6.5 kilometers wide. In 95 A.D., the Apostle John was banished to this island by the Roman Emperor Domitian. While he was there, God gave John the vision which he recorded in the Book of Revelation. (Rev. 1:9.)

Paul

Saul was a Pharisee who hated the Christians. He did not believe that Jesus rose from the dead. But one day Jesus spoke to him from heaven and Saul himself became a Christian. With a new life came a new name and he was called Paul. Paul became an apostle, as well as the first missionary. Many of the Books of the New Testament are letters written by Paul. (Acts 9:1–9; I Timothy 1:1.)

Peacock

Many unusual things were brought home by Solomon's trading ships. From Tarshish he received a cargo of stately peacocks, probably the first such birds to be seen in Palestine. The peacock originally came from India. The hen lays about ten eggs in the spring and they are hatched out in 30 days. The cock has lovely plumage. (I Kings 10:22.)

Pekah

"He did that which was evil in the sight of the Lord." That is the summary of Pekah's rule as king of Israel. To become king he murdered King Pekahiah at Samaria. To keep strong he allied himself with other kings. Isaiah the prophet warned the king of Judah not to join Pekah. Pekah angrily tried to capture Jerusalem but failed. (II Kings 16.)

Pelican

The lonely psalmist cried out, "I am like a pelican of the wilderness." The pelican, a large water bird, was a lonely sight. After feeding on fish along the shores of Galilee or the Nile River of Egypt, the pelican flew to a desolate spot where it stood for days until it became hungry again. The Israelites were not to eat a pelican because it was an unclean animal. (Lev. 11:18; Ps. 102:6.)

Pen

Fountain pens and ball point pens were invented in recent years. Pens in Bible times were usually made from reeds. The ends were split or cut to form a broad flat point. This made it possible to write in thick or thin strokes. A pen would have to be dipped into ink every few words. Pens were used to write on papyrus or parchment. (III John 13.)

Peniel

For 20 years Jacob had not seen his twin brother Esau. But he was afraid to meet Esau because he had cheated him out of his birthright. The night before they met, Jacob wrestled with God through the night. Jacob named the place where he wrestled Peniel, or Penuel, which means "face of God." Esau was friendly when they met and so Jacob said, "Your face is like the face of God." (Gen. 32:24–32.)

Pentecost

"When the day of Pentecost was fully come," Luke wrote about that special day when the Holy Spirit came. As the Christians prayed in the upper room, the Holy Spirit came upon them and gave them power to work for Christ. The Feast of Pentecost was on the fiftieth day after Passover. The name means "fiftieth." It marked the beginning of the harvest thanksgiving. (Acts 2:1.)

Peor

Balak and Balaam stood at the top of Peor, a high mountain peak in Moab by the valley in which the people of Israel were camped. Balak, king of Moab, was afraid of the Israelites who had come out of Egypt. "Curse them!" he told the prophet Balaam. But Balaam blessed the Israelites instead, because he insisted on doing what God told him to do. (Num. 23:28; Deut. 3:29.)

Perga

On their first missionary journey, Paul and Barnabas passed through Perga twice, once on the way and once coming home. John Mark left the two at this point and went home to Jerusalem, and so Paul refused to take him on future trips. Perga was the capital city of Pamphylia in Asia Minor, which is Turkey today. (Acts 13:13, 14; 14:24, 25.)

Pergamos, Pergamum

"I know thy works," the Lord said to the church at Pergamos. He spoke of holding the doctrine of Balaam and the doctrine of the Nicolaitans, "which thing I hate." Pergamos was a great city in Asia Minor, which is Turkey today. It had a large library and beautiful buildings. Parchment received its name from Pergamos, where it originated. (Rev. 2:12–17.)

Persecution

"Blessed are ye, when men shall persecute you . . . for My sake," Jesus told His disciples. He told how the prophets were mistreated because they worked for God. Jezebel persecuted the true believers and forced the prophet Elijah to run away. Saul persecuted the Christians until Christ spoke to him and changed him. Later, the Romans tortured and killed the Christians. (Matt. 5:11, 12.)

Persia

The great Persian Empire, which at its height extended from India to the Mediterranean Sea, was set up by Cyrus II after his capture of Babylon in 539 B.C. Cyrus gave back to the Jews the precious vessels which Nebuchadnezzar had looted from the Temple. He also allowed the Jews to return to Jerusalem and rebuild the Temple. Ezra and Nehemiah organized this work. (Ezra 1:1, 2.)

Peter

Andrew brought his brother Simon Peter to see Jesus. From that time on, Peter followed Jesus and became one of His three closest disciples. Peter means "rock," a man of firm faith. But one time Peter went to meet Jesus, who was walking on water. Peter's doubts caused him to sink until Jesus caught his hand and saved him. (Matt. 14:28–31; 16:18, 19; John 21:15–17; The Epistles from Peter.)

Pharaoh

During the time of the Old Testament, the ruler of Egypt was known as Pharaoh. It was a title used instead of king and means "great house." Pharaoh's court included wise men, magicians, and priests who offered him advice by consulting ancient documents and interpreting dreams. The Egyptians thought that Pharaoh was a god. (Gen. 41:37–44.)

Pharisee

The Pharisees hated Jesus because He healed and cared for people even if it meant breaking some of their harsh rules. The Pharisees were a Jewish sect that did not mix with ordinary people. Even their name means "separated one." Jesus scolded the Pharisees for pretending to be godly when they were trying to make people follow rules instead of pleasing God. (Matt. 5:20.)

Philadelphia

"Thou hast kept My word and hast not denied My name," the Lord wrote to the church at Philadelphia. This was one of the seven churches addressed in the Book of Revelation. Philadelphia was a city in Asia Minor, which is Turkey today. In 17 A.D., the city was destroyed by earthquake but was rebuilt by the Roman emperor. (Rev. 3:7–13.)

Philip the Apostle

It was Philip who introduced Nathanael to Jesus. Both men became apostles. Philip had come from Bethsaida, a fishing village on the shores of the Sea of Galilee. He was probably a fisherman like Peter, Andrew, James, and John. In the latter part of Jesus' ministry, some Greeks came to see Jesus and so Philip took them to Him. (John 1:45–48; 12:20–22.)

Philemon

Philemon's slave Onesimus robbed him and ran away to Rome. There Onesimus heard Paul preach about Christ and became a Christian. Onesimus helped Paul greatly in Rome but Paul decided that he must send Onesimus back to Philemon who was a Christian in Colossae. He sent a letter, the Epistle to Philemon, back with Onesimus asking Philemon to forgive him. (The Epistle of Paul to Philemon.)

Philip the Evangelist

The 12 apostles were spending too much time caring for the believers' food and clothing and not enough time preaching the Word of God. So the believers chose seven men to care for these things. One was Philip. Later Philip preached in Samaria and many came to Christ. Then he went on the Gaza road and led the treasurer of Ethiopia to Christ. (Acts 6:2–6; 8:26–40.)

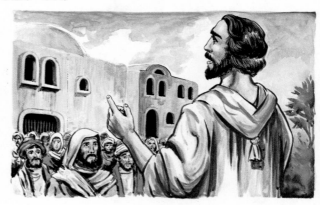

Philippi, Philippians

When Philip of Macedon took the city of Philippi about 300 B.C., he enlarged the gold mines and minted thousands of gold coins with his own portrait on them. When Paul came to Philippi, he was thrown into prison, but God set him free with an earthquake. Paul's letter to the Philippians is much more important today than Philip's gold coins. (The Epistle of Paul to the Philippians.)

Philistines

The warlike Philistines were originally known to the Egyptians as the Sea Peoples. They finally settled along the coast between Egypt and Mt. Carmel. Their five main cities were at Gaza, Ashkelon, Ashdod, Ekron, and Gath. After David had conquered the Philistines and ended their power, some of them joined his bodyguard. (Josh. 13:3; I Sam. 6:17.)

Phinehas

There were three men of the Bible named Phinehas. One was the son of Eleazar and grandson of Aaron. When the Israelites camped near Moab, the people began to sin with the Moabite women and worship their gods. One day Phinehas killed an Israelite who had openly brought one of these women into camp. After his father died, Phinehas became the High Priest. (Num. 25:6–13.)

Phoebe

Phoebe had worked hard among the Christians and Paul spoke warmly of her in his Epistle to the Romans. She probably carried this letter to Rome for Paul. He asked the church at Rome to welcome her when she arrived because she had been helpful to him. Phoebe was a deaconess in the church at Cenchrea, the seaport east of Corinth. (Rom. 16:1, 2.)

213

Phoenicia

The Bible speaks of the land of Tyre and Sidon also known as Phoenicia. It is a narrow strip of land along the Mediterranean coast to the north of Palestine. Today it is the land of Lebanon. The Phoenicians were famous for their ships and shipping and the country had many excellent harbors. They helped Solomon develop his seaport of Ezion-geber. (I Kings 9:26–28.)

Pilate

In New Testament times, the Jews could not put a man to death for a crime. They had to get the permission of the Roman officer in charge. So when they captured Jesus, they sent Him before Pilate to be judged. Pilate was the Roman procurator of Judea from 26 to 36 A.D. It was in his power to free Jesus or put Him to death. To please the Jews he put Him to death. (John 18:29—19:22.)

Phrygia

No one knows for sure exactly where Phrygia began and ended. But it was in the central part of Asia Minor, which is now Turkey. Colossae and Laodicea, which were in Phrygia, had problems. Paul wrote to the Colossians from prison and urged them to put Christ first. In the Book of Revelation, the church at Laodicea was described as lukewarm. Some people at Pentecost were from Phrygia. (Acts 16:6.)

Pilgrim

Thousands of Jews came to Jerusalem as pilgrims. A pilgrim was a person who traveled to a holy place or to a religious feast. Each male was expected to attend the Feasts of Passover, Pentecost, and Tabernacles each year. When Jesus was 12, Mary and Joseph took Him with them to the Passover, which they attended each year. (Luke 2:41.)

Pillar

From earliest times, pillars of wood, stone, or mud-brick were used to support large roofs and balconies in palaces and houses. The pillars which Samson pulled down on the Philistines were probably made of wood and set on stone bases. The word *pillar* is also used to refer to a monument such as a pile of stones. (Gen. 28:18; Judg. 16:25–31.)

Pillar of Cloud

After the Israelites escaped from Egypt into the trackless wilderness, they needed help to know where they should go. God provided them with a pillar of cloud by day and a pillar of fire by night. When the pillar moved forward, the people packed up their tents and followed. When the pillar stopped, the people once again camped. (Exod. 13:21, 22.)

Pisidia

Paul visited two cities named Antioch. One was Antioch in Syria, where he was sent forth on his missionary journeys. The other was Antioch of Pisidia. Pisidia was a mountainous Roman province in Asia Minor, which is now Turkey. It had many bands of robbers who attacked travelers. On one occasion, Paul went throughout Pisidia, strengthening the believers. (Acts 14:21–24.)

Pit

Joseph's brothers were very jealous because their father loved Joseph more than them. "Let's kill him and throw him into some pit," they said. The pit may have been an old well or cistern, probably dry. Or it may have been a deep hole in the ground. Men sometimes dug a pit to trap wild animals, covering it with twigs and earth. (Gen. 37:18–24.)

Pitch

The ancients used pitch or bitumen to waterproof their boats and ships. Pitch is black substance related to oil. It was used by Egyptians in embalming. Noah covered the ark with pitch. Jochebed waterproofed the little basket boat for baby Moses with pitch. Lakes of steaming pitch have been found near Mt. Hermon and near the Dead Sea. (Gen. 6:14; Exod. 2:3.)

Pitcher

A pitcher, or a waterpot, was a large earthenware jar which a woman filled with water and carried on her head. Earthenware is porous and so it absorbs some of the water, which helps to keep the contents cool. Gideon and his men covered their torches with these pitchers when they went to fight the Midianites at night. (Judg. 7:16, 20.)

Pithom

While the Hebrews were slaves in Egypt, they built many things for Pharaoh. One was a store city called Pithom, which was in Goshen in the delta of northeast Egypt. Some of the walls of the storehouses are still standing. They were made of bricks without straw as mentioned in the Book of Exodus. Pithom means "the house of Atum," an Egyptian sun god. (Exod. 1:11.)

Plagues

Plagues came often in the ancient world, bringing disease and death to thousands of people. Several such plagues are mentioned in the Bible. The ten plagues of Egypt were sent by God to show Pharaoh His great power. After the tenth and final plague, when the oldest son in every Egyptian family died, Pharaoh sent the Israelites from the land. (Exod. 7—12.)

Plaster

The inside and sometimes the outside walls of buildings were covered with a plaster, usually made of clay. A finer plaster was obtained by heating crushed limestone. This gave rough stones or brickwork a smooth surface which could then be painted or inscribed. When a hand wrote strange words on Belshazzar's palace wall in Babylon, it wrote on plaster. (Lev. 14:42.)

Pledge

As a pledge or promise that a debt would be repaid, an Israelite left some article with the person to whom he owed the money. A creditor could not take millstones as a pledge, since these were needed every day to grind grain for bread. A pledged cloak had to be returned at sunset for its owner to sleep in. The creditor could not go into the borrowers house to get the pledge. (Exod. 22:25–27.)

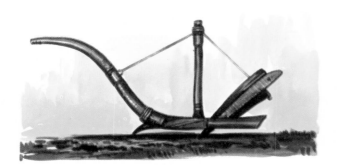

Plow

In Bible times, a plow was made of wood and had a sharp point to break up the ground so that seeds could be planted. The plowman guided it with a wooden handle. The front end was fastened to a yoke which bound a pair of oxen to the plow. Later, metal plowshares were used. Plowing was done as soon as the first rains softened the land. (I Kings 19:19; Job 1:14.)

Plumb Line

Masons used a plumb line to build their walls straight from bottom to top. A plumb line was a long cord with a heavy piece of metal or stone attached to one end. The weight kept the cord straight so the mason could lay the wall up beside it. Amos had a vision of the Lord standing with a plumb line in His hand. It showed that the people of Israel were not living upright lives. (Amos 7:7–9.)

Pomegranate

The pomegranate tree is quite small, almost a shrub, but it bears a lovely fruit, shaped something like an apple. Its name means "an apple with grains." The skin is red, covering many seeds, each in a little sack filled with delicious juice. The pillars of Solomon's Temple and the hem of Aaron's robe were decorated with pomegranates. (Exod. 28:33, 34; I Kings 7:18–20.)

Pontus

On the day of Pentecost, some Jews who were in Jerusalem from Pontus, a Roman province in northeastern Asia Minor, heard Peter's sermon, and became Christians. The land today is in Turkey. Peter addressed his first epistle to Christians in Pontus, among other places. Paul's helper Aquila had been born in Pontus. (Acts 2:9; 18:2; I Pet. 1:1.)

Pool of Siloam

"I am the light of the world," Jesus told a blind man one day. Then he put some clay on the man's eyes and told him to wash in the Pool of Siloam. When the man did, he could see again. The pool was just inside the southeast corner of old Jerusalem. To bring more water to the pool, King Hezekiah had made a tunnel from the Gihon spring. (John 9:5–7.)

Porch

Along the Court of the Gentiles in Herod's Temple was a wide area known as Solomon's Porch. It was covered with a roof, supported by pillars. Standing in Solomon's Porch, Jesus told the Jews that He and His father were one. The pool of Bethesda had five porches, which sheltered the sick who waited to be healed in its waters. Solomon's palace also had porches. (I Kings 6:3; 7:6; John 10:23.)

Potiphar

When Joseph was sold as a slave in Egypt, his first master was the captain of Pharaoh's guard, who was named Potiphar. It did not take Potiphar long to recognize that God was with Joseph and so he put him in charge of his household. God blessed Potiphar because of Joseph. But Potiphar's wife lied about Joseph and Potiphar threw him into prison. (Gen. 39:1–20.)

Potsherd

Pottery was often made of clay and so it was easily broken. The potsherds, or broken pieces, were sometimes used as "paper" for notes and short messages and even school exercises. Whenever ancient ruins are dug up, thousands of these potsherds are found. From them we can learn much about everyday life in ancient times. (Job. 2:8; Ps. 22:15.)

Pottage

A thick broth called pottage was made by boiling meat with lentils or other vegetables. A hungry family gathered around the cooking pot in the open air to eat. Each person took a piece of bread, doubled it into a spoon shape, and dipped it into the pot. Jacob bought Esau's birthright with some pottage. (Gen. 25:29–34; II Kings 4:38, 39.)

Potter

The potter was in demand in Bible times because his clay pots were widely used and easily broken. To make a pot, he mixed his clay thoroughly, sometimes for hours, to remove all the air bubbles. Then he put the clay on his potter's wheel, spun it rapidly, and fashioned the pot. The finished pot was fired in a kiln or open flame. (Jer. 18:1–6.)

Pottery

There were many kinds of clay pottery in the Eastern home—pitchers, bowls, great jars for storing grain, lamps, toys, and even writing tablets. Over the centuries, potters gradually made changes in the shape and decoration of their wares, and this helps to date the articles when they are found in the ruins of ancient buildings. (Jer. 18:1–6.)

Praetorium

At first, the praetorium was the tent of the Roman praetor, or commander-in-chief. Later the name was used for the residence of the governor of a Roman province. When Pilate released Jesus to his soldiers, they took Him into the praetorium and mocked Him. Paul was also guarded by soldiers in the praetorium in Jerusalem. (Mark 15:16.)

Praise

Again and again the Psalms repeat the phrase, "Praise ye the Lord!" The people of God were commanded to show how grateful they were to Him by offering their praise in words and song. In the Temple, the Levites led the public praise. The people sang hymns of praise in their services and the processions at their festivals. (Ps. 112:1.)

Prayer

"Pray without ceasing," Paul wrote to the Christians at Thessalonica. He was telling them to be always in the spirit of prayer, ready and willing to talk to their Father in heaven. Jesus prayed often. So should His people. Prayer is talking personally to God. When we pray, we may thank Him, praise Him, ask Him, confess to Him, or just talk with Him. (I Thess. 5:17.)

Preaching

To preach is to tell people the good news that Jesus came into the world and died to take away their sins. In New Testament times Jesus and the disciples preached during services in synagogues, in the open air, on the mountainside, and by rivers, and the seashore. They preached wherever people were to be found. Peter preached at Pentecost and 3,000 people came to Christ. (Acts 2.)

Priest

In the time of the Old Testament, God's people approached Him through priests. All of the priests were of the tribe of Levi. Priests presented the people's requests to God and made known His will to the people. When Jesus arrived, He became our High Priest, and He made all Christians a royal priesthood. (Exod. 28–29; Rev. 1:5, 6.)

Prince

The word "prince" is today used for the son of a king. But in the Bible it is used for an important person who has royal authority. It is sometimes also used for others. Daniel calls Michael and the other guardian angels of the nations princes. Isaiah prophesied that one of Jesus' names would be Prince of Peace. Satan was called the prince of the power of the air. (Isa. 9:6; Eph. 2:2.)

Prison

When Joseph was put into prison in Egypt, he was probably placed in a dungeon in Potiphar's house. In the early days of Israel, prisoners were kept in a deep pit. By the time of the kings, prison rooms were built onto the palace. Jesus' parable of the unmerciful servant shows how men and their families could be imprisoned for debts. (Gen. 39:20; Matt. 18:28–30.)

Proconsul

The Roman empire was divided into provinces. Those provinces that did not need military forces to keep order were under the command of a civil governor appointed by the Senate in Rome. He was given the title of proconsul and usually held office for one year. Sergius Paulus was proconsul of Cyprus when Paul and Barnabas visited the island. (Acts 13:7.)

Procurator

Jesus was brought to trial before Pilate, procurator of Judea, Samaria, and Idumea. Pilate had that title because the Roman emperor personally had appointed him to govern a province. None of the procurators won the support of the Jews and their failure led to the Jewish-Roman war of 66-70 A.D. Procurator is translated "governor" in some Bible versions. (Matt. 27:11–13.)

Promise

God gave many promises throughout the Bible. The greatest of all was the promise of His Son, the Lord Jesus. In the right time, God did send His Son to save us. Jesus promised that He would send the Holy Spirit after He returned to heaven, which He did at Pentecost. He has also promised that He will some day return. (I Kings 8:56.)

Promised Land

The Hebrew slaves were freed from Egypt and walked toward a land they had never seen, a land God had promised to them. The land of Canaan had been promised to their ancestor Abraham and his family centuries before. At last they claimed that promise for their own and occupied the land for hundreds of years. God always keeps His promises. (Gen. 12:7; Deut. 9:28; 19:8.)

Prophets, Prophecy

The prophet spoke to the people for God, sometimes telling the people things that would happen in the future. Hundreds of years before Christ came, Micah prophesied that He would be born in Bethlehem. Zechariah foretold that He would come riding on a donkey, which Jesus did at the Triumphal Entry. Prophets also told the people how God wanted them to live. (Mic. 5:2; Zech. 9:9.)

Prophetess

Some women in the Bible had the same gifts that a prophet had. Miriam, Moses' sister, was called a prophetess. So was Isaiah's wife. Deborah judged Israel during the days of the judges, but she was also known as a prophetess. Huldah, wife of the keeper of the royal wardrobe, was consulted by Josiah about the Book of the Law found in the Temple. (Judg. 4:4; II Kings 22:14.)

Proselyte

Wherever Jews were to be found in all parts of the known world, they tried to persuade pagans to seek the true God and to become Jews. All who came to the services in the synagogue and kept at least some of the Jewish practices were called "God-fearers." Those who decided to become full Jews were called proselytes. (Matt. 23:15; Acts 2:10.)

Proverbs

"Wisdom is better than rubies," we read in the Book of Proverbs. Since King Solomon was the wisest man who had ever lived, he put some of his wisdom into a book. It is a collection of sayings about how a wise man or woman is able to live a successful life for God. Some of the proverbs were written by Agur and Lemuel, but these may be other names for Solomon. (The Book of Proverbs.)

Providence

The Bible tells of God's love, not only in making the world and all that is in it, but also in taking care of the world. Each day God provides for His people and His world. This provision of God is called providence. He provides some things for all, for the rain falls on the just and the unjust. But He provides some things especially for those who trust Him. (Matt. 5:45; Rom. 8:28.)

Psalms

The meaning of the word psalms is "the twanging of harp strings." Many psalms or songs were written by David as he twanged his harp strings for his sheep. He probably sang his psalms to King Saul to drive away the evil spirit. The Jews sang psalms in their Temple worship which became their "songs of praise" book. Jesus quoted many psalms, as we do today. (The Book of Psalms.)

Psaltery

Originally the psaltery came from Phoenicia. This musical instrument was often played to accompany singing. It was something like a harp and was played by plucking the strings. Samuel told Saul to watch for a band of prophets playing psalteries and other instruments. This band would be a sign from God that Saul was going to become king. (I Sam. 10:5; I Kings 10:12.)

Publican

One day Jesus saw Levi, a publican, sitting at his customs house where he collected taxes for Rome. "Follow Me!" Jesus said. Levi, or Matthew as he was later called, became one of Jesus' disciples. Publicans were tax collectors for Rome. Since most of them cheated, the people hated them. But Jesus ate with publicans and some believed in Him. (Luke 5:27; 18:10.)

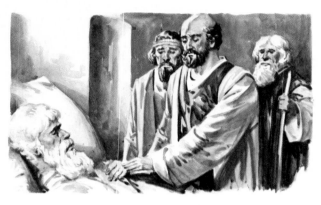

Publius

A cold rain fell on the island of Melita or Malta. When Paul's ship was wrecked along the shore, Paul and his fellow sailors had nowhere to go and built a fire. The chief man of the island, whose name was Publius, took the shipwrecked men into his home and fed them. While there, Paul healed Publius' father. The people of Melita were very good to Paul. (Acts 28:7, 8.)

Pudens

At the close of his second letter to Timothy, Paul sent greetings from Christian friends in Rome. One of those friends was Pudens. The name means "modest" and was a common name among Roman soldiers. Pudens may have been a Roman soldier who guarded Paul in prison where he awaited his death at the hands of Nero. (II Tim. 4:21.)

Punon

On their way to the Promised Land, many years after leaving the slavery of Egypt, the Israelites camped for a while in the desert at Punon. It was east of the mountains of Edom and the home of an Edomite chief. The area had many copper mines. After the copper was smelted at Punon, much of it was taken to Egypt. (Num. 33:42, 43.)

Purification

Purification means eliminating uncleanness by washing with water or by sacrifice. Before an Israelite could go into the Temple, he had to be purified by taking a special bath and changing his clothes. Priests had to wash their feet and hands before going on duty in the sanctuary. After the birth of her baby, a mother was purified by offering a year-old lamb or a pigeon as a sacrifice. (Num. 19:17–19.)

Purim

In the days when the Jewish people were exiled, a wicked ruler named Haman plotted to kill all the Jews in the Persian Empire. But Mordecai, a Jew learned about the plot and encouraged his cousin, Queen Esther, to help stop it. She did and Haman was hanged. The Feast of Purim, March 14 and 15, celebrates the wisdom of Mordecai and the heroism of Esther in saving the Jewish people. (Esther 9:20–32.)

Purse

There were two kinds of purses mentioned in the Bible. One was a leather bag or pouch drawn together at the neck. It had leather straps or cords so that it could be carried easily. The other type was a wide belt, made of leather, woven camel's hair, or cloth. Leather belts sometimes had slots to hold coins. Money was carried in the folds of the cloth belts. (Luke 10:4; 12:33.)

Purple

When Paul arrived in Philippi, he went to see Lydia, who had come from Thyatira. Lydia was a seller of purple, the expensive purple dye that came from a shellfish called murex. Kings and rich men wore robes of purple. Purple cloth was used in the Tabernacle. When Jesus was on trial, the Roman soldiers dressed Him in a purple robe to mock Him. (Exod. 25:4; Acts 16:14.)

Puteoli

On his way to Rome for trial, Paul stopped for a week at Puteoli. There he enjoyed a time with Christian friends and then went on to Rome. Puteoli was an important harbor because it was very safe. It had been founded by Greeks in the Bay of Naples. Today it is called Pozzuoli and is situated near the city of Naples, Italy. (Acts 28: 13, 14.)

Quails

The people of Israel often complained to Moses as they were led through the wilderness. Once they complained for meat and God sent vast swarms of quail. These brown birds often migrate from southeast Europe and cross Sinai to the north Africa coast. God sent them to the Israelites at exactly the time Moses promised He would. (Exod. 16:13.)

Quirinius, Cyrenius

"This taxing was first made when Cyrenius was governor of Syria." These words have been read again and again at Christmas time. It was the taxing that took Mary and Joseph to Bethlehem, where Jesus was born. Quirinius, or Cyrenius, was the Roman governor of Syria from 4 B.C. (the year Christ was born) to 1 A.D. He was governor a second time from 6 to 9 A.D. (Luke 2:2.)

Quiver

Archers carried their arrows in a case called a quiver. It was made of leather or skin and was hung over the shoulder or at the left side. Charioteers fastened quivers to the sides of their chariots. The psalmist said that a man whose home is filled with children is as secure as a warrior whose quiver is full of arrows. (Gen. 27:3; Ps. 127:3–5.)

R

Raamses

The people of Israel built store cities for Pharaoh while they were slaves in Egypt. Two of these store cities were Pithom and Raamses. Raamses was in Goshen in the delta of northeast Egypt. Pharaoh made it his capital city. It was from Raamses that the people of Israel set out on their long journey to the Promised Land. (Exod. 1:11; 12:37.)

Rabbi

Rabbi, which means "master," was a title of respect given to a teacher of the Jewish law. The term Rabboni, which means "my lord, my master," was used to show even greater respect. Jesus was called Rabbi by His disciples and sometimes by others who spoke to Him. The Greek form of the word means "teacher." The scribes (scholars) of Jesus' day were experts on the Jewish law. (John 3:2; 20:16.)

Rabshaken

Sennacherib, King of Assyria, had attacked the city of Lachish. While there, he wanted Jerusalem to surrender too. So he sent an official to Jerusalem to urge the people to give up without fighting. The official's title was Rabshaken, which meant "chief cup-bearer." He talked to the people in their own language, but could not persuade them to surrender. (II Kings 18:17–37.)

Rachel

Rachel must have been a very beautiful young lady because Jacob worked 14 years to marry her. She was the younger of La- ban's two daughters. Rachel had two sons, Joseph and Benjamin. Because of Jacob's deep love for Rachel, these were his two favorite sons. Rachel died when giving birth to Benjamin and was buried near Bethlehem. (Gen. 29:6–18.)

Rahab

Rahab's house was built on the wide city wall of Jericho. She hid Joshua's two spies under the flax drying on the flat roof. After dark, she let them down outside the wall by a rope. She marked her house by tying a scarlet rope in the window. When Joshua's army attacked Jericho, Rahab and her family were kept safe and joined the people of Israel. (Josh. 2.)

Rain

Most of the rain in Palestine falls between October and April and less rain falls in the south and east. In desert areas a few winter storms may cause flooding, but the water quickly runs away and leaves the ground as hard as ever. The first and last rains in the winter are called the former and the latter rain. One of God's most se- vere punishments was to withhold rain. (Deut. 11:17; Lev. 26:4.)

Rainbow

After Noah and his family were saved, God promised that He would never again de- stroy the earth with a flood. As a sign of His promise, God placed a rainbow in the sky for Noah to see. Both in the prophecy of Ezekiel and in the Book of Revelation the rainbow of mercy appears around the throne of God's glory and judgment. (Gen. 9:8–17; Rev. 4:3.)

Raisins

Most foods spoiled easily in the hot climate of Palestine. Dried foods were very important because travelers could carry them for many days without spoiling. Raisins are dried grapes and were widely used because they were easily carried and were nourishing. Abigail gave David a hundred clusters of raisins with some other food. (I Sam. 25:18.)

Ram

The Old Testament frequently mentions the ram, which is a male sheep. Most of the time, it gives instructions about using the ram in sacrifices. When Abraham was about to sacrifice Isaac, God provided a ram caught by its horns in the bushes. The skins of rams, dyed red, formed part of the covering for the Tabernacle. (Gen. 22:13; Exod. 26:14.)

Ramah

A woman of Ramah named Hannah begged God to give her a son. "I will give him unto the Lord," she vowed. God gave her a son and she named him Samuel. She gave young Samuel back to the Lord to work in the Tabernacle at Shiloh with Eli the priest. When Samuel became a prophet, he made his home at Ramah and went out from there to judge Israel. (I Sam. 1:19; 2:11.)

Ramoth-gilead

East of the Jordan River in the territory of Gad there was a walled city named Ramoth-gilead. It was one of the cities of refuge. Benhadad, King of Syria, captured the city from Israel. When King Ahab of Israel and King Jehoshaphat of Judah tried to retake it, Ahab was killed. The name means "heights of Gilead." (I Kings 22:1–37.)

Rams' Horns

Trumpets made of rams' horns were blown to announce the approach of danger and to give signals in time of war. Priests blew rams' horn trumpets to proclaim the appearance of the new moon at the beginning of the month and to mark the opening of the great religious feasts. Rams' horn trumpets were blown at the battle of Jericho. A ram's horn was also used to hold the oil for anointing. (Josh. 6:4–8.)

Ransom

A payment was often required to release a prisoner or to free a slave from bondage. This payment was called a ransom. The Lord required payment of a ransom from every Israelite. When Jesus laid down His life by dying on the cross, He gave it as a ransom to set us free. His life was the price necessary to free us from the power of sin and death. (Exod. 21:30; 30:12; I Tim. 2:6.)

Raven

"Consider the ravens," Jesus said to His disciples. It was a lesson in God's provision. Jesus told how the ravens never sow nor reap, but God provides for them. God also used ravens to feed His prophet, Elijah, during a famine. The raven is a large black bird in the crow family. Its nest is a massive structure of sticks, lined with scraps of cloth and paper. (I Kings 17:4–6; Luke 12:24.)

Rebekah

It was time for Isaac to marry, but his father Abraham wanted his wife to be a godly woman, not one of the neighboring Canaanite girls. So Abraham sent his steward Eliezer to his relatives in Mesopotamia. Eliezer asked God's help in choosing the right bride for Isaac. There he met Rebekah, the daughter of Bethuel, Abraham's nephew. Rebekah and Isaac had twin sons, Esau and Jacob. (Gen. 24.)

Rechabites

The Rechabites had certain rules which set them apart from their neighbors. They refused to drink wine, build houses, or sow seed. Instead, they lived simply in tents. They believed that it was a sign of luxury to settle in a town and could cause them to forget God. Jeremiah commended them for their faithfulness but not necessarily for their rules. (Jer. 35:2–10.)

Recorder

The title "recorder" meant "one who reminds," for it was his job to remind the king of important matters he must consider. He was a high official, probably the president of the council. He was in charge of government and public records. In Josiah's time the recorder was put in charge of Temple repairs. (II Sam. 8:16; II Kings 18:18.)

Red Sea

When God led the people of Israel from Egypt, the waters of the Red Sea stood in their way. But God caused a strong wind to drive back the sea long enough for the Israelites to cross safely. When the Egyptians tried to follow, the waters returned and they were drowned. The Red Sea is shaped like a fork, going along two sides of Sinai. (Exod. 14.)

Redeemer

Prisoners of war were sometimes bought back, or redeemed, with a payment. Slaves could also be redeemed, or purchased, so that they could be set free. Paul reminds the Corinthian Christians that they have been bought with a price, and so they must now live for God. Jesus is our Redeemer, for He paid the price for our freedom from sin. (I Cor. 6:19, 20.)

Reed

The tall marsh reed carries a dense, silky head of purple blossoms. Pens for writing on parchment were cut from the stem. Because it is straight and light, the stem was also used as a measuring rod. Isaiah warned Israel that to depend upon Egypt was like leaning heavily on a reed. The reed would buckle and cut the hand. (Isa. 36:6; Ezek. 40:3.)

Refiner

It was important to clean the impurities from a precious metal such as gold or silver. This was the job of the refiner. He heated the metal in a crucible or pot until the impurities burned away, leaving the pure gold or silver. God also uses this method with His people. He uses fiery trials to purify us and clean sin from our lives. (Isa. 1:25; Mal. 3:2, 3.)

Rehoboam

The old men who counseled King Rehoboam advised him to lighten the load of taxes so that the people would serve him. But the young counselors advised him to make the load heavier. Rehoboam listened to his young counselors. The ten northern tribes of Israel rebelled and made Jeroboam their king. Rehoboam remained king of two tribes only, Judah and Benjamin. (I Kings 12:1–20.)

Rehoboth

Isaac needed water because he had many sheep and goats. But each time Isaac's men dug a well, the men of Gerar claimed it as their own. Each time Isaac moved on and dug a new well rather than fight his neighbors. At last he dug a well which the men of Gerar did not claim. Isaac called the well Rehoboth, which means "room," for he said there is room for us at last. (Gen. 26:17–22.)

Rehum

Rehum and other officials of the Persian government in Samaria wanted to stop the Jews from rebuilding Jerusalem. So they wrote a letter to the Persian king Artaxerxes, complaining about these things. In his letter, Rehum claimed that the Jews would defy the Persian officers and refuse to pay their taxes. Artaxerxes gave Rehum permission to stop the work. (Ezra 4.)

Remnant

The prophets often warned the people of Israel that they would be sent into exile if they did not live godly lives. But God would not let all His people be destroyed. Some of them, the remnant, would be faithful to God and be brought back to their own land. Isaiah called one of his sons Shear-jashub, which means "a remnant shall return." (Isa. 7:3.)

Repent, Repentance

"Repent ye, and believe the gospel," Jesus preached. To repent is to be sorry for sin and to turn away from it to God. Jesus said that the people of Nineveh repented when Jonah preached to them. Therefore God did not destroy the city. When Peter preached at Pentecost telling the people to repent, about 3,000 turned from their sin to Christ. (Mark 1:15; Acts 2:38–41.)

Rephaim

Even before Abraham came into Canaan, there was a race of giants called the Rephaim in the land. The word means "giants." King Og of Bashan was one of the last of these giants. He had a great bed about 14 feet or 4.5 meters long and 6 feet or 1.8 meters wide. God told Abraham that the land of the Rephaim would some day be given to his descendants. (Gen. 15:18–21.)

Rephidim

On their way to Mt. Sinai, the people of Israel stopped at Rephidim. But there was no water and so the people complained to Moses. The Lord told Moses to strike a rock with his rod. When he did, water came from it. While the people of Israel were at Rephidim, the Amalekites attacked, but God gave the Israelites the victory. (Exod. 17.)

Reservoir

There is little rain in Palestine from May through September and so it was important to collect water during the rainy season. Pits were cut into the rock to hold water. These pits, called cisterns or reservoirs, were often pear-shaped with a small hole at the top. Some houses had a private reservoir, but there were also public reservoirs for those who could not afford their own. (II Kings 18:31.)

Restitution

The Jewish law required a penalty for taking things unjustly. The wrongdoer not only had to repay what he had taken but had to add another one-fifth. This was called restitution, giving back what was taken wrongfully. When Zacchaeus followed Jesus, he did much more. He gave back four times as much as he had taken unjustly. (Luke 19:8.)

Resurrection

"I am the resurrection and the life," Jesus told His friends. "Whoever believes in Me will never die." Jesus proved this when He rose from the dead and presented Himself alive to His disciples. For a short while it seemed hard to believe, but then they realized that He was God's Son. Jesus' resurrection shows us that He has the power to raise us from the dead also and give us a life that never ends. (John 11:25.)

235

Reuben

"Unstable as water" was the way Jacob spoke of his firstborn son Reuben. Jacob realized some weaknesses in his son. But he must have also been pleased with Reuben's strengths. It was Reuben alone who tried to keep Joseph from being harmed. And it was Reuben who pledged his own two sons for Benjamin's safe return from Egypt. Leah was Reuben's mother. (Gen. 37:21, 22.)

Reubenites

The descendants of Reuben, oldest son of Jacob and Leah, formed one of the twelve tribes of Israel. By the time of the wilderness wanderings, they numbered more than 43,000. The Reubenites and Gadites requested the territory east of the Jordan because it was good grazing ground for their cattle. The Jordan River isolated them from the rest of the nation and Israel's history. (Deut. 3:12.)

Revelation

The word revelation means "unveiling." It is the last book of the Bible and in it God unveils many of the great events to come. It tells of the struggle between the forces of God and the forces of Satan and the final triumph of Christ and His own. There are seven letters to seven churches in Asia Minor. The Book closes with a description of the heavenly city and Jesus' promise to return. (The Revelation of John.)

Reward

"He shall reward every man according to his works." Jesus was speaking about what He will do Himself when He comes again some day. Good deeds without faith in God will not get people into heaven. But Jesus had promised to reward those who do them. Jesus also spoke of a special great reward in heaven for those who are persecuted for His sake. (Matt. 5:12; 16:27.)

Rezeph

The Assyrian King Sennacherib's commander demanded that King Hezekiah surrender Jerusalem to him. He reminded Hezekiah that even fine cities like Rezeph, which was on the Euphrates near Haran, had given in. The gods of Rezeph were quite unable to resist the Assyrians. So it was useless for Hezekiah to hold out because even the Lord God of Israel could not save him. (II Kings 19:8–12.)

Rezin

In the days of the prophet Isaiah, King Rezin of Syria joined King Pekah of Israel. Together they went to fight Ahaz, King of Judah, setting a siege around Jerusalem. King Ahaz immediately sent Temple treasures to Assyria and asked for help. The Assyrians captured the Syrians and took them back with them. Rezin was killed in the fighting. (II Kings 15:37—16:9.)

Rhoda

When Peter was freed from prison by an angel, he decided to call at John Mark's house to tell his friends who were praying there what had happened. A girl named Rhoda, which means "Rose," came to answer his knock. She was so overjoyed at hearing Peter's voice that she forgot to open the door before rushing back inside to share the good news with the others. (Acts 12:13.)

Rhodes

Between the coast of Greece and Palestine there is a large island called Rhodes. Ships sailing the Mediterranean Sea often stopped at Rhodes and so it became an important place. A great statue was built there called the Colossus. It was one of the seven wonders of the ancient world. Paul visited Rhodes as he returned to Caesarea from Troas. (Acts 21:1.)

Riblah

The king of Egypt, Pharaoh Necho II, had defeated King Josiah at Megiddo. From there he moved northward and set up military headquarters at Riblah. Later, King Nebuchadnezzar defeated the Egyptians and set up his headquarters at Riblah. When he captured King Zedekiah, he killed Zedekiah's sons before his eyes at Riblah. He then blinded Zedekiah and took him to Babylon. (II Kings 25:6, 7.)

Righteousness

If someone could always do exactly what was right, he would be righteous. But he would have to do exactly what God's rules or law says because God's law was given to show us what is right. The Bible teaches that no one except Jesus has done this and so we become right or righteous by accepting Jesus into our hearts and lives and following Him. (Rom. 3:10; 5:18, 19.)

Rimmon

Rimmon "the thunderer" was the Syrian form of the god Baal. It was a god of storms and war. Naaman, commander-in-chief of the Syrian army, worshiped in Rimmon's temple in Damascus. But when Elisha healed him of leprosy, Naaman no longer wanted to bow down to Rimmon. He took two mule-loads of dirt from Israel so that he could build an altar to the Lord. (II Kings 5:17-,18.)

Ring

People today sign their names on checks and letters and others recognize their signature. In Bible times important people had a ring or seal with certain signs or pictures on it called a signet ring. When this was pressed into clay, people recognized the owner's signature. Signet rings were a sign of authority. Pharaoh gave one to Joseph. Haman also received one. (Gen. 41:42, 43; Esther 3:10.)

River

Several great rivers are mentioned in the Bible. When Moses was a baby, he was placed in the Nile River in a basket. The land of Haran, which had been the home of Rebekah and Rachel, was between the Tigris and Euphrates Rivers. Jacob wrestled with the Angel of God beside the Jabbok River. Jesus was baptized in the Jordan River. (Matt. 3:13.)

Road

There were no roads in Palestine before the Romans came. Caravans and armies moved on the great caravan routes, which were merely tracks across the land. Sudden storms could quickly make these tracks dangerous or impossible to use. The Romans were famous for their roads, which made it possible for the first time for wheeled vehicles to move quickly and safely across the land.

Robbers

Most travelers banded together in caravans because it was dangerous to travel through the countryside alone. There were many caves in Palestine which provided good hiding places for robbers. On the road from Jerusalem to Jericho, the Good Samaritan found a man who had been attacked and injured by robbers. This road was especially dangerous for travelers. (Luke 10:30.)

Robe

Both men and women wore a long outer garment which we would call a robe. Robes of many colors were worn by tribal chiefs or princes. Jacob gave Joseph a robe of many colors. It showed that he put Joseph above his brothers. Jesus wore a simple robe made without a seam. Priests wore special robes which set them apart from common people. (Gen. 37:3; Matt. 27:28, 35.)

Rod and Staff

"Thy rod and thy staff they comfort me," David sang to the Lord. David knew about a rod or staff because as a shepherd he carried one. The rod or staff was a long stick or club which the shepherd carried to fight wild animals. He also used it as a walking stick. God used Moses' rod for many miracles. God's rod or staff is His protection, which is always a comfort for us. (Exod. 4:17; Ps. 23:4.)

Rome, Romans

In the days when Jesus was on earth, Rome was the world's most important city. The Roman emperor and his highest officials lived there. They controlled much of the world. Paul was put into prison in Rome on two occasions. Once he wrote a letter to the Christians in Rome, reminding them that the gospel is powerful to change lives. (The Epistle of Paul to the Romans.)

Roman

A Roman citizen had special rights that others did not have. He could not be bound or beaten without permission, as Paul reminded some Roman officers on two occasions. The Roman citizen also could vote, become a magistrate, or own property. He was someone who had Roman parents or had bought his citizenship. (Acts 16:37–39; 22:27, 28.)

Roof

Most houses in Palestine had a flat roof where people often stored items or slept when the evenings were hot. The roof of a poor man's home was often made of boughs or rafters covered with clay. A better house had a stone or tile roof. Rahab hid the spies of Israel on her roof. Samuel and Saul talked on the roof of Samuel's house. (Josh. 2:6; I Sam. 9:25, 26.)

Rope

When the spies of Israel visited Rahab, she hid them until it was dark and then let them down with a scarlet rope. Later, Rahab saved herself and her family by hanging the rope from her window. That was the signal to Joshua's army not to harm the people of that home. Rope at that time was made from twisted strands of flax or the hair of camels and goats or even bulrushes. (Josh. 2:15, 18.)

Rose of Sharon

"I am the rose of Sharon and the lily of the valley." So it was written in the Song of Solomon. The Rose of Sharon was probably the red tulip that grows wild in the Plain of Sharon, especially after the spring rains. Some believe the term "Rose of Sharon" refers to Christ. The "Lily of the Valley" could have been the bright red lily that grew in King Solomon's garden, a symbol of true beauty. (Song of Sol. 2:1.)

Rudder

It was obvious to everyone on board that the ship on which Paul was sailing would be wrecked. So the sailors loosed the rudders, pulled up the anchors, drifted toward shore with the wind, and crashed onto the island of Melita. The rudder was like a large oar which guided the ship. Sometimes there was one rudder at the back and sometimes two. (Acts. 27:40.)

Rue

Jesus scolded the Pharisees because they were careful to tithe such herbs as rue but they were careless about the love and judgment of God. Rue was a garden herb with a strong smell and taste. It was often scattered around public buildings as a disinfectant. Sometimes it was used as a medicine or food flavoring. The plant has lemon-colored flowers and grows almost as tall as a person. (Luke 11:42.)

Ruler

Cities had rulers, who often sat at the city gate to do their work. Moses appointed rulers over hundreds to lead his people. The rulers over cattle were the head herdsmen. Jairus was ruler of the synagogue at Capernaum. The ruler was an official who led others under him. But even the rulers, such as Jairus and the Roman centurion came to Jesus for help. (Luke 8:41.)

Runner

When officials had urgent news, they had to send runners because there were no telephones or postal service. Sometimes a runner went ahead of a royal chariot to test the road and protect the king. John the Baptist was called a forerunner because he prepared the way for the King of kings, the Lord Jesus. (II Sam. 18:19; Matt. 3:3.)

Rushes

Some 20 different kinds of rushes grow by streams and rivers in the Holy Land. The common soft or bog rush is a plant as tall as a man. The round whip-like leaves are still cut today and used to make baskets, mats, chair seats, and snares to catch game. Isaiah prophesied that one day even parched ground will become a pool lined with rushes. (Isa. 35:7.)

Ruth

When Naomi left Moab to return to her home in Bethlehem, her daughter-in-law Ruth went with her. Ruth went into the fields to gather stalks of grain which the reapers left behind, providing food for herself and Naomi. Later Ruth married Boaz, the owner of the fields. Their son became the grandfather of King David. Ruth's lovely story is written in the book which bears her name. (The Book of Ruth.)

Sabbath

"The sabbath was made for man, and not man for the sabbath," Jesus said. The Jewish Sabbath was a day of rest, from sunset on Friday until sunset on Saturday. No work was done on the Sabbath. The Pharisees had many burdensome rules for the Sabbath. They even complained when Jesus healed and helped people. But Jesus said it was important to use the Sabbath for God. (Mark 2:27.)

Sabbath Day's Journey

The Jews of Jesus' time were not permitted to travel far on the Sabbath. A Sabbath day's journey was only 2,000 cubits, about a third of a mile or half a kilometer. This was the distance between the Ark of the Covenant and the people while marching through the wilderness. The Mount of Olives was a Sabbath day's journey from Jerusalem. (Acts 1:12.)

Sabbatical Year

As the Sabbath day was the seventh day of the week, so the sabbatical year was the seventh year. Both the seventh day and the seventh year were holy, set aside because the Israelites were a chosen people. During the sabbatical year the people were to let their fields rest, without planting or harvest. God promised that the sixth year would provide enough to last through the sabbatical year. (Lev. 25:1–7.)

Sabeans

Only one of Job's men escaped to tell him that Sabeans had attacked his flocks and servants. Sabeans were slave traders who lived in Saba, or Sheba, in West Arabia. The Sabeans had many camel caravans, bringing goods from India to Bible lands. They often brought such things as gold, precious stones, perfumes, and spices. (Job. 1:15; Joel 3:8.)

Sackcloth

In times of trouble, people often put on sackcloth and sometimes sprinkled ashes on their heads. It was a sign of mourning or sorrow for sins and a prayer for deliverance. Prophets wore sackcloth to remind people of their message of repentance. Sackcloth was a coarse material made from goats' hair. It was usually black. (Luke 10:13.)

Sacrament

Some Christians refer to baptism and the Lord's Supper as sacraments. A sacrament is an outward visible sign of something with spiritual meaning. The water used in baptism is a sign of cleansing from sin. The bread and wine in the Lord's Supper represent the body and blood of Jesus. The Bible commands Christians to be baptized and to celebrate the Lord's Supper. (Matt. 26:26–28.)

Sacrifice

In the Old Testament, a sacrifice was something given up to win God's favor or forgiveness. Burnt offerings were animal sacrifices whose lives were given as a way to ask God to forgive sin. Jesus' death on the cross was a sacrifice for sin, for He gave up His life so that God would forgive our sins. Sacrifices we make today are in thanksgiving to God for what Jesus has done. (Exod. 20:24; Rom. 12:1.)

Sadducees

While some Pharisees accepted Jesus, we do not know of any Sadducees who did. The Sadducees were a group of priests who did not believe in life after death or the resurrection. They also did not accept all of the rules of the Pharisees, only the law of Moses. The Sadducees were always working against Jesus. After Jesus returned to heaven, they arrested the apostles and put them in prison. (Acts 5:17, 18.)

Salamis

Paul and Barnabas began their first missionary journey by sailing from Selevcia to Salamis, a city on the east coast of Cyprus. There was a fine harbor at Salamis at that time but it has since filled with mud. Paul and Barnabas visited the Jewish synagogues at Salamis and on the rest of the island and preached to the people there. (Acts 13:5.)

Salome

John the Baptist had told King Herod Antipas that it was wrong for him to marry Herodias, his brother Philip's wife. So Herod put John in prison. At a birthday party for Herod, Herodias' daughter Salome danced for the king. Herod was so pleased that he offered her a gift of her choice. She chose the head of John the Baptist on a silver plate. (Matt. 14:1–12.)

Salt

Along the Dead Sea, people found abundant salt but it was a poor quality. Better salt was shipped into the land or taken from sea water that evaporated in rocky holes. People seasoned their food with salt and preserved dried fish, olives, and vegetables with it. They also sprinkled salt on the offerings sacrificed to God. Jesus called His disciples the "salt of the earth." (Matt. 5:13.)

Salvation

"God is the God of salvation," the psalmist wrote. That is because God alone can save people from their deepest troubles. Salvation means to be saved or rescued from something. God saves us from our sin through His Son, Jesus Christ. Through His death on the cross, Christ made peace between God and us so that we can be saved. (Ps. 68:20; Acts 4:12; Rom. 1:16; 10:10.)

Samaria

Samaria was another name for the northern kingdom of Israel or Ephraim after the nation split into two. Samaria was also the name of the capital. The city was founded by Omri on a hill about five miles or eight kilometers from Shechem. Samaria was named after Shemer who sold the site to Omri for two talents of silver. (I Kings 16:24; John 4:4–5.)

Samaritan

After the Assyrians captured Samaria in 722 B.C., they took the leading citizens of the land back home with them. Then they brought other people into the land and these intermarried with the poorer Israelites who were left. This mixed race became known as the Samaritans. Later, the Jews hated them and tried to avoid them. Jesus told a parable about a good Samaritan. (Luke 10:30–37; John 4:9.)

Samson

God gave Samson greater strength than any other man. But Samson did not always use his strength for God. A Philistine woman named Delilah betrayed Samson and he was captured and blinded. Samson became a slave until his strength returned. Then he destroyed a great building, killing himself and about 3,000 Philistines. (Judg. 16.)

Samuel

Hannah begged the Lord for a son. She made a promise to give this son to the Lord if He would answer her prayer. Hannah did have a son and named him Samuel. As a child, Samuel helped Eli the priest take care of the Tabernacle. Later, he became the last and greatest of the judges of Israel. It was Samuel who anointed Saul and David as kings. (I Sam. 1:27, 28.)

Sanballat

Nehemiah had come back to Jerusalem to rebuild the walls. But Sanballat, an important official in Samaria, tried many times to stop him. He often sneered at the work and the workers. Then he tried to lure Nehemiah to Ono, where he plotted to kill him. But Nehemiah refused to stop work to go. Sanballat married a daughter of the High Priest Jehoiada. (Neh. 6:2.)

Sanctuary

For many years the people of Israel worshiped the Lord at His house the Tabernacle. It was a great tent which they had made in the wilderness. But it was God's house, their only sanctuary or place of worship. Later the Temple became their sanctuary, the house of God. In both places the Holy of Holies was considered the holiest place in the sanctuary. (Exod. 25:8.)

Sandal

People of Bible times thought of their shoes and sandals as the lowest form of clothing. Because the paths were so dusty, their feet and shoes were almost always dirty. Shoes were made of soft leather. Sandals were hard leather straps with soles made of wood, cane or palm bark. They were tied with thongs called shoe latchets. It was a slave's job to tie the shoe latchets. (Mark 1:7.)

Sanhedrin

During the time of Jesus, the Jewish high court was called the Sanhedrin. At first it judged matters over all the land. But later, under Herod Archelaus, it had authority only in Judea. It was this court that judged Jesus and then later Peter and John. Stephen was condemned by the Sanhedrin. After Jerusalem was destroyed in 70 A.D., the Romans abolished the Sanhedrin. (Mark 15:1.)

Sapphire

The sapphire mentioned in the Bible is different from our sapphire today. It was a dark blue stone flecked with gold. Some say it was lapis lazuli, others say it was lazurite. The sapphire was one of the precious stones in the High Priest's breastplate. Moses and the elders of Israel saw a vision of God standing on a sapphire pavement more blue than the sky. (Exod. 24:10.)

Sarah

Sarah was a very beautiful woman. Her name meant princess. Although she was Abraham's half sister, they were married in Ur. Through the years she traveled with Abraham to Canaan and Egypt. When she was 90 years old, God promised her a son, which was born the next year. This son, Isaac, became the father of Jacob and Esau. Sarah died at Hebron at the age of 127. (Gen. 17:15–22.)

Sardis

"I know your works," God said to the church at Sardis. "You have a name that lives, but you are dead." Sardis was a city in Asia Minor, which is now Turkey. It was a rich city because of its textile and jewelry trade. But the wealth of the city caused the church there to rest on its reputation. The letter to the church called upon it to wake up. (Rev. 3:1–6.)

Sargon

Shalmaneser V, king of Assyria, besieged the city of Samaria in 724 B.C. But he died before it was captured. Then Sargon II became king and captured Samaria. He built a royal city northeast of Nineveh which we know today as Khorsabad. Sargon was murdered in 705 B.C. and his son Sennacherib became king of Assyria. (Isa. 20:1.)

Satrap

Darius I, king of Persia, divided the Persian Empire into 20 provinces. Each had its own governor called a satrap, a Persian word meaning "a protector of the empire." Satraps, chosen from noble families, had much power. They are mentioned in the Books of Ezra, Esther, and Daniel. Some versions call them princes or lieutenants. (Dan. 3:2.)

Satan

"We would have come to you, but Satan hindered us," Paul wrote to the Thessalonians. Satan, the Devil, is a powerful spirit who is at war against God and His people. He is a person of great evil, leading the forces of evil. Satan sometimes comes as a "roaring lion" who violently seeks to overthrow God's people and His work. But he also disguises himself as an "angel of light," seeking to deceive people into following him while he plots to destroy them. Satan, with God's permission, took away all that Job had so that he could test him. But Job remained faithful to God. To help him fight his evil battles, Satan has a vast army of evil angels. Satan once tried to convince Jesus to sin against God. In three efforts, he promised Jesus food for His hunger, power over the nations, and honor from the multitudes. But Jesus restrained Satan by quoting the Word of God to him. Satan sent many demons into the world during Jesus' earthly life and ministry, but Jesus showed His great power over them. Satan is also called Apollyon, Beelzebub, Belial, the great dragon, the father of lies, the evil one, the old serpent, the prince of this world, and the tempter. The Bible tells of Satan's doom when he will be thrown into a lake of fire and brimstone, "tormented day and night for ever and ever." (Zech. 3:1, 2; Matt. 4:1–11; 25:41; Eph. 2:2; Rev. 20:1–3, 7–10.)

Saul

Samuel's sons were not fit to rule the nation and so the people cried out for a king. They wanted to be like other nations. God told Samuel to anoint Saul as the first king of Israel. Saul won great victories, but he disobeyed God. Saul became insanely jealous of David and tried several times to kill him. In the end Saul died while fighting the Philistines. (I Sam. 11:15.)

Savior

When Jesus was born, an angel announced, "To you is born a Savior, who is Christ the Lord." Jesus came to save us from our sins and bring us to God. Thus He is known as our Savior. But God the Father is also called Savior because He planned our salvation and sent His Son to make it happen. A savior is anyone who saves, but Jesus is THE Savior. (Luke 1:47; 2:11; John 4:42.)

Scapegoat

On the Day of Atonement Aaron took two goats to the Tabernacle. One goat was sacrificed to the Lord as a sin offering. Aaron put his hands on the head of the other goat, called a scapegoat, and confessed the sins of the people over it. Then the scapegoat was sent into the wilderness, a sign that the sins were removed. (Lev. 16:8, 10, 26.)

Scarlet

"Though your sins be as scarlet, they shall be as white as snow," the prophet Isaiah wrote. Scarlet dye was almost impossible to remove. But God's forgiveness is so complete that it will remove every sin. Scarlet dye was obtained from the eggs of an insect that lived in the oak trees of Palestine. It was used for the clothing of the wealthy and the hangings of the Tabernacle. (Isa. 1:18; Dan. 5:29.)

Scepter

Ancient kings often held a rod or staff in their hands as a sign of authority. It was sometimes covered with gold or jewels and was called a scepter. When Esther went to see the king, she knew she was safe when he held out his golden scepter to her. At Jesus' trial, Roman soldiers mocked Jesus because He claimed to be King. They put a reed in His hand and called it His scepter. (Esther 5:1, 2; Matt. 27:29.)

School

Before the time of the exile, Jewish children were educated by their parents in the home. But after the Jews returned from the exile, they set up synagogues throughout the land which became the schools for both children and adults. By the time of Jesus, almost every important community had a synagogue school. Paul attended a school taught by Gamaliel. (John 18:20.)

Scorpion

No loving father would give his son a scorpion when he asked for an egg. It was Jesus' way of telling how a good God gives good gifts to those He loves. A scorpion looks like a small lobster, although some grow as long as ten inches or 25 centimeters. It has a long tail with a stinger to poison its victim. A scorpion eats beetles and locusts and people fear its sting. (Luke 11:11, 12.)

Scribes

Two kinds of scribes are mentioned in the Bible. Jewish scribes, who were teachers of the law of Moses, were also called lawyers in the New Testament. They taught the law in the synagogues. Ezra was an important scribe. The other kind of scribe was a writer who was hired to keep accounts, write letters, or rewrite old records. Baruch was Jeremiah's scribe. (Jer. 36:32.)

Scripture

When Paul and Silas taught in Berea, the people "searched the Scriptures daily." At that time, the Scriptures were the writings that are now in our Old Testament. Later, Scripture included all writing inspired by God, both the Old and New Testaments. The Scripture is our Bible, the Word of God. It is given to help us know God and how to live. (Acts 17:11; II Tim. 3:16.)

Scroll

In Bible times, books were not made like ours today. Instead, they were made as scrolls, long strips of parchment or papyrus which were rolled up at either end. The writing was in columns and was read as the parchment was rolled from one side of the scroll to the other. Scrolls were in use in Egypt several thousand years before Christ. (Isa. 34:4; Rev. 6:14.)

Scythians

In the days of Jeremiah and Zephaniah, the Scythians lived in the region north of the Black Sea and Caspian Sea. They were a warlike and barbaric tribe who swept down on the coast at Ashkelon and plundered the temple of Venus. They threatened to invade Egypt and Judah also, but turned back when Egypt gave them large sums of money. (Col. 3:11.)

Seal

Written signatures were not widely used in Bible times. An important person had a seal made of stone, either a small cylinder or one shaped like a beetle. These stone seals had pictures or words on them. When someone wished to sign a document or article, he pressed the seal into soft clay and left its mark. The seal was either worn as a ring or hung about the neck. (I Kings 21:8.)

Seat

Chairs and couches were common in ancient Egypt but they were not practical in the tents of the Israelites. The people of Israel sat on the ground or on mats. Thrones were beautiful seats for kings and queens. The chief seats at a banquet were the places of honor for the most important guests. Synagogue seats were important places for the scribes and merchants. (Mark 12:38, 39.)

Seir

"Esau returned that day on his way unto Seir." He and his twin brother Jacob had just met for the first time in 20 years. Now he was going home to Seir, the mountainous region south of the Dead Sea. Esau's descendants, the Edomites, lived there for many years. When the people of Israel came from Egypt, the Lord appeared in great glory to them on Mt. Seir. (Gen. 33:16; Deut. 33:2.)

Seleucia

When Paul and Barnabas left the church at Antioch to go on their first missionary journey, they went first to the seaport of Seleucia, not far from Antioch. From there they sailed in a ship for Cyprus. Seleucia was founded in 300 B.C. by Seleucus Nicator as a seaport for Antioch. There was another Seleucia on the Tigris River. (Acts 13:4.)

Sennacherib

Not long after Sennacherib became king of Assyria in 705 B.C., he invaded Judah. In his records, he boasts that he shut up King Hezekiah like a caged bird in his royal capital of Jerusalem. But Sennacherib could not capture the city and so he went back home. Sennacherib was murdered by two of his sons in 681 B.C. (II Kings 19:35–37.)

Sepulchres

The people of Israel buried their dead in tombs or sepulchres cut into the rocky hillsides. A great stone was rolled in front of the sepulchre to keep animals from getting in. Only the wealthy used coffins. Sepulchres were often whitewashed on the outside so people would know they were burial places. Jesus called the Pharisees "whitewashed sepulchres." (Matt. 23:27.)

Seraiah

Seraiah, an official of King Zedekiah, was captured with the king and taken to Babylon. But Jeremiah wrote the evil things that would happen to Babylon on a scroll which he gave to Seraiah. The "quiet prince," as he is called, read them aloud in Babylon, then threw the scroll in the Euphrates River. It was a sign that Babylon would some day sink and never rise again. (Jer. 51:59–64.)

Seraphim

Isaiah wrote of a strange and wonderful vision in which he saw the Lord upon a throne. Above the throne there were heavenly creatures called seraphim. Each had six wings. Two wings covered its face, two covered its feet, and two were used for flying. These creatures cried "holy, holy, holy" to one another. One of the seraphim touched Isaiah's lips with a burning coal to remove his sin. (Isa. 6:1–7.)

Sergius Paulus

When Paul and Barnabas visited Cyprus on their first missionary journey, the Roman proconsul, Sergius Paulus, invited Paul to tell him about Jesus. But a sorcerer in the court of Sergius Paulus named Elymas tried to make fun of Paul's message and was suddenly struck blind. This miracle caused Sergius Paulus to believe in Jesus. (Acts 13:7–12.)

Seth

Seth was born after Cain killed his brother Abel and was driven away from his home. He was the third son of Adam and Eve. The name Seth means appointed or substituted, for Eve said, "God has substituted another child instead of Abel." He was 912 years old when he died. Mary, Jesus' mother, descended from Seth. (Luke 3:23–38.)

The Seven

The apostles had become too busy caring for the needs of the believers. They did not have enough time to tell others about Jesus. So the believers chose seven men to care for their daily needs and take care of the poor and the widows. These were called The Seven or the seven deacons. Stephen and Philip were two of the best known of the seven deacons. (Acts. 6:1–7.)

Seveneh, Syene

"From the tower of Seveneh" was another way of saying the entire length of Egypt. Seveneh was the Hebrew name for Syene, a town in Egypt at the place where Aswan stands today. It was a fortress built on the east bank of the Nile River and was at the boundary of Egypt and Ethiopia. Red granite for Egyptian monuments came from Seveneh. (Ezek. 29:10; 30:6.)

Shadow

The sun in Palestine is so fiercely hot during the day that anything which causes a shadow is welcome. Job pointed out that servants who work in the sun desire a shadow. Jonah was grateful for the cool shade of a plant as he sat outside Nineveh waiting to see what would happen. God's protecting hand is said by Isaiah to be like the shadow of a great rock in a weary land. (Job 7:2; Isa. 25:4; Jon. 4:5–6.)

255

Shadrach, Meshach, and Abednego

Hananiah, Mishael, and Azariah had been captured, brought to Babylon, and given new names: Shadrach, Meshach, and Abednego. When they refused to bow to a large statue, the king became angry and threw them into a fiery furnace. But God miraculously saved them. (Dan. 1:7; 3:1–30.)

Shallum

In the days of Hosea the prophet, Shallum plotted with others against King Zechariah and killed him. This brought an end to the reign of King Jehu's family, as God had predicted a hundred years earlier. Shallum became the sixteenth king of Israel, but he reigned for only a month. Then he was murdered by Menahem who became the next king of Israel. (II Kings 15:10–15.)

Shalmaneser

Although there were five Assyrian kings with the title Shalmaneser, only one is mentioned in the Bible. Shalmaneser V received tribute from King Hoshea of Israel until Hoshea joined with the king of Egypt. Then Shalmaneser V put Hoshea in prison and besieged Samaria for three years. Earlier, Shalmaneser III and King Ahab fought, but this is not mentioned in the Bible. (II Kings 17:3–5.)

Shamgar

Shamgar lived during the time of the judges of Israel. Because of the danger from wandering bands of Philistines, travel by road had become almost impossible. But Shamgar attacked the Philistines with an oxgoad and killed 600 of them and so gave peace and security to the country. Shamgar is praised as a hero in the Song of Deborah. (Judg. 3:31.)

Shammah

Samuel had come to Bethlehem to anoint one of Jesse's sons as the next king of Israel. But Samuel did not know which son. One by one they came forward. Shammah was third, but he was not chosen. With his two older brothers, Shammah later served in Saul's army and saw his youngest brother David kill the Philistine giant Goliath. (I Sam. 16:9; 17:13.)

Shaphan

When King Josiah decided to repair the Temple, he put Shaphan the scribe, an important official, in charge of the money. As the work was going on, Hilkiah the High Priest found the Book of the Law and Shaphan took it and read it to the king. Josiah sent Shaphan to ask Huldah the prophetess about the meaning of the book. (II Kings 22:3–20.)

Sharon, Saron

For eight years Aeneas had been paralyzed. But Peter came and healed him. When the miracle was known in his own village of Lydda and the surrounding Plain of Sharon, many turned to the Lord. The Plain of Sharon lies between Joppa and Mt. Carmel and is the most fertile plain in the land. The plain was once covered with oaks but now in the spring abounds in wild flowers. (Acts 9:34, 35.)

Shaving

Although Egyptians and Romans usually shaved their faces, the men of Israel did not except for some special reason. Job shaved his head as a sign of mourning. Foreign women who were taken captive had their heads shaved before becoming wives of Jews. Some of David's servants were insulted by having their beards shaved on one side by the Ammonites. (II Sam. 10:4.)

Shearing

There were many shepherds in Palestine in Bible times. The sheep provided meat, milk, and wool. Wool was sheared from the sheep at the beginning of summer. First the sheep were dipped in water to clean the fleece, which was then cut off. The wool was washed again to remove the grease. Wool brought much money and so shearing was celebrated by a feast. (I Sam. 25:2.)

Shear-jashub

Isaiah named his oldest son Shear-jashub, which means "a remnant shall return." Shear-jashub went to see King Ahaz with Isaiah when the prophet had a message from God. Isaiah warned Ahaz that the kingdom of Judah would be judged and its people taken away but that some day a remnant (some of them) would come home. (Isa. 7:3.)

Sheba

In the days of King Solomon, the Queen of Sheba came to visit and learn of his wisdom. Sheba was the land of the Sabeans in southwest Arabia. Much of its wealth came from the caravans which passed through, carrying gold, frankincense, spices, and jewels. The queen's trip was probably about 1,200 miles or 2,000 kilometers. (I Kings 10:1–13.)

Shebna

The prophet Isaiah scolded Shebna for his pride. Shebna had been given much, for he was not only a high government official under King Hezekiah but a wealthy man as well. But Shebna used his wealth to build an expensive rock-hewn tomb as a monument to himself. Isaiah predicted that Shebna would lose his position and be replaced by Eliakim. (Isa. 22:15–25.)

Shechem

Abraham and Jacob had both camped at Shechem. There Jacob buried the family idols which Rachel had stolen from her father Laban. After Solomon died, Rehoboam assembled the people at Shechem to make him king. After the exile, Shechem became the chief city of the Samaritans, who built a temple there. Shechem was in the hills of Ephraim, beside Mt. Gerizim. (I Kings 12:1–19.)

Sheep

The Bible gives more attention to sheep than any other animal. That's because sheep were so important. Sheep provided milk, meat, and wool, as well as skins for leather. The horns of rams were used as trumpets or anointing horns. The Tabernacle covering was made of the skin of rams. Sheep were also sacrificed for sin. That's why Jesus was called the Lamb of God. (Lev. 1:10; John 1:29.)

Shekel

Long before coins were used as money, people paid for goods by giving the seller a certain amount of gold or silver. This was decided and checked before witnesses. The shekel was a unit of weight that was used widely and was less than half an ounce or about 11 grams. Abraham paid 400 shekels of silver, about ten pounds, for the field of Machpelah. (Gen. 23:14–16.)

Shem

The Semitic people are descended from Shem, Noah's oldest son. These people include the Arabs, the Israelites, and the Canaanites. Shem was 98 at the time of the Flood. His first child, Arphaxad, was born two years later. Shem lived to be 600 years old, living longer than nine generations of his descendants, except for Abraham and Eber. (Gen. 11:10–26.)

Shepherd

"I am the Good Shepherd," Jesus told His disciples. A good shepherd cared for his sheep, leading them, helping them find food, protecting them, and taking them into the sheepfold at the end of the day. A good shepherd knew his sheep by name and if necessary, would even give his life for his sheep. Jesus did all of this and more for us. (Ps. 23; John 10:11, 14.)

Sheshbazzar

When King Cyrus of Persia permitted the Jews to go back to rebuild the Temple, he made Sheshbazzar, a Jewish prince, governor of Judah. King Cyrus returned to him the gold and silver vessels which Nebuchadnezzar had taken from the Temple. Sheshbazzar laid the Temple foundation and his work was completed by Zerubbabel, the next governor. (Ezra 1:8, 11; 5:14, 16.)

Shield

The Israelites used two kinds of shields. The large shield carried by the heavily armed footsoldier was rectangular in shape like a door, and big enough to cover the whole body. Archers carried a smaller shield. Shields were first made of wood or wicker-work overlaid with leather. Later, bronze was used, especially for shields of soldiers guarding the king. (II Chron. 25:5.)

Shiloh

For almost 400 years the Tabernacle stood at Shiloh, about 12 miles or 19 kilometers northeast of Bethel. Hannah and her husband came to Shiloh each year to worship. It was here that she prayed for a son; and, when Samuel was born, she gave him to serve the Lord in the Tabernacle with Eli. Later, the Philistines won a battle nearby and captured the Ark of God. (I Sam. 1:3.)

Shimei

Shimei, a relative of King Saul, came from his home at Bahurim to curse David as he was fleeing from his son Absalom. Shimei also threw stones and dirt at David. But David would not let his cousin Abishai kill Shimei for this. When David won the battle against Absalom and returned, Shimei came to meet him, begging for forgiveness. (II Sam. 16:5–14.)

Ship

King Solomon was the first Israelite to do much with shipping. With the help of the Phoenicians, who were skilled sailors, Solomon had a fleet of ships which sailed from Ezion-geber, near the present-day city of Elat. When Jonah tried to run away from God, he boarded a ship at Joppa. Paul was taken to Rome as a prisoner by ship. (I Kings 10:11, 22.)

Shishak

Shishak was a prince of Libya who became Pharaoh of Egypt from about 945 to 924 B.C. When Jeroboam fled from Solomon, Shishak let him stay in Egypt. Jeroboam later became king over Israel and King Rehoboam of Judah became his enemy. Shishak then invaded Judah and carried off the Temple treasures. He put up a great monument at Thebes to celebrate his victories. (I Kings 11:40; 14:25, 26.)

Shittim

The shittim tree is also known as acacia. It is a thorny tree found in the Sinai desert and around the Dead Sea. The tree has a gnarled trunk and twisted branches. The wood of the shittim tree was used for the Tabernacle and its furniture. The wood is hard with a fine grain. As it ages, it changes from a yellow-brown color until it becomes almost black. (Exod. 27:1.)

Shovel

Shovels of copper or bronze were used to clear away ashes from the altar after burnt offerings were made. Hiram made the shovels for Solomon's Temple, but they were captured by Babylon in 586 B.C. A wooden shovel was also used for winnowing. The threshed grain was thrown into the air so the wind would blow away the chaff. This may have been different from the winnowing fork or fan. (Isa. 30:24.)

Showbread

Moses was told by God to put showbread on a special table inside the Tabernacle opposite the candlestick. The showbread consisted of 12 baked loaves made of fine flour and set out in two rows each of six loaves. Every Sabbath day the priest placed fresh bread on the table. Aaron and his sons were allowed to eat the old bread. (Exod. 25:30.)

Shunammite

Whenever Elisha the prophet visited Shunem, a generous lady who lived there invited him and his servant to eat with her and her husband. One time she and her husband made a room for Elisha so he could stay there whenever he was in town. When her son died, Elisha raised him to life. She was called a Shunammite because she lived at Shunem. (II Kings 4:8–37.)

Shushan

The great Persian kings, including Esther's husband Ahasuerus, made their winter home at Shushan. Darius began a beautiful palace there and the kings that followed him enlarged it. It was famous for its cedar wood, silver, gold, ivory, and colored glazed brick. The city received its name from the fields of lilies that grew nearby. Nehemiah and Esther both lived at Shushan. (Esther 1:2; 4:8; Neh. 1:1.)

Sickle

At harvest time the farmer cut the wheat or barley with a sickle, a curved blade with a short handle. With one hand, a reaper held a sheaf of grain while he cut it with the other hand. The earliest sickles, before Abraham's time, were made of wood with the cutting edge made of flint. Later they were made of iron or bronze. The sickle also was a symbol of God's judgment. (Deut. 16:9; Mark 4:29.)

Siege

Any city which would not surrender to an invading army was at once surrounded. This method of making a city surrender is called a siege. Water and food supplies from outside were cut off. Attempts were made to burn down the city gates, and to dig under the city walls. The attackers used battering rams to try to break holes in the walls so that their soldiers could pour through. (II Chron. 32:9.)

Sieve

"I will sift Israel among the nations, as grain is sifted in a sieve," the Lord told His people. The sieve was used in harvesting. After the grain was winnowed, or separated from the chaff, it was sifted through a sieve. The sieve was a wood frame with string, rushes, hair, or leather thongs woven across it. Grain fell through it, while chaff and stones remained behind. (Amos 9:9.)

Sign

People were often not sure about God's message for them, and so they asked for a sign, something they could see. Moses was afraid the Egyptians would not listen to him and God gave him two signs to show them. One sign was that his rod turned to a snake when he threw it down. Miracles were often used as signs to show that God was involved. (Luke 11:29, 30.)

Sihon

It was necessary for the Israelites to pass through the land of King Sihon and the Ammonites on their way to the Promised Land. But Sihon refused to let them go through his land. He attacked the Israelites and was killed. The land was captured and given to the tribes of Reuben and Gad. This victory is mentioned often in the Old Testament. (Num. 21:21–29.)

Silas

Paul and Barnabas had a quarrel about John Mark. The young man had deserted them on their first missionary journey. Paul did not want to take him on another trip. Barnabas did. So Paul took Silas with him on his next trip and Barnabas took Mark. Like Paul, Silas was a Roman citizen. Both he and Paul were beaten by the officials at Philippi. (Acts 16:19–40.)

Siloam

Siloam was famous for its pool which supplied Jerusalem with much of the city's water. On the Ophel ridge above the pool was a tower. One day the tower collapsed and 18 people were killed. Jesus said that the victims did not die because they were more wicked than other people. But unless those that listened to Him repented, they would "likewise perish." (Luke 13:4; John 9:7.)

Silver

Silver was used for many things in Bible times. Joseph hid his silver cup in Benjamin's grain sack. Abraham bought the field of Machpelah with silver. Demetrius was a silversmith who made silver images of the goddess Diana. In earliest Bible times, silver was used as money by weighing it. Later there were silver coins. Jesus was betrayed for 30 silver coins. (Matt. 26:15.)

Simeon

When Mary and Joseph brought the infant Jesus to the Temple to present Him to the Lord, old Simeon recognized Him as the Messiah, God's Son. Simeon gave a hymn of praise which some know as the Nunc Dimittis. He told Mary what the coming of Jesus would mean. Another Simeon in the Bible was one of Jacob's 12 sons, who became head of one of the 12 tribes of Israel. (Exod. 1:1–4; Luke 2:25–35.)

Simon Magus

The miracles which Philip did through the power of the Holy Spirit impressed Simon Magus because he was a magician. Simon had been a sorcerer at Samaria and had great power and influence over the people. Simon claimed to become a believer, was baptized, and followed Philip. But later he tried to buy the gift of the Holy Spirit and Peter condemned him. (Acts 8:9–24.)

Sin, Sinner

A sinner is not merely a person who does something wrong. By doing wrong, he separates himself from God, for a holy God cannot live with sin. Sins are wrongs and a sinner is a wrong-doer. Jesus died to pay the penalty for sin and thus to bring us back to God, but we must accept that payment by accepting Him into our lives. (Rom. 5:12–21; I Pet. 2:24; I John 3:4.)

Sinai

The Wilderness of Sinai is a desolate area on the Sinai peninsula. Mt. Sinai is a tall mountain in this wilderness. By this mountain God spoke to Moses from a burning bush. Later Moses led the people of Israel to this mountain, where God gave him the law. Mt. Sinai is sometimes called Horeb. Elijah came here when he ran away from Jezebel. (Exod. 19:20; I Kings 19:8.)

265

Slave

"We were Pharaoh's bondmen in Egypt." Moses often reminded his people that they had been slaves, but that God had set them free. A slave was not set free very often. He was owned by his master and could be bought and sold like property. Many people were made slaves when captured in war. Paul sent Onesimus, a slave, back to his master, Philemon, with a letter asking Philemon's forgiveness. (Deut. 6:21.)

Sleep

The way a person slept in Bible times depended on his wealth. A poor person used a mat on the ground, wrapped in the cloak he wore during the day. A person who could afford more slept on a mattress stuffed with wool. The very wealthy person often had an ornate bed. Kings and queens sometimes had beds made of ivory, gold, or silver. (Esther 1:6; Amos 6:4.)

Sling

The sling which a shepherd used was much different from the slingshots we know today. The sling was a piece of leather which held a stone. On each side a leather "string" was tied. The slinger held the two ends of the string and whirled the sling around and around. Then he released one end of the string which let the stone go flying. David killed Goliath with a sling. (I Sam. 17.)

Smith

There were many needs for metal objects in Bible times. Soldiers needed swords, spears, and knives. Farmers used plows, tips for ox goads, forks, and axels. Housewives enjoyed metal pots and pans when they could afford them. The smith was a metal craftsman who made these things. Tubal-cain was the first smith mentioned in the Bible. (Gen. 4:22; Isa. 2:4.)

Smyrna

One of the seven letters in Revelation was written to Smyrna, a Roman city on the coast of Asia Minor, which is now Turkey. Smyrna became known for a circle of beautiful public buildings on Mt. Pagos which looked like a crown. "Be faithful and I will give you a crown of life," the Lord promised His church there. He was telling them of a much greater crown than their beautiful buildings. (Rev. 2:8–11.)

Snow

Snow rarely falls in Palestine south of Hebron and is never found along the seacoast or in the Jordan valley. But Mt. Hermon and Mt. Lebanon ("mountain of snow") are often capped with frozen snow. God promises through the prophet Isaiah that though our sins are like scarlet, they shall be as white as snow if we love and obey Him. (Isa. 1:18.)

Sodom and Gomorrah

Sodom and Gomorrah have become associated with God's judgment. When Abraham gave Lot his choice of land, Lot chose the land near Sodom. He moved into the city and became one of its prominent men. But Lot was rescued by some angels just before God destroyed Sodom and Gomorrah with fire and brimstone because they had become so wicked. (Gen. 19:1–28.)

Soldier

"Put on the whole armor of God," Paul wrote to the believers at Ephesus. He was in Rome, guarded by Roman soldiers. He probably watched his guard as he wrote of the shield of faith, the breastplate of righteousness, the helmet of salvation, and the sword of the Spirit. Through Paul, God was telling believers that they should stand firm against evil as good soldiers for Him. (Eph. 6:11–18.)

Solomon

After King David died, his son Solomon became king of Israel. Of all the kings mentioned in the Bible, he was the wisest and richest. Solomon built the great Temple in Jerusalem and set up a fleet of ships to trade with other nations. But he foolishly married many foreign women and let them bring their pagan gods into the land for others to worship. (I Kings 4:34.)

Solomon's Porch

A magnificent porch, surrounding the court of the Gentiles in the Temple, was known as Solomon's Porch. The porch was a walkway covered by a roof which was supported by great columns. It was a favorite meeting place for the early Christians. Here a crowd gathered to see a lame man whom Peter and John had healed. (Acts 3:11.)

Song of Solomon

"The song of songs, which is Solomon's," the book begins. It is an Old Testament book of beautiful poetry, telling of the love between a man and woman. It is also a picture of the love between the Lord and His people, a love like that between husband and wife but much greater. It was written by Solomon, King of Israel. (The Book of Song of Solomon.)

Sower

"A sower went forth to sow," Jesus said in a parable. It was a familiar scene in the land, for that was the way men planted their wheat and barley. From October until February, the sower scattered the seed by hand, taking it from a bag which he carried. Jesus compared the sower to a person who shared the Word of God with others. (Matt. 13:3–8, 18–23.)

Sparrow

Sparrows were not worth much in the market. If a buyer took four, he could have a fifth free. But even though these small birds had little value, Jesus said that God knew about each one. He was telling His disciples that they were worth much more than sparrows. The God who cared for the sparrows would do much more for them. (Matt. 10:29–31.)

Spices

Spices were highly valued in Bible lands. Cummin, cinnamon, dill, and mint were used for flavoring food and wine. Cosmetics and ointments were made from aloes, spikenard, saffron, and cassia. Spices were also put in graveclothes when bodies were prepared for burial, like the mixture of myrrh and aloes which Nicodemus brought for Jesus' burial. (John 19:39, 40.)

Spikenard

Jesus had been invited to dinner at the house of Simon the leper in Bethany. While He was eating, Mary poured a pound of spikenard upon Him. It was an act of love, for she could have sold the ointment for almost a year's wages. Spikenard was a fragrant oil from a plant in northern India. It was shipped in sealed alabaster jars which were opened only for special occasions. (John 12:2–8.)

Spinning

Wool, flax, and goats' hair had to be spun into thread before being used by a weaver. Spinning was done with a distaff and spindle. Wool was hooked onto a distaff, a small wooden rod held under the arm. Wisps of wool were drawn and attached to the spindle, which was then twirled. Clever spinners could spin while walking about. (Exod. 35:25.)

Spoils

After capturing a city, the victors took away as spoils anything they wanted. The spoils included gold, silver, clothing, animals, and goods of every kind. It even included men, women, and children who were kept or sold as slaves. When the Israelites invaded Canaan, they were commanded not to take captives. Goods captured were shared between the army and the people. (II Chron. 15:11.)

Staff

A big heavy stick was called a rod or staff when used for certain purposes. A shepherd protected his sheep with his staff, fighting off wild animals. A rod or staff was used by parents to punish their children or servants. The rod or staff came to be known as a symbol of authority and so the scepter became the king's staff. (Num. 22:27; I Sam. 17:40; Ps. 23:4.)

Stable

There had not been many horses in Palestine until Solomon became king because God warned against them. But Solomon had stables at Megiddo, Hazor, and Gezer where he kept 4,000 chariot horses and 12,000 riding horses. Some remains of Solomon's ancient stables have been found. Each was a long covered hall with stalls on both sides. (Deut. 17:16; I Kings 4:26.)

Star

"He telleth the number of the stars; he calleth them all by their names." The psalmist reminded his readers that the One who made the stars knows each one. Abraham could not count the stars but God could. The most famous star in the Bible guided the Wise Men to Jesus in Bethlehem. It was a special star which God provided for that purpose. (Ps. 147:4; Matt. 2:1–10.)

Stephanas

Stephanas lived at Corinth. He was one of the first Christians in Greece and was baptized by Paul. Paul speaks highly of Stephanas and his family because of their devoted service to the Lord. Stephanas visited Paul at Ephesus and gave him a letter from the Corinthian Christians. The First Epistle to the Corinthians is Paul's answer. (I Cor. 1:16; 16:15, 17.)

Stephen

Seven men were chosen to help care for the needs of the early Christians. Stephen, one of the seven, was "a man full of faith and the Holy Spirit." But some jealous men lied about Stephen and brought him to court. Stephen bravely told the court about the Lord Jesus and was then dragged outside the city and stoned to death. Thus Stephen became the first Christian martyr. (Acts 6—7.)

Steward

The households of wealthy men had many servants. A steward was in charge of the household and servants, taking care of things for his master. Eleazar of Damascus was Abraham's steward. When Joseph was sold as a slave, he became Potiphar's steward. Christians are God's stewards in this world because He expects us to make good use of time, talents, and treasures which all belong to Him. (Titus 1:7.)

Stocks

Prisoners were sometimes punished by putting them in stocks. These were large blocks of wood with holes in which the hands or feet were fastened. The prophet Hanani was put in stocks for rebuking King Asa of Judah. Jeremiah was punished in stocks also for preaching God's message. So were Paul and Silas when they visited Philippi. (Jer. 20:2; Acts 16:24.)

Stone

Palestine was a land of stones and so the people found many uses for them. Stones were used as landmarks to show the boundaries of fields. Large stones closed the entrances of caves. Stones covered wells and formed the walls of buildings. Stones were made into altars, memorials, and even weapons. David killed Goliath with a stone. (Josh. 15:6.)

Storehouse

Taxes were often paid to the king in goods such as oil, grain, and wine because money was not used as much as it is today. The king had to have storehouses where he collected these goods and stored them for his use. When the people of Israel were slaves in Egypt, they built great storehouses for Pharaoh at Pithom and Raamses. (Exod. 1:11; Deut. 28:8.)

Stork

The white stork migrates in large numbers each spring across Palestine, going from its winter home in Africa and Arabia to its summer home in Europe. The black stork comes through alone or in small groups. Storks feed in muddy places, eating frogs, mice, fish, and insects. They are large birds, standing about three feet or almost a meter tall. (Ps. 104:17; Jer. 8:7.)

Storm

Thunderstorms are most frequent in Palestine in November and December and occur most commonly in the Jordan valley. Hailstorms, which take place mostly between December and March, often do great damage to the growing crops. Windstorms from the hills can suddenly sweep down upon the Sea of Galilee, whipping up great waves and catching fishermen by surprise. (Ps. 107:25.)

Stranger

In the Bible a stranger is another name for a foreigner or someone of another race. The people of Israel were told by God's law that they must look after strangers who live in their country. Some of the harvest must be left for strangers to collect. In return, strangers in Israel must keep the Sabbath and not worship idols. Ruth was a stranger in Israel when she gleaned in the fields of Boaz. (Exod. 23:9.)

Straw

When the people of Israel made bricks for Pharaoh, they used chopped straw mixed with clay. But Pharaoh's taskmasters punished the Israelites by making them find their own straw. Straw, the stems of wheat or barley after the grain has been removed, is mentioned with the other food for horses, cattle, and camels. Worthless straw and chaff was often burned. (Exod. 5:7; Judg. 19:19.)

Street

The streets of Bible-time cities were narrow and crooked with room only for an ox cart or chariot. People threw their garbage into the streets and so they were usually very dirty, cleaned only by scavenger dogs. Streets were filled with ruts and mud and had houses built next to them. Near the gates there were open spaces where markets and courts were held. (Isa. 10:6; Nah. 2:4.)

Succoth

After 20 years, Jacob and his twin brother Esau renewed their friendship. Then Esau went home to Seir while Jacob went on to Succoth, east of the Jordan River. There Jacob built a house and made booths for his animals, giving Succoth its name, meaning "booths" or "huts." Many years later, Gideon punished the people of Succoth for refusing to help him as he fought the Midianites. (Gen. 33:17; Josh. 13:27.)

Sun

Before the Israelites arrived in Palestine, some Canaanites worshiped the sun. But it was not until many years later that the people of Israel practiced sun-worship. Manasseh erected altars in the Temple to make offerings to the sun. Just before Jerusalem was captured and destroyed, Ezekiel the prophet saw men in the Temple facing east to worship the rising sun. (Ezek. 8:16.)

Surety

Jacob's sons had to return to Egypt to buy grain. But they could not buy grain without Benjamin and Jacob refused to let him go. "I will be surety for him," Judah promised. That meant that Judah would be responsible for anything that happened. Surety also meant that a person would be responsible for another's debts. But the Bible warns that this could lead to trouble. (Gen. 43:9; Prov. 11:15.)

Swaddling Clothes

When Jesus was born, Mary "wrapped him in swaddling clothes." At that time, a baby was placed on a square piece of cloth with one corner below its feet. This corner was joined with the corner on each side. The baby's entire body was covered except for its face. Then the baby was wrapped in long bands of cloth called swaddling bands. (Job 38:9; Luke 2:7, 12.)

Swallow

The swallow knows God's ways, Jeremiah told his people, so why can't God's people know them? Each year the swallow, a small, swift bird, knows when to return to the land. But God's people did not know His judgment. The psalmist told of the swallow nesting in the Temple, God's house. This bird often nests in buildings. (Ps. 84:3; Jer. 8:7.)

Swine

The Jewish people thought the pig or swine was a very low animal. The law forbid them to eat the meat of swine. Foolishness was compared to "casting pearls before swine," or to put "a gold ring in a swine's nose." When Jesus cast out some demons, He let them go into a herd of swine. And when the Prodigal Son found no other work, he fed a herd of swine. (Prov. 11:22; Matt. 7:6.)

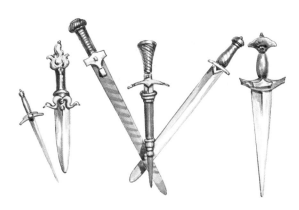

Sword

Many different kinds of swords have been found in Bible lands, some long and some short. Blades were made of iron, bronze, copper, or steel, and could be single or double-edged. A Philistine sword factory, with its smeltery and furnace, has been found at Gerar. For the Christian, the sword of the Spirit in fighting evil is the Word of God. (I Sam. 21:9; Eph. 6:17.)

Sycamore, Sycomore

The prophet Amos had two jobs in addition to his work as a prophet. He was a shepherd and a gardener who took care of sycamore fig trees. The figs had to be cut or pricked so they would ripen well. Zacchaeus climbed a sycamore fig tree one day to see Jesus. The tree is an evergreen. It produces figs which can be eaten, but they are not very good. (Amos 7:14; Luke 19:4.)

Sychar

While Jesus was resting by Jacob's well, not far from Sychar, a Samaritan woman came to get water. Jesus talked with her and told her that He was the Water of Life. As He talked, she began to realize that He was the Messiah, God's Son. Quickly the woman brought her neighbors from Sychar and many believed. Sychar was a town in Samaria near Shechem and Mt. Gerizim. (John 4:5.)

Synagogue

From the time of King Solomon until the time of the exile, the Israelites worshiped at the Temple. But when they were taken away to Babylon, they began to meet together to pray and read the Scriptures. When they returned, the Israelites built synagogues, or meeting houses, where they could worship and teach the Scriptures. Jesus and Paul went often to the synagogues. (Luke 4:16.)

Syracuse

While Paul was on his way to Rome as a prisoner, his ship stopped for three days at Syracuse. This was a prosperous port on the east coast of Sicily. Syracuse had two good harbors which brought it much wealth from shipping. One Roman writer said that Syracuse was the most beautiful of all cities. At the time of Paul, it was under the control of Rome. (Acts 28:12.)

Syria

The boundaries of Syria have changed much through the years. In the days when Paul sailed from Antioch in Syria on his missionary journeys, it included the territory north of Galilee and east from the Mediterranean Sea. Damascus, the capital, is one of the oldest cities in the world. Paul became a Christian in Syria near Damascus. (Acts 9:1–25.)

Syrophoenicia

In the days of Jesus, Phoenicia was part of the Roman province of Syria and so was called Syrophoenicia. When Jesus was preaching there, near Tyre and Sidon, a woman from Syrophoenicia begged Him to heal her daughter. She would not take no for an answer and Jesus praised her great faith. Returning home, she found her daughter well. (Mark 7:26.)

T

Tabernacle

While the people of Israel camped by Mt. Sinai, the Lord gave Moses the exact plans for the Tabernacle, a large tent where the people would worship. During the years in the wilderness, the Israelites carried the Tabernacle from place to place. When they entered the Promised Land, they set it up at Shiloh where it remained for about 400 years. (I Sam. 1:3, 9.)

Talent

The talent was a large amount of gold, silver, lead, bronze, or iron. The weight was not the same from country to country or even from metal to metal. The Hebrews thought of a talent as the amount a man could carry, about 75 pounds or 34 kilograms. Naaman loaded two talents of silver on two of his servants to carry to Elisha. (II Kings 5:23.)

Tanner

The tanner made leather from the skins of sheep and goats. He did this by beating the hide in water to remove the dirt, then soaking it in a solution made from various plants, and stretching the wet hide to dry. Tanning caused a bad smell and so tanners were not welcome in town. Peter once stayed at the home of a tanner named Simon near Joppa. (Acts 9:43; 10:6, 32.)

Tares

Bible-time people spoke of their weeds as tares. One type of tare, the bearded darnel, caused much trouble because it looked like the wheat until harvest time. In a parable, Jesus told how a man's enemy sowed tares in the man's wheat field. The man let the tares grow with the wheat until harvest and then gathered them and burned them. (Matt. 13:24–30, 36–40.)

Tarsus

Paul mentioned with pride that he was from Tarsus, the capital city of Cilicia. Today this area is in southeastern Turkey. Tarsus was an important city of about half a million people. It was a university city, with an emphasis on higher learning. Tarsus was also on an important trade route between the eastern and western countries. (Acts 21:39; 22:3.)

Tax Collector

Most people hated tax collectors, or publicans, for they were Jews who worked for the Romans. People hated taxes but they hated their Roman captors even more. The Romans gave tax collectors a certain amount of the money they collected, but many collected some more for themselves. Matthew and Zacchaeus were both tax collectors before they followed Christ. (Matt. 17:25; 22:17.)

Tekoa

The area around Tekoa was a harsh, stony region with few trees. Amos the prophet was born there. In addition to his work as a prophet, he took care of sheep and some sycamore fig trees. Tekoa was high in the hills of Judah. Rehoboam fortified the town and in the days of Jeremiah it was a station for trumpet signals to warn of approaching danger. (Amos 1:1; 7:14.)

Temple

Three temples were built on Mt. Moriah in Jerusalem. Solomon built the first, which was destroyed about 400 years later by Nebuchadnezzar. After the Jews returned from the exile, Zerubbabel built the second. The third was an enlargement of this second Temple and was begun by Herod the Great in 20 B.C. It was destroyed by the Romans in 70 A.D. (II Chron. 3:1.)

Temptation

It is not a sin to be tempted, for Jesus was tempted. But it is a sin to yield to the temptation to do wrong. Jesus did not do that. Satan tested Jesus to get Him to do wrong but Jesus resisted Satan with the Word of God. The Bible speaks of temptations, or testings, for a good purpose too. Abraham's faith was tested with God asked him to sacrifice Isaac. (Matt. 4:1–11.)

The Ten Commandments

God wrote the Ten Commandments with His own hand on Mt. Sinai. Then He gave them to Moses who passed them on to the people of Israel. These tablets were placed inside the Ark of the Covenant in the Holy of Holies of the Tabernacle. The Ten Commandments are the heart of God's covenant or agreement with His people. (Ex. 20; 31:18.)

Tent

In the days of the patriarchs, many Bible-time people lived in tents because they were shepherds, moving about from place to place. As their animals ate the grass in one place, they had to move on. During the 40 years the people of Israel spent in the wilderness, they had to live in tents because they were often on the move. The apostle Paul was a tentmaker. (Gen. 9:27.)

Teraphim

Laban was angry because someone had stolen his household gods, or teraphim. These were small statues. While he searched through Jacob's baggage, his daughter Rachel sat quietly on her camel, for the teraphim were hidden under her. Laban wanted the teraphim back because whoever had them also had the right to inherit his property. (Gen. 31:34.)

Tertullus

Because of the uproar in Jerusalem, Paul was arrested and taken to Caesarea. There he was put on trial before the Roman governor Felix. But the Jewish leaders hired Tertullus, a lawyer, to speak against Paul. In his speech, Tertullus praised Felix with glowing words and then skillfully tried to suggest that Paul had been responsible for the trouble in Jerusalem. (Acts 24:1.)

Tetrarch

The title tetrarch was originally given to a ruler of the fourth part of a kingdom. Philip of Macedon divided Thessaly into four tetrarchies. Later the Romans adopted the title and gave it to a ruler of any small country. When Herod the Great died in 4 B.C., the Roman emperor Augustus divided Herod's territory into tetrarchies among his three sons. (Luke 3:1.)

Thaddaeus

Thaddaeus was only one of his names. He was called "Lebbaeus, whose surname was Thaddaeus." But he was also called "Judas the brother (or son) of James." Not much is known of this man except that he followed Jesus and became known as one of the twelve apostles. He once asked Jesus how He would show Himself to the Apostles and not to the world. (Matt. 10:3; Mark 3:18; Acts 1:13.)

Thank Offering

One way to show gratitude to God was through the thank offering. It was the same as the peace offering or sacrifice. The man making this offering led an animal to the altar, laid his hand on its head, and killed it. Part of the animal was given to the priest, part was burned on the altar, and the rest was used in a great feast. (Lev. 3:1–5.)

Thebez

When Abimelech attacked Thebez, a city on Mt. Ephraim, many of the people took refuge in a strong tower. He tried to set fire to the door of the tower and a woman dropped a heavy millstone down upon him from the roof. Abimelech ordered his armor-bearer to kill him with the sword so that men might not say that a woman had killed him. (Judg. 9:50–57.)

Theophilus

"It seemed good to write to you, most excellent Theophilus," Luke wrote as he opened his Gospel. He also addressed the Acts of the Apostles to Theophilus. Luke's friend must have been a high Roman official, undoubtedly one who had become a Christian. His name means "friend of God," but nothing else is known about him. (Luke 1:3; Acts 1:1.)

Thessalonica, Thessalonians

Thessalonica is one of the chief cities of Macedonia. Paul visited Thessalonica on his second missionary journey. Some Jews living there became Christians as a result of Paul's preaching, but others grew jealous and Paul had to leave. Paul sent two Epistles to the Thessalonian Christians. (The Epistles of Paul to the Thessalonians.)

Thief

Thieves and cattle rustlers were in trouble when caught. If the thief still had the animal he had stolen, he had to repay the owner double. If he had sold the animal, he had to repay four or five times as much—five times for an ox, four times for a sheep. If he could not pay, the thief could be sold as a slave. Two thieves were crucified with Jesus. (Exod. 22:1–4.)

Thomas

Thomas, one of the 12 apostles, could not believe that the Lord had risen from the dead. He had not been with the other apostles in the Upper Room when Jesus had appeared to them. He would not believe, he said, unless he saw Jesus and touched His wounds. A week later Jesus appeared again in the Upper Room. Thomas saw Him and touched His wounds. Then he believed. (John 20:26–29.)

Thorns

If thorns were allowed to grow, they quickly choked the crops, trees, and vineyards. But thorns did have some good uses. Thorn bushes were grown or piled up as hedges, making a good fence to keep out wild animals. Thorn bushes were used also as fuel, especially for shepherds who moved from place to place. Jesus was crowned with thorns by the Roman soldiers. (Gen. 3:17, 18.)

Threshing Floor

Grain was not threshed with machines, as it is today. The harvester cut the grain with sickles and brought it to the threshing floor, a flat circle of rock or hard ground. After the grain was separated from the stalks, it was winnowed, or thrown up into the air so the wind would blow away the chaff. Ruth visited Boaz one night at his threshing floor. (Ruth 3:1–7.)

Threshold

People often considered the threshold of a door to be sacred. The priests of Dagon avoided stepping on the threshold of his temple when they found that their idol had fallen upon it. The threshold of the Temple in Jerusalem shook when Isaiah saw a vision of the Lord. The threshold was often a plank or stone on the ground across the doorway. The threshold of the Temple was gold. (I Sam. 5:4, 5; Isa. 6:4.)

Tiberias

Herod Antipas founded Tiberias just a few years before Jesus was born and named it after the Roman emperor Tiberius. The city was on the west bank of the Sea of Galilee, also called the Lake of Tiberias. Because of the warm springs it became popular, but good Jews avoided it because it was a Gentile city. Tiberias is still a thriving city today. (John 6:1, 23.)

Throne

People in high offices sat on ornate chairs called thrones. These included such people as kings, queens, judges, governors, or emperors. Solomon had an unusually beautiful throne made of ivory overlaid with gold. There were six steps leading up to the throne, each guarded by a pair of great carved lions. In Isaiah's vision, he saw God sitting on a throne. (I Kings 10:18–20; Isa. 6:1.)

Tiberius

The Caesar mentioned in the Gospels was the second Roman emperor, Tiberius Caesar. He was a successful military leader for many years. At the age of 56, he succeeded Augustus and ruled Rome from 14 to 37 A.D. Tiberius was a stern and rather gloomy man and so was not very popular. But he had a great fear of treason and tried a number of people whom he suspected. (Luke 3:1.)

Tiglath-pileser

When Israel and Syria joined forces to fight Judah, King Ahaz of Judah asked Assyria for help. Tiglath-pileser, king of Assyria, sent his army against Israel and Syria and defeated them. Ahaz rewarded Tiglath-pileser, who was also called Pul, by giving him silver and gold from the Temple. Tiglath-pileser was king from 745 to 727 B.C. (II Kings 16:5–8.)

Tigris

Sometimes the Tigris River was called the Hiddekel. It was one of four rivers which watered the Garden of Eden. The Tigris and the Euphrates were the two great rivers which formed the boundaries of Assyria and Babylonia. The city of Nineveh stood on the banks of the Tigris, which were lined with palms, pomegranates, and jungles of reeds. (Gen. 2:14.)

Timbrel

The people of Israel were safely through the Red Sea. It was a time to dance and sing! So Miriam and her friends took timbrels in their hands and danced with joy. The timbrel was like a small drum with discs on the side. The player could beat it, shake it, or rattle it. This instrument was probably the same as the tambourine. (Exod. 15:20; Judg. 11:34.)

Timothy

Timothy's father was Greek, but his mother Eunice was Jewish and taught him the Word of God. Timothy's home was at Lystra and it was there that Paul helped him come to know Christ. Then Timothy became one of Paul's faithful helpers. In his two letters to Timothy, Paul gives suggestions about the care of the believers. (The Epistles of Paul to Timothy.)

Tithe

"Bring ye all the tithes into the storehouse," the prophet Malachi wrote. In Bible times, the people of Israel were required to give a tenth of their harvests or flocks to the Lord. Since the Levites served the Lord in the Tabernacle and Temple, this tithe was given for their support. They had no other income, because they had received no inheritance in the Promised Land. (Lev. 27:30–33.)

Titus

When trouble broke out among the Christians at Corinth, Paul sent Titus, a trusted companion, to solve the problem. Titus was also given the job of collecting money for the poor Christians in Jerusalem. Titus was a Gentile, the son of Greek parents. When Paul wrote to him, he told about the way believers should conduct themselves. (The Epistle of Paul to Titus.)

Torch

On the night when Judas betrayed Jesus, he came with a band of men who carried lanterns and torches to Gethsemane. A Bible-time person used a torch when he needed more light than an oil lamp would give. The torch was often made from pieces of wood held together and coated with oil or pitch. During the Feast of Tabernacles, Jerusalem was lit by blazing torches on tall pillars. (John 18:3.)

Tower of Babel

Babel was another name for Babylon. People who had been nomads in the east arrived and decided to settle down. They proudly began to build a city and also a great tower, which they boasted would be as high as heaven. God scattered the builders by making them speak other languages so that they could not understand one another. (Gen. 11:1–9.)

Transfiguration

High in a mountain, Jesus was suddenly changed before His three closest disciples, Peter, James, and John. This change is called the transfiguration of Jesus. His clothes became as white as light and His face shone as the sun. "This is My Son," God's voice called out. "Listen to Him!" God Himself was saying that Jesus was His Son and that people should pay attention to Him. (Matt. 17:1–8.)

Treasury

In the treasury of the Temple, which was also the Court of the Women, there were 13 chests where worshipers put their offerings. They were shaped like trumpets and so they were called a Hebrew word which meant trumpets. One day Jesus watched a poor widow put two tiny coins into a chest. From that, Jesus taught His disciples that true giving is not how much you share, but how much you keep. (Luke 21:1–4.)

Tribute

A weaker country often paid tribute to its strongest neighbor or to a country that conquered it in war. This was usually paid in money, treasure, goods, or slaves. It kept the stronger country from destroying the land. Tribute was often paid each year. If it did not arrive on time, it was a sign of rebellion and an army was sent to punish the rebels. (I Kings 9:21.)

Troas

One night, in Troas, Paul had a vision of a Macedonian begging for help. He sailed for Macedonia, where he took the Gospel to Europe for the first time. Troas was a port in northwest Asia. Both the city and the region around it were called Troas. Once while Paul was preaching at Troas, a young man named Eutychus went to sleep and fell from a third story window. (Acts 16:9–12.)

Trumpet

"When the people heard the sound of the trumpet, and they shouted with a great shout, the wall fell down flat." So the great city of Jericho fell to Israel. The long ram's horn trumpet was also used to summon people to religious occasions and to war. Moses made two silver trumpets to signal the time to break camp in the wilderness. (Num. 10:2–10; Josh. 6:20.)

Tychichus

Paul was fortunate to have many close friends who helped him share the Gospel on his missionary journeys. Tychichus was one of those friends. He was probably from Ephesus. While Paul was imprisoned in Rome, Tychichus was with him and carried Paul's letter to the Ephesian believers. He is remembered as a faithful helper even in time of trouble. (Eph. 6:21; Col. 4:7.)

Tyrannus

In the mornings, Tyrannus taught in his own school at Ephesus. But when school let out, probably about 11 A.M., he let Paul use his school as a meeting place. When Paul first went to Ephesus, he spoke in the synagogue for three months. But the Jews said evil things about him and he went to the school of Tyrannus. He stayed there for two years. (Acts 19:8, 9, 10.)

Tyre

Both David and Solomon worked closely with King Hiram of Tyre. The king provided the cedars for Solomon's Temple and helped Solomon build his merchant fleet. Tyre was a Phoenician seaport about 35 miles or 56 kilometers north of Mt. Carmel. When Hiram died, Ethbaal became king. His wicked daughter Jezebel married King Ahab and encouraged the people to worship Baal. (I Kings 5:10, 11; 16:31.)

U

Unclean Animals

God commanded that certain animals could not be used for food or sacrifice. These included animals which had a divided hoof or chewed the cud. Pigs, camels, the coney, eagles, mice, owls, and vultures were all considered unclean. In addition, any animal which was strangled, died by itself, or was killed by another animal was considered to be unclean. (Lev. 11:1–8.)

Unleavened Bread

When the people of Israel were freed from their slavery in Egypt, they left so fast that they had no time to bake leavened bread. After that time, the Israelites were forbidden at Passover time to eat bread made with leaven. This was to remind them of their hurried freedom from Egypt. Leaven was like yeast and helped the bread rise. Unleavened bread was flat and thick. (Exod. 12:39.)

Upper Room

The night before He was crucified, Jesus ate supper with His disciples in a large upstairs room. It was the last Passover they would eat together. This upper room may have been a guest room in the home of John Mark's mother in Jerusalem. After Jesus rose into heaven, the disciples met in this room to pray. While there, the Holy Spirit came upon them in tongues of fire. (Matt. 26:17–19; Acts 1:13; 2:2–4.)

Ur

When Abraham was a boy he lived at Ur. It was a great city, with temples, palaces, and schools. Many beautiful golden objects have been found buried in the royal cemetery there. Abraham and his family migrated from Ur to Haran. There God told Abraham to leave his family for Canaan and He would make a great nation of his descendants. (Gen. 11:27—12:2.)

Uriah

David wanted Uriah's beautiful wife Bathsheba for himself. But he could not marry her as long as Uriah was alive. So David gave orders for Uriah to be sent on a dangerous attack during the siege of Rabbath-ammon. As expected, Uriah was killed in the fighting and David married Bathsheba. Bathsheba later became the mother of King Solomon. (II Sam. 11.)

Urim and Thummin

Nobody knows for sure what the Urim and Thummin looked like, but the High Priest kept them in a pocket in his breastplate. The High Priest found God's will by choosing or throwing the Urim and Thummin a certain way. They were probably stones. This may have been the same as "casting lots." Urim means "lights" and Thummin means "perfections." (Exod. 28:30; Lev. 8:8.)

Uzziah

Uzziah was only 16 years old when he was chosen to be king. For 52 years, Judah enjoyed prosperous times under his rule. King Uzziah, who was also called Azariah, was proud of his good career because he had not only ruled well but had also fought successful wars. But when Uzziah tried to burn incense on God's altar, he was suddenly stricken with leprosy. (II Kings 14:21; II Chron. 26:16–23.)

V

Vashti

King Ahasuerus of Persia was proud of his beautiful queen Vashti. But when he commanded her to show off her beauty before all his guests at a great banquet, she refused. The king was so angry with Vashti's disobedience, and his advisers feared that all the women of Persia would disobey their husbands. Ahasuerus took away Vashti's right to be queen and made Esther queen instead. (Esther 1:10–19.)

Veil

Before Rebekah met her future husband Isaac, she covered her face with a veil. The veil was a piece of cloth to hide the face or to protect someone from the sun. Veils were sometimes used by shepherds, farmers, and travelers to keep the hot sun from the back of the head. Ruth's veil was large enough to hold a bushel and a half of barley. (Gen. 24:65; Ruth 3:15.)

Village

A village was usually smaller than a city, and had no wall, moat, or ramparts for protection. But villages, also called towns, were usually built around fortified cities and so the villagers could reach those cities for protection in time of danger. Bethphage, Bethany, and Bethlehem are all called villages in the New Testament. (Lev. 25:31; I Sam. 6:18; Luke 8:1.)

Vine

Melons, gourds, and cucumbers are all called vines in the Bible. But the word usually referred to a grapevine. Grapes were one of the main crops in Palestine and the climate produced excellent fruit. The spies of Israel who came into the Promised Land found a cluster of grapes so large that two men carried it on a pole between them. (Num. 13:23.)

Vinegar

The vinegar of the Bible was not the same as our vinegar today. It was a sour, over-fermented wine or palm juice. Poor people and soldiers often drank vinegar diluted with water. When Jesus was dying on the cross, the Roman soldiers offered Him vinegar mixed with gall or myrrh. This mixture would have deadened pain, but Jesus refused to drink it. (Matt. 27:34.)

Vineyard

Grapevines required a great amount of care to help them bear the best grapes. The ground in a vineyard was cultivated and weeds cut from among the vines. Vines were pruned or cut back to keep the best part bearing. A watchman stayed in a stone tower to protect the grapes as the harvest time drew near. Thorny hedges were often planted to keep out animals. (Num. 22:24; Isa. 5:4–6.)

Viper

On a cold, wet morning the ship carrying Paul to Rome was wrecked on the coast of Malta. As Paul gathered firewood, a viper wriggled from the heat and fastened on his hand. The islanders were surprised that Paul did not die because the viper was a poisonous snake. But God had cared for the apostle, for He had much for him to do. (Acts 28:3–6.)

Vision

Many visions are mentioned in the Bible. They were something like a dream but appeared while the person was awake. God often spoke to people through visions. Ezekiel and Daniel described a number of their visions. The Roman soldier Cornelius had a vision of an angel while he prayed. The angel told Cornelius to send for Peter, who came and taught him about Jesus. (Acts 10:1–6.)

Vow

When Jacob came to Bethel, he made a vow to worship God and give Him a tithe of all his goods if God would be with him and look after him. A vow was a solemn promise, usually to God. Frequently the person making the vow said he would keep his promise only if God would do something. God did not require the vow; but, when it was made, He required that it be kept. (Gen. 28:20–22.)

Wages

The law required an employer to pay his workers at the end of each day. The amount of the wage was anything the employer and worker agreed upon before the work was begun. The prophets often denounced dishonest employers for cheating their workers. In one of Jesus' parables, the denarius was considered the proper wage for a day. It is sometimes called a "penny" in some translations. (Lev. 19:13.)

Wagon

Ancient wagons or carts had two solid wooden wheels and were pulled by oxen, horses, or mules. The wagons were used for light loads, especially at harvest time. Most wagons were not strong enough for long journeys, but Joseph sent some sturdy Egyptian wagons to carry Jacob and his family to Egypt. The Tabernacle was carried in covered wagons. (Gen. 45:21–28.)

Wailing

In times of great sadness, people often wept, wailed, and beat their breasts. When someone died, mourners were often paid to wail or cry loudly. It was considered an insult to the dead to have a funeral without loud wailing. When Jesus went to Jairus' home, He put all of the professional mourners out and then raised Jairus' daughter from the dead. (Mark 5:38–40.)

Wall

The cities were enclosed with great walls to keep out invaders. Nearby villages did not have walls and so the villagers prepared to run into the cities when warned of an attack. The walls of houses were often made of sun-baked brick but sometimes they were made of stone in an area where stone was plentiful. Rahab's house was built on top of the wall of Jericho. (Josh. 2:15.)

War

Jesus spoke of wars as part of this evil world, something we must learn to expect. Wars were mostly hand to hand fighting, for there were few machines of war in ancient times. Some nations used chariots and horses, but the Israelites did not have these until the time of Solomon. Enemy armies often put a siege around a city, cutting off the food supply until people starved or fought. (I Sam. 17.)

Wash

When guests arrived at a house, the host provided them with water to wash their feet, which were hot and dusty from the road. Before taking part in a service, priests washed their hands and feet in a special basin so as to be ceremonially clean. Pilate washed his hands in public to show that he was clean from guilt. (Lev. 14:8; Matt. 27:24.)

Watchtower

As harvest time neared and grapes ripened, thieves and wild animals found the vineyards a temptation. By this time, vineyard owners or a watchman moved into a stone watchtower in the vineyard until the harvest was completed. On top of the tower was a rough shelter made of branches. This kept the hot sun from beating upon the watchman. (Isa. 1:8.)

Water

The winter months in Palestine were rainy, but the summer months were dry. It was important for people to build their towns near springs and wells so that they could have water throughout the year. Cisterns were cut into rock to hold rainwater through the dry months. Drought was a serious problem because crops would not grow without rain and famine would follow. (I Kings 17.)

Waterpot

Women and girls carried waterpots gracefully balanced on their shoulders or heads. The pots were made of clay and had one or two handles. They held the water as it was carried home from wells, cisterns, springs, or streams. The waterpots at Cana were large, holding as much as 20 gallons or 75 liters, because they were used for purification rites. (John 2:6.)

Weaving

There were no stores to buy clothing or cloth in Bible times and so every family did its own weaving at home. Everything from clothing to tents was hand made. Paul was a tentmaker. So were his friends Aquila and Priscilla. Babylonian weavers were especially skillful. That is why Achan wanted to keep the beautiful Babylonian cloak he found when the Israelites captured Jericho. (Josh. 7:21.)

Weights

In Bible times, weights were usually stones carved in shapes such as animals. But there was no system to keep them exactly the same and over the years weights probably changed in value. Small weights were often carried in a buyer's pocket so that he could check the weights used by the merchants. Micah denounced those who carried a bag of false weights. (Micah 6:11.)

Wedding

After the harvest had been gathered, Autumn was a popular time for a wedding. The autumn nights were still warm enough for merrymaking. Many relatives and friends attended the wedding and the celebrations lasted a week or more. During the feasting, the bridegroom and bride sat on thrones and were considered a king and queen by the village people. (Gen. 29:22–27; Matt. 25:1–13.)

Well

Because water was so scarce in Palestine, it was necessary to dig wells. But quarrels often broke out over the ownership and use of the wells. Isaac dug several wells near Gerar rather than quarrel with his neighbors. A well was often handed down from father to son. Jesus was sitting by Jacob's ancient well when He talked with the woman of Samaria. (Gen. 26:17–25.)

Wheat

From the earliest times, wheat has been used to make bread. The grains of wheat were often roasted over a fire and eaten whole. This was called "parched corn" in some versions of the Bible. In Palestine, wheat is sown in winter after the barley and reaped in May and June. To thank God for providing this important food for the people of Israel, wheat was used as a cereal offering in the Temple. (Lev. 23:14.)

Wheel

The earliest wheels were made of wood. But by the time of Solomon, wheels had become more highly developed. The wheels on the base of the great "sea" of Solomon's Temple had axles, spokes, rims, and hubs. Daniel had a vision in which God was seated on a throne with wheels of fire. A potter's wheel was really two stone discs used in making pottery. (I Kings 7:20–33.)

Whip

Some crimes were punished by whipping. The whip was usually made of cords attached to a handle. Roman whips had pieces of lead or bone at the end to cut the skin when someone was whipped. Jesus was scourged or punished with a Roman whip. When Jesus drove the money-changers from the Temple, He used a whip made of cords. (Matt. 27:26.)

Widow

When her husband died, a widow usually faced a very hard life, especially if she had a family of young children to bring up. Special laws tried to help widows by allowing them to glean any harvest that remained in fields and orchards and to share in village sacrifices and feasts. The first Christians made special arrangements to care for widows. (Exod. 22:22; I Tim. 5:3.)

Wilderness

There were not many plants in the wilderness, for it was a dry part of the land. Large stretches of wilderness went southward from Beersheba and into the Sinai peninsula. Occasionally an oasis such as Elim could be found. But away from an oasis there were only tough trees like acacia and tamarisk and a few scattered bushes or desert plants. (Gen. 21:14.)

Willow

Several kinds of willow trees are found near water and along streams in Palestine, especially by the river Jordan. Branches from willows were used to build the shelters put up during the Feast of Tabernacles. The Jews exiled from their homes to Babylon were so sad that they refused to sing songs and hung up their harps on the willow trees. (Ps. 137:2.)

Wind

The south wind brings scorching heat to Palestine but a wind from the north gives cool refreshing breezes. The wind blowing from the Mediterranean to the mountains and back again produces dew which gives moisture to vegetation in summer. A strong east wind drove back the waters of the Red Sea and let the Israelites cross. (Exod. 10:13.)

Window

Glass window panes had not been developed in Bible times. The window of a house was only a narrow opening, just enough to let in some air. It was often covered with a mat, curtain, or panel of wood. Most houses did not have many windows on the ground floor because it was easier to heat or cool the house without them. Windows facing a street had a lattice on them. (I Sam. 19:12.)

Wine

The use of wine in Bible times was common. Good drinking water was hard to find and grapes were plentiful. Grapes were squeezed in a large pit called a winepress. The juice was stored in earthenware jars or in animal skins sewed around the edges. Old skins were not used because wine expanded with age and would burst them. Jesus turned water into wine at Cana. (John 2:1–11.)

Winepress

When workmen brought baskets of grapes from the vineyards, they dumped them into a winepress. This was a large tank, about three feet or one meter deep, cut in solid limestone. Near the bottom, a hole allowed the juice to flow into a basin. The juice was squeezed from the grapes as workers stamped on the grapes with their bare feet. (Neh. 13:15.)

Winnowing

After heads of grain had been beaten from the stalks, they were piled on the threshing floor to wait for a wind. At the right time, the grain was tossed into the air with a winnowing fork or shovel. As the wind blew the straw and chaff away, the grain fell back to the ground. After that, the grain was sifted through a sieve. (Ruth 3:2; Isa. 30:24.)

Wisdom

"Give your servant an understanding heart," Solomon asked the Lord. God was pleased with Solomon's request and gave him great wisdom. One time two women claimed the same baby. But God gave Solomon the wisdom to know how to find out which was the true mother. The Bible speaks of wisdom as a gift from God for those who fear Him. The Word of God is the source of wisdom. (Ps. 111:10.)

Wise Men

Matthew does not tell how many Wise Men came to see Jesus, nor exactly where they began their long trip. They came from the east, possibly Mesopotamia or Persia. They had studied the stars and found the message that a great king had been born. God provided a special star for them to follow to Bethlehem. Advisers in courts of kings were also called wise men. (Dan. 2:13; Matt. 2:1–12.)

Witness

In court at least two witnesses whose evidence agreed were required to prove a charge. If the sentence was one of stoning, the witnesses had to throw the first stones. Women, children, slaves, and shepherds were not accepted as witnesses. A false witness who was found out suffered the same punishment as that which he hoped to bring upon the prisoner. (Deut. 19:18, 19.)

Withered Hand

One day in a synagogue, Jesus met a man with a withered hand. The Pharisees watched Him to see if He would heal the man because it was the Sabbath. That would be considered working on the Sabbath. Jesus told the man to stretch out his withered hand and it was healed. A withered hand was one which had shrunk from disease or lack of use. (Luke 6:6–11.)

Wolf

Jesus described a cowardly shepherd who was hired to watch sheep but ran away when a wolf came. He told how the wolf caught some sheep and scattered the others. Wolves were fierce animals and great enemies of shepherds and sheep. Isaiah speaks of a day in God's kingdom when such great peace will come that a wolf and lamb can feed together. (John 10:12.)

Woodcutter

When the Gibeonites realized that Joshua would conquer them, they tricked him into signing a peace treaty with them. Joshua did not kill the Gibeonites because of the treaty, but he forced them to be woodcutters, supplying the wood for the burnt offerings. Solomon hired expert woodcutters from Tyre to help build the Temple. (Josh. 9:27; II Chron. 2:8–10.)

Work

According to the Fourth Commandment, people are to work six days in the week. All Jewish boys were taught a trade and even rabbis were not ashamed to work with their hands to earn their living. Paul was a tentmaker and Peter a fisherman. Jesus Himself worked as a carpenter at Nazareth for many years before beginning His ministry. (Exod. 20:9, 10.)

Word

The Word of God is what God says to the world and us. Jesus is the living Word. The Bible is the written Word. Before Jesus came, God spoke through patriarchs and prophets, through Moses and kings. Then He spoke to us through His Son, Jesus. Later, God spoke through the apostles. The Word of God tells us what God wants and we are to obey it. (Ps. 119:89; John 1:1.)

Writing

Pens, pencils, typewriters, and paper were not part of the Bible-time household. Most people could not write because there were not many schools in ancient times. Some early writing was on clay tablets. Jeremiah's book was written on a scroll. Zacharias wrote on a writing tablet, probably made of wood covered with wax. Some writing was on broken pieces of pottery. (Jer. 36:27, 28.)

Y

Yoke

An acre was considered the amount of land a yoke of oxen could plow in a day. The yoke was a large piece of wood fastened to the necks of two animals. This made it possible for both animals to pull together. Only animals which had never worked with a yoke could be offered in sacrifice. Working for Jesus is like bearing His yoke. But His yoke is gentle. It does not chafe. (Num. 19:2; Matt. 11:29, 30.)

Youth

Bible-time people often looked for wisdom among the elders, or older men. There was great respect for old age and the wisdom that often went with it. But there were times when this was not so. Solomon had great wisdom as a young man. David was anointed to be king when he was young. And King Rehoboam listened to the counsel of his young men instead of his older men. (II Chron. 10:8.)

Z

Zacchaeus

Zacchaeus' neighbors did not like him because he was a rich tax collector who gathered money for the Romans. When Jesus came to Jericho, Zacchaeus wanted to see him, but he was too short to see over the crowds. So Zacchaeus climbed a tree by the side of the road. When Jesus saw him, He called for Zacchaeus to come down so that He could visit with him. (Luke 19:1–10.)

Zacharias

While burning incense in the Temple one day, the priest Zacharias suddenly saw an angel nearby. The angel promised Zacharias that he and his wife Elizabeth would have a son, even though they were already old. Zacharias did not believe the angel and so he was unable to speak until the child was born. The baby was John the Baptist. (Luke 1:5–25.)

Zadok

For many years Zadok the priest remained faithful to King David. Together with Abiathar he was in charge of the Ark of the Covenant. When Absalom rebelled against his father, David, Zadok remained loyal to the king. Later Zadok anointed Solomon as king. Zadok and his descendants were High Priests in the Temple until it was destroyed in 587 B.C. (II Sam. 15:24–36.)

Zamzummim

When the Ammonites came to live in the country east of the river Jordan, they found a race of giants already in the land. But even though they were tall, the Ammonites despised them. They gave them the name of Zamzummim, which means "mumblers;" because, when they spoke it sounded like people trying to talk with their mouths full. (Deut. 2:20.)

Zealot

Simon the Zealot (Zelotes) was one of Jesus' disciples. The Jews hated their Roman captors and so some formed a political group called Zealots. Their purpose was to drive the Romans from the land. The Zealots had a leading part in the war against the Romans in 66 A.D. This war brought about the destruction of Jerusalem. The last Zealot stronghold, at Masada, fell in 73 A.D. (Luke 6:15.)

Zarephath

During a severe drought in King Ahab's reign, God told Elijah to go to Zarephath where he would find a widow to care for him. Although the widow had only enough oil and flour for one meal, God worked a miracle so that there was always more each day. When the widow's son died, Elijah brought him back to life. Zarephath was a small Phoenician town between Tyre and Sidon. (I Kings 17:9–24.)

Zebah and Zulmunna

For seven years the Midianites and their two kings Zebah and Zalmunna stripped the land of Israel, taking their crops and animals. But God appointed Gideon to destroy the Midianites. After a great battle near the hill of Moreh, Gideon pursued the Midianites and captured the two kings. Gideon asked a young man to kill them, but he was afraid. So Gideon did it. (Judg. 8:4–21.)

303

Zebedee

Zebedee's name is in the Bible because of his two sons James and John, two of Jesus' disciples. He was a successful fisherman who lived at Bethsaida. Zebedee owned a number of fishing boats which were used on the Sea of Galilee. When Jesus called James and John to follow Him, Zebedee stayed behind to carry on the business. (Mark 1:19, 20.)

Zebul

During the days of Abimelech, Zebul was the governor of Shechem. A man named Gaal began to stir up trouble, telling the people of Shechem that they should have another king instead of Abimelech. Zebul warned Abimelech about the plot and suggested a clever ambush by which Abimelech overthrew the rebels. (Judg. 9:26–48.)

Zebulun

Zebulun, one of the 12 tribes of Israel, was named after the sixth son of Jacob and Leah. Zebulun's territory lay between the Sea of Galilee and the Mediterranean and included Nazareth and Cana. In Deborah's great victory over Sisera and in Gideon's war against the Midianites, the tribe of Zebulun was especially praised for bravery and skill in battle. (Gen. 30:19, 20.)

Zechariah

After the people of Israel returned from the captivity, the Temple remained in ruins for 20 years. At a time when the people were discouraged, God raised up two prophets to lead them. Haggai and Zechariah both moved the people to rebuild the Temple. Zechariah was a member of a priestly family. His prophecies are in a book by his name. (The Book of Zechariah.)

Zedekiah

Nebuchadnezzar took King Jehoiachin to Babylon as a prisoner and left Zedekiah in Judah as the new king. But Zedekiah plotted against Nebuchadnezzar and so the Babylonian army attacked Jerusalem, captured Zedekiah, and killed his sons before his eyes. Then they blinded Zedekiah and put him in prison in Babylon. (II Kings 25:7.)

Zelophehad

When Zelophehad died, he had no sons to inherit his property. His five daughters came to Moses and claimed their father's inheritance. God told Moses to agree and a new law was made that if a man died without sons his goods should go to his daughters. But the daughters must not marry outside their own tribe. (Num. 27:1–4.)

Zenas

Zenas was a friend of Paul's who went with Apollos to deliver a letter to Titus. In the letter, which we know as the Epistle to Titus, Paul urged Titus to look after Zenas and Apollos and make sure they had all they needed for the next part of their journey. Zenas was a Christian who was probably a teacher of the Jewish law before his conversion. (Titus 3:13.)

Zephaniah

Zephaniah's parents may have given him his name, which means "the Lord protects," because he was born during the evil reign of King Manasseh. He preached during the early years of Josiah's reign, encouraging the young king to remain faithful to the Lord and to repair the Temple. Zephaniah was probably related to some of the kings and was a fearless prophet. (The Book of Zephaniah.)

Zerubbabel

The Persian king Cyrus gave Zerubbabel permission to lead the first party of exiled Jews back to their homeland. Zerubbabel's work in Jerusalem was to begin the rebuilding of the ruined Temple. With the king's help in money and materials a start was made. The foundation was laid in the second month of the second year after Zerubbabel arrived. (Ezra 3:2.)

Zeruiah

Zeruiah must have been a remarkable woman because her three sons, Abishai, Joab, and Asahel, became King David's three great generals. Zeruiah must have become a widow early in life and was left to raise her sons alone. Her unnamed husband was buried at Bethlehem. She was an older sister of King David. (II Sam. 2:18; I Chron 2:16.)

Ziba

David and Jonathan had been best friends and so when David became king, he wanted to honor Jonathan's family. Ziba, a servant of Saul, told David about Mephibosheth, one of Jonathan's sons. David brought Mephibosheth to live in the palace and put Ziba in charge of his property. When Absalom rebelled against David, Ziba brought food and donkeys. (II Sam. 16:1–4.)

Ziklag

King Saul wanted to kill David and so David had to escape to the Philistines. King Achish of Gath gave David and his men the city of Ziklag for a home. One day while they were gone, Amalekites destroyed the city, taking the women and children as captives. But David defeated the Amalekites, rescued the women and children, and returned to Ziklag to live. (I Sam. 27:1–7.)

Zimri

Zimri had the strange honor of being king of Israel for a week. Captain of half the king's chariots, Zimri murdered Elah the king so that he could become king. The news reached the army and the soldiers proclaimed Omri king and marched to Tirzah, where Zimri had set up his capital. Zimri hid in the palace and then set fire to it, burning himself to death. (I Kings 16:8–18.)

Zion

At first Zion was the name of a fortified hill in Jerusalem where the Kidron and Hinnom valleys meet. Zion was captured from the Jebusites by David, who built his palace there. Later, the whole city of Jerusalem was sometimes called Zion. In the New Testament Zion is the name given to the future heavenly city of New Jerusalem. (II Sam. 5:6–9.)

Ziph

When David had to run away from King Saul, he escaped to the wilderness near Ziph, a town in the hills of Judah southeast of Hebron. The people of Ziph told Saul that David was hiding nearby and Saul brought his army. But while Saul was on one side of a mountain, David went to the other side and escaped. (I Sam. 23:14–24.)

Zipporah

After Moses killed an Egyptian taskmaster, he ran away from Egypt and went to live in the land of Midian. There he met Zipporah, one of the seven shepherdess daughters of Jethro, a Midianite priest. Moses married Zipporah and they had two sons, Gershom and Eliezer. Moses apparently sent her back home to live during the troubled times leading up to the Exodus. (Exod. 2:15–22.)

Scripture Index

310

Isa. 30:24—Shovel, Winnowing
Isa. 30:28—Bridle
Isa. 33:21—Oar
Isa. 34:4—Scroll
Isa. 35:7—Rushes
Isa. 36:6—Reed
Isa. 38:21—Figs
Isa. 40:31—Eagle
Isa. 47:12ff—Astrologer
Isa. 55:3–5—Jesus
Isa. 55:13—Myrtle
Isa. 61:10—Bride
Jer. 1:1—Anathoth
Jer. 4:21—Banner
Jer. 6:29—Bellows
Jer. 8:7—Stork, Swallow
Jer. 8:22—Balm
Jer. 18:1–6—Potter, Pottery
Jer. 18:6—Clay
Jer. 20:2—Stocks
Jer. 25:10—Mill
Jer. 28—Hananiah
Jer. 32:7ff—Anathoth
Jer. 35:2–10—Rechabites
Jer. 36—Baruch
Jer. 36:27,28—Writing
Jer. 36:32—Scribes
Jer. 38:6–13—Ebed-melech
Jer. 39:14—Gedaliah
Jer. 40:13,14—Johanan
Jer. 41:11–15—Johanan
Jer. 43:3–6—Baruch
Jer. 44:1—Memphis
Jer. 48:2—Carchemish
Jer. 51:27—Ararat
Jer. 51:59–64—Seraiah
Ezek. 1:1—Chebar
Ezek. 3:23—Chebar
Ezek. 4:2—Battering Ram
Ezek. 8:16—Sun
Ezek. 10:15—Chebar
Ezek. 21:22—Battering Ram
Ezek. 23:24—Helmet
Ezek. 23:40—Cosmetics
Ezek. 27:6,29—Oar
Ezek. 27:9—Gebal
Ezek. 27:16—Emerald
Ezek. 27:17—Balm
Ezek. 27:19—Cassia
Ezek. 29:10—Seveneh, Syene
Ezek. 30:6—Seveneh, Syene
Ezek. 40:3—Reed
Dan. 1:1,3—Babylon
Dan. 1:1–4—Captivity
Dan. 1:7—Shadrach, Meshach,
    and Abednego
Dan. 2:5–49—Babylon
Dan. 2:10—Astrologer
Dan. 2:13—Wise Men
Dan. 3—Fiery Furnace, Image
Dan. 3:1–30—Shadrach,
    Meshach, and Abednego
Dan. 3:2—Satrap
Dan. 3:4—Herald
Dan. 3:5–15—Flute
Dan. 3:5,6—Adoration
Dan. 3:28—Angels
Dan. 4:7–33—Babylon
Dan. 5—Belshazzar, Mene,
    Mene, Tekel, Upharsin
Dan. 5:10—Banquet
Dan. 5:27—Balance

Dan. 5:29—Scarlet
Dan. 5:31—Darius
Dan. 6:8—Media
Dan. 6:10—Chamber,
    Chamberlain
Dan. 9:25,26—Messiah
Joel 2:20—Dead Sea
Joel 3:8—Sabeans
Amos 1:1—Earthquake, Tekoa
Amos 1:6–8—Ashkelon
Amos 2:6—Jeroboam II
Amos 3:15—Ivory
Amos 6:4—Bed, Couch, Ivory,
    Sleep
Amos 7:7–9—Plumb Line
Amos 7:14—Sycamore, Tekoa
Amos 8:5—New Moon
Amos 9:9—Sieve
Jon. 1–4—Nineveh
Jon. 1:7—Lots
Jon. 1:17—Fish
Jon. 4:5,6—Shadow
Jon. 4:6,11—Gourd
Micah 5:2—Jesus, Prophets,
    Prophecy
Micah 5:6—Nimrod
Micah 6:5—Balak
Micah 6:11—Weights
Nah. 2:4—Street
Nah. 3:14—Brick
Hab. 3:19—Hart and Hind
Zech. 3:1,2—Satan
Zech. 5:6–10—Ephah
Zech. 9:9—Jesus, Prophets,
    Prophecy
Zech. 9:15—Basin
Zech. 14:1–11—Earthquake
Mal. 3:2,3—Refiner
Mal. 3:5—Hireling
Matt. 1—28—Jesus
Matt. 1:5—Obed
Matt. 1:21—Name
Matt. 1:23—Immanuel
Matt. 2:1—Jerusalem
Matt. 2:1–10—Star
Matt. 2:1–12—Wise Men
Matt. 2:1–19—Herod the Great
Matt. 2:11—Frankincense,
    Gold, Myrrh
Matt. 2:13–15—Egypt
Matt. 2:13–23—Joseph of
    Nazareth
Matt. 2:22—Archelaus
Matt. 2:23—Nazarene,
    Nazareth
Matt. 3:1–6—Confession
Matt. 3:3—Runner
Matt. 3:4—Camel's Hair,
    Leather
Matt. 3:13—Jericho, River
Matt. 3:13–17—Jordan
Matt. 3:16—Baptism
Matt. 4:1—Jericho
Matt. 4:1–11—Devil, Satan,
    Temptation
Matt. 4:20,21—Net
Matt. 4:25—Decapolis
Matt. 5:1—Disciple
Matt. 5:3–12—Beatitudes
Matt. 5:11,12—Persecution
Matt. 5:12—Reward
Matt. 5:13—Salt

Matt. 5:15—Bushel
Matt. 5:17—Law
Matt. 5:20—Pharisee
Matt. 5:22—Fool, Hinnom
Matt. 5:23,24—Forgiveness
Matt. 5:45—Providence
Matt. 6:9—Father
Matt. 6:16–18—Fast
Matt. 6:24—Mammon
Matt. 6:27—Cubit
Matt. 6:28,29—Flowers, Lily
Matt. 7:6—Swine
Matt. 8:5–13—Centurion
Matt. 8:8,9—Capernaum
Matt. 8:14,15—Fever
Matt. 8:16—Demons
Matt. 9:2–7—Healing
Matt. 9:3—Blasphemy
Matt. 9:9–13—Capernaum
Matt. 9:20—Fringes
Matt. 10:3—Thaddaeus
Matt. 10:29—Farthing
Matt. 10:29–31—Sparrow
Matt. 11:23,24—Capernaum
Matt. 11:29,30—Yoke
Matt. 13:3–8, 18–23—Sower
Matt. 13:10,11—Parable
Matt. 13:24–30—Tares
Matt. 13:31,32—Mustard
Matt. 13:33—Leaven
Matt. 13:36–40—Tares
Matt. 13:55—Carpenter
Matt. 14:1–12—Salome
Matt. 14:17–20—Fish
Matt. 14:20—Basket
Matt. 14:28–31—Peter
Matt. 15:21–28—Dog
Matt. 16:13–17—Caesarea
    Philippi
Matt. 16:18—Church
Matt. 16:18–19—Peter
Matt. 16:27—Reward
Matt. 17:1–8—Transfiguration
Matt. 17:20—Mustard
Matt. 17:25—Tax Collector
Matt. 17:27—Money
Matt. 18:9—Hell
Matt. 18:21,22—Forgiveness
Matt. 18:28–30—Prison
Matt. 19:24—Needle's Eye
Matt. 20:3–6—Market
Matt. 20:17—Jerusalem
Matt. 21:1–20—Bethphage
Matt. 21:12—Money-changers
Matt. 21:42—Cornerstone
Matt. 22:24—Banquet
Matt. 22:17—Tax Collector
Matt. 22:19—Denarius
Matt. 23:15—Proselyte
Matt. 23:27—Sepulchres
Matt. 24:41—Grinding
Matt. 25:1–9—Lamp
Matt. 25:1–13—Marriage,
    Wedding
Matt. 25:41—Satan
Matt. 26:6–13—Bethany,
    Ointment
Matt. 26:7—Alabaster
Matt. 26:15—Silver
Matt. 26:17–19—Upper Room
Matt. 26:26–28—Sacrament
Matt. 26:27—Cup

Matt. 26:30—Hymn
Matt. 26:34—Cock Crowing
Matt. 26:36–56—Gethsemane
Matt. 26:53—Legion
Matt. 26:57—High Priest
Matt. 26:57–68—Caiaphas,
Council
Matt. 27:3–10—Aceldama,
Judas Iscariot
Matt. 27:11–13—Procurator
Matt. 27:12—Elders
Matt. 27:16ff—Barabbas
Matt. 27:24—Wash
Matt. 27:26—Whip
Matt. 27:28,35—Robe
Matt. 27:29—Crown, Crown of
Thorns, Scepter
Matt. 27:32—Cross
Matt. 27:33—Golgotha
Matt. 27:34—Vinegar
Matt. 27:35—Lots
Matt. 27:51–53—Earthquake
Matt. 27:57—Joseph of
Arimathea
Matt. 28:1–8—Mary
Magdalene
Matt. 28:3—Lightning
Mark 1—16—Jesus
Mark 1:4–11—John the Baptist
Mark 1:6—Camel's Hair
Mark 1:7—Sandal
Mark 1:15—Repent,
Repentance
Mark 1:16—Fisherman
Mark 1:19,20—Zebedee
Mark 1:24—Demons
Mark 2:27—Sabbath
Mark 3:17—Boanerges
Mark 3:18—Bartholomew,
Thaddaeus
Mark 4:29—Sickle
Mark 5:20—Decapolis
Mark 5:22–24,35–43—Jairus
Mark 5:38–40—Wailing
Mark 6:3—Carpenter
Mark 6:19–22—Herodias
Mark 6:48—Night
Mark 7:26—Syrophoenicia
Mark 7:31—Decapolis
Mark 7:31–35—Ephphatha
Mark 8:27—9:8—Caesarea
Philippi
Mark 9:3—Fuller
Mark 10:46–52—Beggar
Mark 11:1–14—Bethphage
Mark 11:12–14—Fig Tree
Mark 11:20,21—Bethphage
Mark 12:38,39—Seat
Mark 12:42—Farthing
Mark 13:35—Cock Crowing
Mark 14:3—Alabaster
Mark 14:14–26—Guest Room
Mark 14:22–25—Last Supper
Mark 15:1—Sanhedrin
Mark 15:16—Praetorium
Mark 15:17—Crown of Thorns
Mark 15:30—Cross
Mark 15:38—Curtain
Mark 16:9—Mary Magdalene
Mark 16:19—Ascension
Luke 1—24—Jesus
Luke 1:3—Theophilus

Luke 1:5–23—Holy Place
Luke 1:5–25—Dumbness,
Zacharias
Luke 1:5–57—Elizabeth
Luke 1:11–38—Gabriel
Luke 1:26—Nazareth
Luke 1:26–38—Annunciation
Luke 1:26–56—Mary, The
Mother of Jesus
Luke 1:47—Savior
Luke 2:1—Augustus Caesar,
Caesar
Luke 2:1–5—Census
Luke 2:1–7—Bethlehem
Luke 2:2—Quirinius,
Cyrenius
Luke 2:7—Inn, Manger,
Swaddling Clothes
Luke 2:10—Gospel
Luke 2:11—Savior
Luke 2:12—Swaddling Clothes
Luke 2:21–24—Law
Luke 2:25–35—Simeon
Luke 2:36–38—Anna
Luke 2:41—Pilgrim
Luke 2:44—Day's Journey
Luke 2:46—Doctor
Luke 3:1—Caesar, Ituraea,
Tetrarch, Tiberius
Luke 3:2—Annas
Luke 3:17—Chaff, Granary
Luke 3:23–38—Jacob, Seth
Luke 3:32—Obed
Luke 3:37—Enoch
Luke 4:8—Adoration
Luke 4:16—Synagogue
Luke 4:16–30—Nazareth
Luke 4:31—Galilee
Luke 5:6—Fisherman
Luke 5:17—Doctor
Luke 5:18,19—House
Luke 5:24—Couch
Luke 5:27—Publican
Luke 5:37,38—Bottle
Luke 6:6–11—Withered Hand
Luke 6:13—Apostle
Luke 6:15—Zealot
Luke 6:20–23—Beatitudes
Luke 7:11–17—Funeral, Nain
Luke 7:37—Alabaster
Luke 7:44–46—Guest
Luke 8:2,3—Joanna
Luke 8:26–36—Demons,
Gadara
Luke 8:29—Fetters
Luke 8:30—Legion
Luke 8:41—Ruler
Luke 9:51–55—James the
Apostle
Luke 9:54–56—Boanerges
Luke 10:4—Purse
Luke 10:13—Sackcloth
Luke 10:29–37—Neighbor
Luke 10:30—Robbers
Luke 10:30–37—Samaritan
Luke 10:34—Anointing, Inn,
Medicine
Luke 10:35—Denarius
Luke 10:38–42—Martha
Luke 11:11,12—Scorpion
Luke 11:29,30—Sign
Luke 11:42—Rue

Luke 12:16–24—Granary
Luke 12:20—Fool
Luke 12:24—Raven
Luke 12:33—Purse
Luke 13:4—Siloam
Luke 13:32—Fox, Herod the
Tetrarch
Luke 14:17—Banquet
Luke 15:11–32—Grace
Luke 15:16—Husk
Luke 15:17—Hireling
Luke 16:19–31—Hell
Luke 16:21—Dog
Luke 17:11–19—Leprosy
Luke 18:10—Publican
Luke 18:35–43—Bartimaeus
Luke 19:1–10—Zacchaeus
Luke 19:4—Sycamore
Luke 19:8—Restitution
Luke 19:20—Napkin
Luke 19:29,37—Mount of
Olives
Luke 21:1–4—Mite, Treasury
Luke 22:14–20—Last Supper
Luke 22:50,51—Malchus
Luke 22:52—Guard
Luke 23:7–12—Herod the
Tetrarch
Luke 23:33—Calvary,
Crucifixion
Luke 23:43—Paradise
Luke 23:45—Curtain
Luke 23:55,56—Joanna
Luke 24:13–35—Emmaus
Luke 24:10—Joanna
Luke 24:50–52—Ascension
John 1—21—Jesus
John 1:1—Word
John 1:29—Lamb, Sheep
John 1:32—Dove
John 1:39—Hour
John 1:40—Andrew
John 1:41—Messiah
John 1:44—Bethsaida
John 1:45,46—Bartholomew,
Nazarene
John 1:45–49—Nathanael,
Philip the Apostle
John 2:1–11—Cana, Wine
John 3:1–21—Nicodemus
John 2:6—Waterpot
John 3:2—Rabbi
John 3:14–16—Brazen Serpent
John 4:4,5—Samaria
John 4:5—Sychar
John 4:5–10—Jacob's Well
John 4:6—Hour
John 4:9—Samaritan
John 4:23—Gerizim, Mt.
John 4:25—Messiah
John 4:46–54—Cana
John 4:42—Savior
John 5:1–16—Bethesda
John 6:1,23—Tiberias
John 6:48—Bread
John 7:1—Galilee
John 7:5—Jude
John 9:5–7—Pool of Siloam
John 9:6–15—Clay
John 9:7—Siloam
John 9:8,9—Beggar
John 10:11,14—Shepherd